Mastering the Great Table

Volume II of the Mastering Enochian Magick Series

Scott Michael Stenwick

Volume II
of the
Mastering Enochian Magick Series

Mastering the Great Table

Scott Michael Stenwick

PENDRAIG Publishing
Los Angeles, CA 91040

Mastering the Great Table
Volume II of the Mastering Enochian Magick Series
Scott Michael Stenwick
First Edition © 2013
by PENDRAIG Publishing
All rights reserved.

No part of this publication may be reproduced, stored in a retrieval system or transmitted in any form or by any means, electronic, mechanical, photocopying, recording or otherwise without the prior written permission of the copyright holder, except brief quotation in a review.

Edited by   Tony Mierzwicki

Cover Design & Interior Images
Typeset & Layout   Jo-Ann Byers Mierzwicki

PENDRAIG Publishing
Los Angeles, CA 91040
www.PendraigPublishing.com
Printed in the United States of America

ISBN: 978-1-936922-65-9

For Michele Rockne, Thomas Brenden, Keith Strickland, Whitney Holiday, and Maurine Stenwick, all of whom joined with me in the Great Table workings that led to the writing of this book. May you all accomplish the Great Work and attain the Summum Bonum, True Wisdom, and Perfect Happiness!

Thanks once again to Joseph H. Peterson for his wonderful Enochian artwork, used here with his permission.

Contents

Chapter 1	Introduction	13
Chapter 2	The Great Table	17
Chapter 3	The Temple Arrangement	35
Chapter 4	Great Table Ritual Template	55
Chapter 5	Opening the Temple	61
Chapter 6	The Preliminary Invocation	69
Chapter 7	The Angelic Pronunciation	77
Chapter 8	The Angelic Keys	85
Chapter 9	Tuning the Space	113
Great Table Conjurations		133
Chapter 10	Great Table Conjurations	135
Chapter 11	Great Table Talismans	141
Chapter 12	The Kings and Seniors	173
Chapter 13	The Kerubic Angels	177

Chapter 14	The Lesser Angels	183
Chapter 15	The Cacodemons	191
Chapter 16	The Charge	199
Chapter 17	Closing the Temple	205
Chapter 18	Conclusion	209
Appendix A	Basic Ritual Forms	211
Appendix B	Conselh Ananael Great Table Evocation Ritual	233
Bibliography		243
About the Author		245
Index		247

Figures

Figure 1	Recensa Table English	18
Figure 2	Recensa Table Angelic	20
Figure 3	King Bataivah East	28
Figure 4	Seniors East	29
Figure 5	Controlling Cross	30
Figure 6	Enochian Rings	36
Figure 7	Enochian Lamens	37
Figure 8	Holy Table	38
Figure 9	Sigillum Dei Aemeth	39
Figure 10	Sigillum Bottom	40
Figure 11	Holy Table Ensigns Sigillum	41
Figure 12	Ensign of Venus	42
Figure 13	Ensign of Sun	42
Figure 14	Ensign of Mars	43
Figure 15	Ensign of Jupiter	43
Figure 16	Ensign of Mercury	44
Figure 17	Ensign of Saturn	44
Figure 18	Ensign of the Moon	45
Figure 19	ORO Banner	47
Figure 20	Active Spirit Pentagrams	119

Figure 21	Passive Spirit Pentagrams	120
Figure 22	Pentagrams of Fire	121
Figure 23	Pentagrams of Water	121
Figure 24	Pentagrams of Air	122
Figure 25	Pentagrams of Earth	122
Figure 26	Sigil Marks for Angels Above Controlling Cross	142
Figure 27	Sigil Marks for Angels Below Controlling Cross	143
Figure 28	Sigil Marks Cacodemons	143
Figure 29	Sigil Marks Kings and Seniors	144
Figure 30	Sigil Kings and Seniors of the East	145
Figure 31	Sigil Kings and Seniors of the South	146
Figure 32	Sigil Kings and Seniors of the West	146
Figure 33	Sigil Kings and Seniors of the North	147
Figure 34	Angels of Natural Substances of the East	147
Figure 35	Angels of Natural Substances of the South	148
Figure 36	Angels of Natural Substances of the West	148
Figure 37	Angels of Natural Substances of the North	149
Figure 38	Angels of Transportation of the East	149
Figure 39	Angels of Transportation of the South	150
Figure 40	Angels of Transportation of the West	150
Figure 41	Angels of Transportation of the North	151
Figure 42	Angels of Mechanical Arts of the East	151
Figure 43	Angels of Mechanical Arts of the South	152
Figure 44	Angels of Mechanical Arts of the West	152
Figure 45	Angels of Mechanical Arts of the North	153
Figure 46	Angels of Secret Discoveries of the East	153
Figure 47	Angels of Secret Discoveries of the South	154
Figure 48	Angels of Secret Discoveries of the West	154
Figure 49	Angels of Secret Discoveries of the North	155
Figure 50	Angels of Medicine of the East	155
Figure 51	Angels of Medicine of the South	156
Figure 52	Angels of Medicine of the West	156
Figure 53	Angels of Medicine of the North	157

Figure 54	Angels of Metals and Precious Stones of the East	157
Figure 55	Angels of Metals and Precious Stones of the South	158
Figure 56	Angels of Metals and Precious Stones of the West	158
Figure 57	Angels of Metals and Precious Stones of the North	159
Figure 58	Angels of Transformation of the East	159
Figure 59	Angels of Transformation of the South	160
Figure 60	Angels of Transformation of the West	160
Figure 61	Angels of Transformation of the North	161
Figure 62	Angels of Living Creatures and the Four Elements of the East	161
Figure 63	Angels of Living Creatures and the Four Elements of the South	162
Figure 64	Angels of Living Creatures and the Four Elements of the West	162
Figure 65	Angels of Living Creatures and the Four Elements of the North	163
Figure 66	Cacodemons of Medicine of the East	163
Figure 67	Cacodemons of Medicine of the South	164
Figure 68	Cacodemons of Medicine of the West	164
Figure 69	Cacodemons of Medicine of the North	165
Figure 70	Cacodemons of Metals and Precious Stones of the East	165
Figure 71	Cacodemons of Metals and Precious Stones of the South	166
Figure 72	Cacodemons of Metals and Precious Stones of the West	166
Figure 73	Cacodemons of Metals and Precious Stones of the North	167
Figure 74	Cacodemons of Transformation of the East	167
Figure 75	Cacodemons of Transformation of the South	168
Figure 76	Cacodemons of Transformation of the West	168
Figure 77	Cacodemons of Transformation of the North	169
Figure 78	Cacodemons of Living Creatures and the Four Elements of the East	169
Figure 79	Cacodemons of Living Creatures and the Four Elements of the South	170

Figure 80	Cacodemons of Living Creatures and the Four Elements of the West	170
Figure 81	Cacodemons of Living Creatures and the Four Elements of the North	171
Figure 82	Bataivah Spiral	173
Figure 83	The Six Seniors of the East	175
Figures 84 & 85	The Pentagrams of Earth	212
Figures 86 & 87	The Hexagrams of Fire	216
Figures 88 & 89	The Hexagrams of Earth	217
Figures 90 & 91	The Hexagrams of Air	217
Figures 92 & 93	The Hexagrams of Water	218
Figures 94	The Banishing Pentagram of Earth	221
Figure 95	The Invoking Pentagram of Earth	223
Figure 96	Unicursal Hexagram of Earth — Invoking	225
Figure 97	Unicursal Hexagrams of Fire	225
Figure 98	Unicursal Hexagrams of Air	226
Figure 99	Unicursal Hexagrams of Water	226
Figure 100	Unicursal Hexagrams of Earth	227
Figure 101	Saturn Hexagrams	227
Figure 102	Moon Hexagrams	228

Tables

Table 1	Spirits of the Angelic Keys	57
Table 2	The Conjurations	58
Table 3	The Fundamental Obeisance Associations	72
Table 4	The Angelic Pronunciations	79
Table 5	The Angelic Pronunciations - Hebraic	80-81
Table 6	Planetary Hours of the Day - Sunrise to Sunset	115
Table 7	Planetary Hours of the Day - Sunset to Sunrise	116
Table 8	Correspondences of the Kings	136
Table 9	Sub-quadrant Associations	137-138

Table 10	The Kings	174
Table 11	The Seniors	175
Table 12	Angels of Natural Substances	178
Table 13	Angels of Transportation	179
Table 14	Angels of Mechanical Arts	180
Table 15	Angels of Secret Discovery	181
Table 16	Angels of Medicine	184
Table 17	Angels of Gold and Precious Stones	185
Table 18	Angels of Transformation	186
Table 19	Angels of Living Creatures and the Elements	187
Table 20	Cacodemons of Medicine	193
Table 21	Cacodemons of Gold and Precious Stones	194
Table 22	Cacodemons of Transformation	195
Table 23	Cacodemons of Living Creatures and the Elements	197

Chapter 1
Introduction

The first book in this series, Mastering the Mystical Heptarchy, explored a portion of the sixteenth-century Enochian material received by Dr. John Dee and Edward Kelley that modern magicians have mostly ignored, the Heptarchia Mystica. This book, on the other hand, explores a portion of that same material that has inspired numerous modern magical groups including the various Golden Dawn orders, Aleister Crowley's A∴A∴, and the Aurum Solis. Whereas presenting a functional system for conjuring Heptarchial angels required some elaboration upon the source texts, doing the same for the Great Table angels presents the opposite problem. Every modern group that has worked with this aspect of the Enochian system has created its own version or dialect, including elements and concepts not found in the source material and in some cases directly contradicting the original text. As with the previous volume, the goal of this book is to present a system that includes all of the functional pieces of the original system suitable for both modern and Solomonic working styles.

Generally speaking, you will get the most out of this book if you have already read Mastering the Mystical Heptarchy. In that book, I cover a brief history of the Enochian system, provide more detailed explanations of the various pieces of temple furniture, and cover the use of the opening pentagram and hexagram rituals to create the various magical fields that I have found to facilitate effective practical magick. For convenience, I have included the scripts for both the traditional pentagram and hexagram rituals along with those for my own Aoeveae, Madriax, and Naz Olpirt Enochian rituals in Appendix A. However, I have not reproduced the expositions of those rituals here as these can be found in the previous volume. Similarly, while I have included Joseph Peterson's images of the temple equipment explained in Mastering the Mystical Heptarchy, I have not included the larger images intended for photocopying that you will find in my first book. In addition, the previous volume includes much of my advice to beginning magicians, as I assumed that anyone new to magick and interested in exploring the Enochian system would start at the beginning of the series.

The magick of the Western Esoteric Tradition can be roughly divided into two basic classes, usually referred to as theurgy and thaumaturgy. The term theurgy alludes to the mystical practices of the art, in which the magician invokes the form of a particular deity in order to expand his or her consciousness and eventually experience union with the source of all being. Thaumaturgy, on the other hand, alludes to the practical application of spiritual power with the goal of influencing the material world through the direction of natural forces. Tension sometimes arises between advocates of these two approaches. It is often erroneously asserted that these perspectives conflict with each other, a belief that is rooted in the dualistic illusion of matter and spirit as opposites. Although magick as such is only practiced by a tiny minority in the Western world, this dualistic conditioning runs deep and manifests in religion, politics, and even the scientific establishment. In order to allow realized consciousness to flourish, this worldview must be transcended, regardless of one's initial approach to the magical path.

In order to facilitate this non-dual realization, a comprehensive magical practice should include elements of both classes. An exclusive focus on thaumaturgy can lead to a perspective such as is found in syncretic practical systems like Hoodoo, where effective techniques depend largely upon methods and materials that have little to do with the spiritual development of the practitioner. On the other hand, a pure focus on theurgy is equally problematic because at best it can lead the magician to a perspective that dismisses material concerns as irrelevant, and at worst it can foster serious delusions of exalted realization that are not grounded in anything but the practitioner's imagination – and in fact, for a long time the latter condition has been considered one of the hazards of working with Enochian magick. While reliable information on this subject can be hard to track down, plenty of rumors have circulated regarding practitioners informed of their own unique and cosmically significant destinies while in communication with the Enochian angels. A few of these individuals have gone on to publish these "revelations," only to find them taken far less seriously by anyone else. Since I do not believe that the Enochian system is inherently any more dangerous than other forms of ritual magick, I suspect that this tendency has a lot to do with how the system is usually approached.

In my experience, most Enochian magicians never use the system for anything practical or material, but rather direct their efforts towards achieving some sort of meaningful dialogue with the angels. It is for this reason that I chose to focus my Enochian series on the practical applications of the system. I have no problem with the theurgic approach to the Enochian system, or operations undertaken with the goal of establishing angelic communication. However, too many published Enochian books approach the system as if all you are supposed to do with it is scry and/or meditate. This methodology is extremely limiting, especially when applied to as profound and powerful a system as Enochian magick. While the eventual goal of magick is always spiritual illumination, there is no real conflict between matter and spirit that exists anywhere outside of our own subjective cultural programming. Better life circumstances make a sustained magical practice easier to cultivate, and it is a sustained magical practice that leads to heightened spiritual realization.

In fact, theurgy and thaumaturgy feed off each other. Greater realization should allow you to create stronger probability shifts with your rituals, and if it does not you may want to revise your opinion of how great your realization actually is. People are born with different levels of magical talent, of course, so this does not necessarily mean that a more powerful sorcerer is always going to be a more realized being. Nonetheless, in the context of your own work the principle should hold. As you progress spiritually, the material results you can create with your rituals should likewise become more reliable and more impressive. Similarly, measurable magical successes should strengthen your resolve and your identification with the divine, in addition to facilitating favorable life conditions for your theurgic practices.

With this in mind, I welcome you to explore the Great Table and its angels. They bring to the Enochian system that began with the Heptarchia Mystica, a whole new set of powers and properties for you to draw upon in your pursuit of the Great Work, the Summon Bonum, True Wisdom, and Perfect Happiness.

Scott Michael Stenwick

Minneapolis, MN

Chapter 2
The Great Table

The initial form of the Great Table was received by John Dee and Edward Kelley on June 25, 1584. It was preceded by the Leaves of Liber Loagaeth and the Angelic Keys, which in turn followed the Heptarchial material. The order of the Keys and attributions of the Thirty Aires followed, though the parts of the Earth that the Aires represent are drawn from a network of sigils traced over the Great Table itself. In addition, the Angelic Key that opens them was received along with the other Keys. As such, the Aires seem more closely related to the Great Table than the Kings and Princes of the Heptarchia Mystica, which follow their own separate schema.

Like most of the books and tables received by Dee and Kelley, the Great Table consists of a large grid of letters. It has four quadrants, each made up of 12 x 13 squares, and the "black cross," two perpendicular rows that bind the four quadrants together into a single large 25 x 27 grid. Dee related the quadrants to the four cardinal directions and referred to them as the four castles or watchtowers. The latter term

r	Z	i	l	a	f	A	y	t	l	p	a	e	T	a	O	A	d	v	p	t	D	n	i	m
a	r	d	Z	a	i	d	p	a	L	a	m		a	a	b	c	o	o	r	o	m	e	b	b
c	z	o	n	s	a	r	o	Y	a	v	b	x	T	o	g	c	o	n	x	m	a	l	G	m
T	o	i	T	t	z	o	P	a	c	o	C	a	n	h	o	d	D	i	a	l	e	a	o	c
S	i	g	a	s	o	m	r	b	z	n	h	r	p	a	t	A	x	i	o	V	s	P	s	N
f	m	o	n	d	a	T	d	i	a	r	i	p	S	a	a	i	x	a	a	r	V	r	o	i
o	r	o	i	b	A	h	a	o	z	p	i		m	p	h	a	r	s	l	g	a	i	o	l
t	N	a	b	r	V	i	x	g	a	s	d	h	M	a	m	g	l	o	i	n	L	i	r	x
O	i	i	i	t	T	p	a	l	O	a	i		o	l	a	a	D	n	g	a	T	a	p	a
A	b	a	m	o	o	o	a	C	u	c	a	C	p	a	L	c	o	i	d	x	P	a	c	n
N	a	o	c	O	Tt	tT	n	p	r	n	T	o	n	d	a	z	N	z	i	V	a	a	s	a
o	c	a	n	m	a	g	o	t	r	o	i	m	i	i	d	P	o	n	s	d	A	s	p	i
S	h	i	a	l	r	a	p	m	z	o	x	a	x	r	i	n	h	t	a	r	n	d	i	l
m	o	t	i	b			a	T	n	a	n		n	a	n	T	a			b	i	t	o	m
b	O	a	Z	a	R	o	p	h	a	R	a	a	d	o	n	p	a	T	d	a	n	V	a	a
u	N	n	a	x	o	P	S	o	n	d	n		o	l	o	a	G	e	o	o	b	a	u	a
a	i	g	r	a	n	o	o	m	a	g	g	m	O	P	a	m	n	o	V	G	m	d	n	m
o	r	p	m	n	i	n	g	b	e	a	l	o	a	p	l	s	T	e	d	e	c	a	o	p
r	s	O	n	i	z	i	r	l	e	m	v	C	s	c	m	i	o	o	n	A	m	l	o	x
i	z	i	n	r	C	z	i	a	M	h	l	h	V	a	r	s	G	d	L	b	r	i	a	p
M	o	r	d	i	a	l	h	C	t	G	a		o	i	P	t	e	a	a	p	D	o	c	e
O	c	a	n	c	h	i	a	s	o	m	t	p	P	s	u	a	c	N	r	Z	i	r	Z	a
A	r	b	i	z	m	i	i	l	p	i	z		S	i	o	d	a	o	i	n	r	z	f	m
O	p	a	n	a	l	a	m	S	m	a	P	r	d	a	b	t	T	d	n	a	d	i	r	e
d	O	l	o	P	i	n	i	a	n	b	a	a	d	i	x	o	m	o	n	s	i	o	s	p
r	x	p	a	o	c	s	i	z	i	x	p	x	O	o	D	p	z	i	A	p	a	n	l	i
a	x	t	i	r	V	a	s	t	r	i	m	e	r	g	o	a	n	n	P	A	C	r	a	r

Figure 1. The Great Table (1587 Tabula Recensa, English)

is most common amongst modern magicians, as it was the preferred terminology in the Golden Dawn Enochian system that most modern groups draw upon.

Several versions of the Great Table exist, and deciding which one to work with is the first question any magician who wishes to explore this area of the Enochian system must answer. Dee himself received two versions, the original and a later revision "reformed by Raphael" in 1587. This later version is referred to by Enochian magicians as the Tabula Recensa, or "reformed table," and is the version with which I primarily work. Some magicians who prefer the initial version, point out that the 1587 revision was obtained by Kelley scrying Raphael on his own, and thus should be regarded more skeptically than the previous version obtained in Dee's presence. However, according to the spirit diaries, Dee immediately accepted the revised Table, and furthermore much of the suspicion toward Kelley implied by early biographers of Dee has been questioned by more recent scholarship.

A third version of the Great Table was developed in the late nineteenth century as part of the curriculum of the original Hermetic Order of the Golden Dawn. This Table is widely used, but unfortunately has significant problems. The first and most obvious of these is that the Golden Dawn Table is usually rendered with multiple letters per square in many places. Rather than accepting the Tabula Recensa or even going with Dee's final version of the letters, the Golden Dawn system takes no chances and includes every letter named by the angels for each square, even though it is clear from the diaries that some of them were simply errors that arose during the scrying process. Considering other works of the period, such as Agrippa's Three Books of Occult Philosophy, it is clear that no other source presents a grid of letters such as the Great Table in any configuration other than that of a single letter drawn per square.

A fourth version of the Great Table was proposed by modern occult author Donald Tyson in Tetragrammaton, published in 2003, and reiterated in Enochian Magic for Beginners, published in 2008, both by Llewellyn. Tyson goes so far as to describe his revision as the "Great Table of Tyson," even though it is relatively easily derived from the source documents and displays little inventiveness on his part. The Tyson revision essentially consists of the Tabula Recensa with the upper right and lower left quadrants swapped relative to Dee's diagram (cite from Tyson). This, in turn, allows the Table to conform to a second diagram found in document 3191 of the British Museum's Sloane collection of Dee's dairies that shows the banners bearing the twelve names of God arranged by direction (cite from James). Initially, I thought Tyson might be onto something and played with his arrangement for about a year. However, I eventually that concluded it did not work nearly as well as recensa and switched back.

As I mentioned in my previous book, I am a strong proponent of probability testing magical rituals – that is, performing multiple versions of the same ritual against known probabilities to see which one produces on average the greatest probability shift. When I was first trying to work out which version of the Table to use, this is the method that I chose to employ. I took a known probability, cast against it, and recorded the results over a reasonably large sample size of rituals. The results were that the Tabula Recensa produced the largest probability shifts, followed in order by the Golden Dawn revision, the initial Dee arrangement, and finally the "Table of Tyson." I was actually quite surprised to see Tyson's version fare so poorly, as aside from the two transposed quadrants, the letters on it are the same as on the Tabula

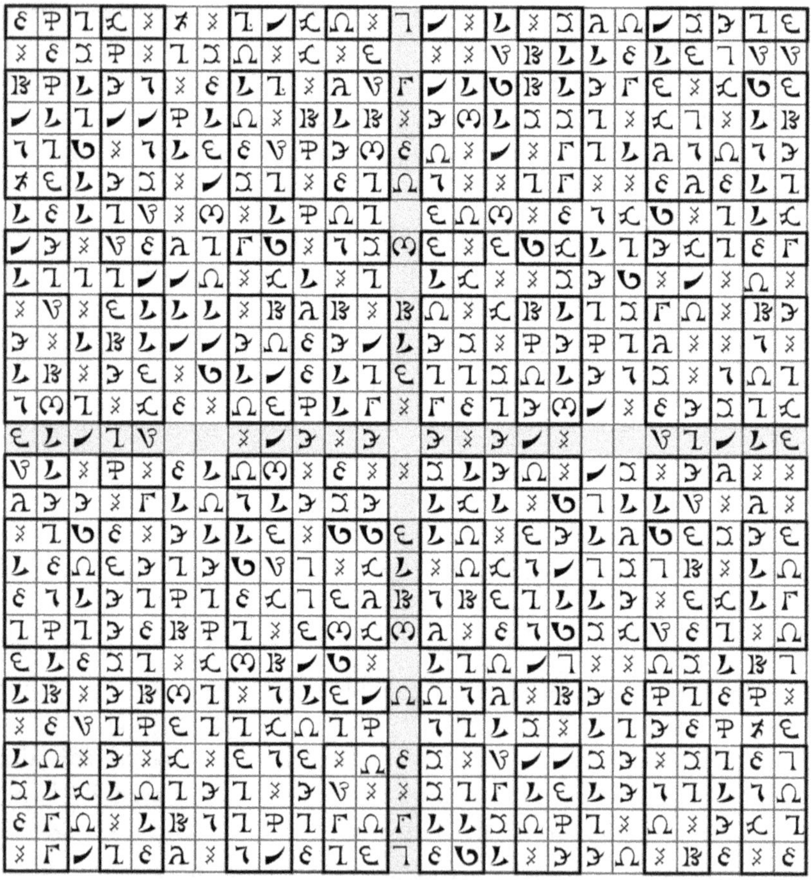

*Figure 2. Tabula Recensa lettered in Angelic.
Note the absence of structures such as truncated pyramids,
which are specific to the Golden Dawn Enochian system.*

Recensa, and to this day I am unsure why it did not perform better. I was also surprised that the Golden Dawn version worked as well as it did since it differs so much from both of the Dee versions. This suggests to me that some real practical experimentation went into its construction, rather the design being merely the result of syncretic metaphysical speculation.

When transposed from English into Angelic letters, the upper and lower case of the English letters is not represented in any way. The English version of the Great Table is more of a reference document than a magical sigil, and when Dee drew it up, he chose to use capital letters to note the first letter for each of the names of the 91 parts of the Earth. These names represent the various regions of the physical world as understood by the spirits of the Enochian system. These names can be extracted from the Great Table by means of a complex grid of sigils, each of which begins with one of the capital letters that appear on the English transliteration. These names are unrelated to the spirits of the quadrants and sub-quadrants covered in this book, but are extremely important when working with the magick of the Aires or Aethyrs which will be addressed in the third book of this series, Mastering the Thirty Aires.

The structure of the Great Table is based on the four elements and, by extension, the four Qabalistic worlds. The four elements date back to the ancient Greeks, and the doctrines associated with them were further elaborated upon over the centuries. Modern physics students have been known to ridicule the ancient Greeks for believing in only four elements when in fact more than a hundred have now been discovered, but this attitude is mostly based on semantic confusion. The four elements of the ancients do not map onto the list of elements that includes substances like hydrogen, nitrogen, and oxygen, but rather the four states in which matter is usually found – solid, liquid, gas, and plasma.

To the original four elements, the Golden Dawn magical system added two others, called Active and Passive Spirit. These map well to the two fundamental states of material in the universe, matter and energy, and if we represent them that way, it becomes clear how the other four are generated. Matter completely devoid of energy – that is, at zero degrees Kelvin – takes a form that physicists describe as Bose-Einstein condensate, and recent research shows that this condition represents a discrete state separate from that of a solid. A solid is the next step in density order, in which enough energy has been applied to a Bose-Einstein condensate to cross the energetic transition barrier and alter its state. The next of these transitions is from a solid to a liquid, then from a liquid to a gas, and finally from a gas to a plasma. The energy applied may be represented as Active Spirit and the matter that receives it may be represented as Passive Spirit. I sometimes simply refer to these "elements" in scientific terms as Energy and Matter, though for consistency with the magical tradition, I will retain the Active and Passive Spirit designations.

One very important point to keep in mind with this schema is that the esoteric element corresponding to a substance is based on its state, with the material of which it is composed treated as largely irrelevant in this context. Lava is formed from stone, but while it is in liquid form its esoteric element is Water. Similarly, the substance we colloquially refer to as water can be found in nature as a solid, a liquid, and a gas. The solid form corresponds to the esoteric element of Earth, the liquid form to that of Water, and the gaseous form to that of Air, even though all of them have the same molecular structure. These distinctions can be important in planning magical rituals. For example, a ritual to govern the behavior of clouds or fog should work with Air rather than Water for maximum effect, and a spell to conjure rain could focus on the transition from Air into Water rather than simply trying to make Water manifest.

In Hermetic Qabalah, the universe is believed to be divided into four discrete "worlds" or levels of reality that correspond to the four elements. The highest of these is the Archetypal World, called Atziluth in Hebrew. This is the world of Plato's ideal forms, in which objects exist only as generalized abstractions. The next is the Creative World, called Briah. This is the world in which the process of creation for a particular object begins. The next is the Formative World, called Yetzirah. This is the world in which the process of forming the object first conceptualized in Briah unfolds. Finally, the fourth is the material world, called Assiah, in which the object takes on physical characteristics.

This process of manifestation is actually quite similar to the instantiation of objects found in my own professional field of object-oriented computer programming. The level of Atziluth represents the code corresponding to a particular class or object; the level of Briah the method call that creates a new instance of the object; the level of Yetzirah the allocation of memory and so forth that renders the new object usable by the program; and finally the level of Assiah corresponds to method calls or property references on the new instance issued by the program. I sometimes have wondered whether the creators of the object-oriented computer programming methodology knew anything about Hermetic Qabalah, or if the pattern simply conforms to basic logic and seemed obvious at the time.

From a microcosmic perspective each of these worlds is also thought to represent a particular aspect of the physical and subtle body of the magician. Atziluth is the realm of the Yechidah, or Self, and the Chiah, or Life-Force. Briah is the realm of the Neschamah, or Intuition, Yetzirah that of the Ruach, or Intellect, and Assiah is the realm of the Nephesch, or Animal Soul. This association with Assiah, the physical world, and the findings of modern neuroscience suggest that the Nephesch is less a "soul" in the usual sense of the word but rather a symbolic term for those aspects of the physical world that give rise to perceptions, moods, and sensations. For example, this suggests that in order to heal a thought disorder rooted in a chemical imbalance in the brain, the magician should target the Nephesch rather than the Ruach even though the symptoms of the disorder may permeate what seems to be the intellect.

The four elements are usually attributed to the four worlds following a pattern based on the Tetragrammaton, YHVH. Yod is related to Fire, Heh to Water, Vav to Air, and final Heh to Earth. So the traditional arrangement looks like this:

> Atziluth — Fire
> Briah — Water
> Yetzirah — Air
> Assiah — Earth

Years ago my magical working group undertook a series of elemental operations in which we invoked the elements in order. Earth went smoothly, as did Air. However, the transition into Water was very difficult. Most of the people in the group developed various problems in their lives at that point, and we had to put the series on hold until those problems could be resolved. This problem is apparently not unusual. Frater W.I.T. published an account of a similar experience in Enochian Initiation and stories like his are commonplace in magical groups that are structured so as to run initiates through the elements in this order. We finally finished our series of invocations, but wondered if there might be a way to work through the elements with less difficulty.

There are those magicians out there who contend that hardship and problems are signs that the magical process is working, but I am not one of them. When I see problems arising in the context of my magical work I assume that I must be doing something wrong, and in fact I usually am able to correct whatever the problem is by carefully contemplating and thinking through my methods. When we decided to do a second series along the same lines, we did some research and made one essential change to our methodology. We came across a European alchemical group called the Philosophers of Nature whose model of the Qabalistic worlds went in density order rather than following the pattern of YHVH, like so:

> Atziluth — Fire
> Briah — Air
> Yetzirah — Water
> Assiah — Earth

We decided that we would perform a second elemental series just like the first, except that it would follow this density order beginning with Earth. One would think that this simple change would make little difference, but in fact the character of our second elemental series was fundamentally changed, even for those participants who had not been part of the first series. Some problems arose in the lives of the participants, as the series spanned most of a year, but there was little correlation with the transitions between elements and most importantly said problems were in every case rapidly resolved rather than lingering on and causing further difficulties. This was even true in one case where the problem in question was a direct result of a longstanding issue that had dragged on for many years. Based on the profound differences between these two series of workings we concluded that the Philosophers of Nature were right – the best and most effective way to work through the elements and by extension the Qabalistic worlds is in density order.

A full discussion of Hermetic Qabalah and the Tree of Life is beyond the scope of this book, but I bring up the four worlds in relation to the elements because they are extremely important in understanding how the Great Table works. In the "round house" vision Kelley saw representations of the elements attributed to each of the four cardinal directions, and the order of those elements follows density rather than any of the other directional arrangements that appear in Renaissance texts such as Agrippa's Three Books of Occult Philosophy. I generally refer to this directional order as the alchemical arrangement, since it allocates the directions clockwise from the east in density order, beginning with Fire and concluding with Earth.

> East — Fire
> South — Air
> West — Water
> North — Earth

This order is particularly relevant to the elemental attributions of the Kings and the structure of the conjurations, which always begin in the east and end in the north. In effect, the Great Table conjurations start with the Angels of Atziluth and then "step down" through the four worlds until the angels have been conjured at every level of reality within a particular sphere of influence. This alone may account for the reputed power of the Enochian system – a full conjuration of one of the classes of angels spans the entire pathway of manifestation from the most divine to the most material. In order to accomplish these sorts of conjurations, the Angels of the Great Table are generally summoned in groups. The four Kings are summoned together, as are the twenty-four Seniors and the sixteen Angels of each of the eight classes found in the sub-quadrants. This even holds true for the thirty-two cacodemons corresponding to each of the four available classes. This is an unusual method in the Golden Dawn system, where working with individual angels is much more widely practiced. However, it should be pointed out that these groupings can be adapted into the Golden Dawn schema, as is done to good effect by Frater W.I.T. in his second book, Advanced Enochian Magick.

This structure also provides a high level of precision, which may be necessary for certain operations. If the change you desire only needs to occur in one of the four worlds, the angels of the corresponding quadrant can be evoked or invoked on their own. This will concentrate the force of the operation upon one particular level of reality. In addition, the sub-quadrant angels themselves have their own elemental attributions. It was explained to Dee that the four Angels of each sub-quadrant group are each attributed to a particular element. Reading down the list of names, the first is attributed to Air, the second to Water, the third to Earth, and the fourth to Fire. So this means that you could construct a Great Table ritual that summons a single angel representing one element of one world within a particular sphere of influence. It should be noted, though, that this is rarely necessary with Enochian angels. One of the advantages that these angels have over some of the other types of spirits that I have worked with is that they tend to be smarter about finding paths of manifestation and therefore better at making things happen.

In the Golden Dawn Enochian system these elemental attributions are different and much more complex. In your research you may come across a version of the Great Table that shows each square of the grid drawn as a truncated pyramid with assorted elemental colors on the four sides. While I have spoken to a number of Golden Dawn Enochian magicians who find those structures useful, it should be pointed out that they have nothing to do with the original Dee Enochian system. It is believed that they were derived from "Enochian Chess," an intricate game designed and played by Samuel Liddell MacGregor Mathers and Wynn Wescott of the original Hermetic Order of the Golden Dawn. It is extremely difficult to play and supposedly encodes the occult secrets of the "Concourse of Forces," the Golden Dawn text that outlines attributions such as those of the truncated pyramids. Like the pyramids themselves this game has nothing to do with anything found in Dee's diaries and you need not know anything about it in order to become an effective Enochian magician.

In addition to assigning elements to the quadrants, which is relatively clear from the "round house" vision, the Golden Dawn system also assigns sub-elements to the sub-quadrants. So, for example, the upper right sub-quadrant (Fire) of the upper left quadrant (Air) would represent the Fiery part of Air. This sub-element schema is derived from the Treatise on Angel Magic, a late seventeenth-century text that attempted to syncretize the Great Table with the signs of geomancy and includes other questionable concepts such as mapping the various Goetic demons onto Dee's Ensigns of Creation. However, as you can see from a simple survey of the powers allocated to the various classes of spirits, this sub-element schema does not hold as the powers themselves do not fall along strict elemental lines. Even if they did, the powers allocated to the two groups of angels found in each sub-quadrant are also not consistent. After much experimentation, I finally decided that the best solution was to eliminate the sub-element associations altogether, so that each quadrant simply represents a single element according to the alchemical density-order arrangement of the four Qabalistic worlds.

Taken as a whole, the Great Table encodes the names of the following classes of spirits:

The Four Kings
   Rulership of the Four Elements and Qabalistic Worlds
The Twenty-Four Seniors
   Knowledge and Judgment in Human Affairs
The Kerubic Angels
   Mechanical Arts
   Transportation
   Natural Substances
   Secret Discovery
The Lesser Angels
   Medicine
   Gold and Precious Stones
   Transformation
   Living Creatures
The Cacodemons
   Medicine
   Gold and Precious Stones
   Transformation
   Living Creatures

Each quadrant of the Great Table is ruled over by a King and six Seniors. These may be thought of as analogous to the King and Prince of each day in the Heptarchial system, at least up to a point. In the Heptarchial system the King is generally conjured to obtain some sort of knowledge or realization, and the Prince is generally conjured to perform some practical action. When working with the Great Table this order is inverted. The Seniors are conjured to obtain "knowledge and judgment in human affairs," and while Dee's diaries assign no particular powers to the Kings I have found them quite effective for practical elemental operations. The names of the Kings are extracted by tracing a spiral in the center of each quadrant. The example shown here is from the Tablet of the East with the letters of the name of King

r	Z	i	l	a	f	A	y	t	l	p	a
a	r	d	Z	a	i	d	p	a	L	a	m
c	z	o	n	s	a	r	o	Y	a	v	b
T	o	i	T	t	z	o	P	a	c	o	C
S	i	g	a	s	o	m	r	b	z	n	h
f	m	o	n	d	a	T	d	i	a	r	i
o	r	o	i	b	A	h	a	o	z	p	i
t	N	a	b	r	V	i	x	g	a	s	d
O	i	i	i	t	T	p	a	l	O	a	i
A	b	a	m	o	o	o	a	C	u	c	a
N	a	o	c	O	Tt	tT	n	p	r	n	T
o	c	a	n	m	a	g	o	t	r	o	i
S	h	i	a	l	r	a	p	m	z	o	x

Figure 3. The name of King Bataivah shaded on the Tablet of the East

Bataivah shaded in dark gray. The spiral starts on the left-hand letter B and proceeds clockwise to spell the name.

The names of the Seniors are extracted from the cross that unites the four sub-quadrants together. The names are all read out from the center, overlapping at the two squares in the very center of the quadrant (in this case the A and H that form the last two letters of

r	Z	i	l	a	f	A	y	t	l	p	a
a	r	d	Z	a	i	d	p	a	L	a	m
c	z	o	n	s	a	r	o	Y	a	v	b
T	o	i	T	t	z	o	P	a	c	o	C
S	i	g	a	s	o	m	r	b	z	n	h
f	m	o	n	d	a	T	d	i	a	r	i
o	r	o	i	b	A	h	a	o	z	p	i
t	N	a	b	r	V	i	x	g	a	s	d
O	i	i	i	t	T	p	a	l	O	a	i
A	b	a	m	o	o	o	a	C	u	c	a
N	a	o	c	O	Tt	tT	n	p	r	n	T
o	c	a	n	m	a	g	o	t	r	o	i
S	h	i	a	l	r	a	p	m	z	o	x

Figure 4. The name of the six Seniors shaded on the Tablet of the East

Bataivah). The names of the six Senoirs of the East are thus Habioro (read from right to left), Aaozaif (read from bottom to top), Htmorda (read from bottom to top), Ahaozpi (read from left to right), Hipotga (read from top to bottom), and Avtotar (read from top to bottom).

Each sub-quadrant is divided by two controlling names that appear in the shape of a cross. The four letters that appear above the horizontal arms of this cross represent a class of four angels that the Golden Dawn system refers to as the Kerubic Angels. The sixteen letters that appear below the horizontal arms form the names of a class of four angels that that Golden Dawn system refers to as the Lesser Angels. Combined with letters from the Black Cross they also form the names of a class of eight demons that Dee called the Cacodemons. In general, the powers of the Cacodemons correspond to those of the

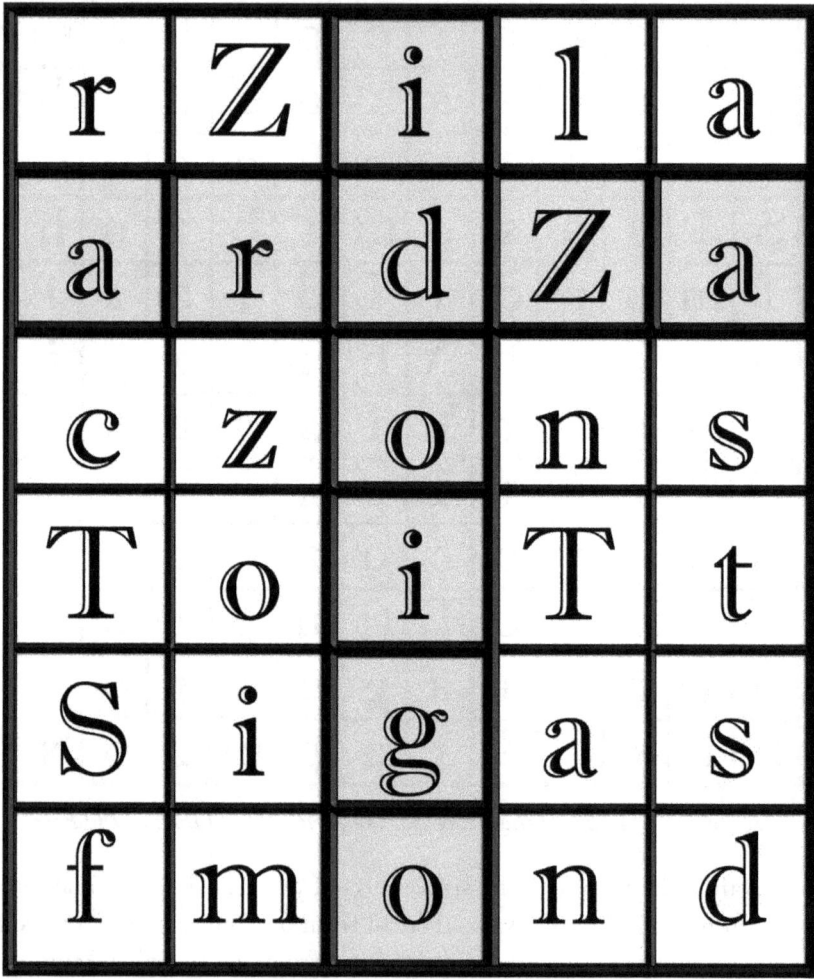

Figure 5. The controlling cross, showing squares above and below the horizontal arm.

Lesser Angels but in negative or destructive terms. For example, the Cacodemons corresponding to the Lesser Angels of Medicine are conjured in order to cause diseases.

In addition to the elemental attributions of the four quadrants, the spirits of the sub-quadrants also have sub-elemental attributions. In the Dee system these are figured quite differently than in the Golden Dawn system. Reading the names below the horizontal arms of the cross from top to bottom for each sub-quadrant, the first row is attributed to Air, the second row to Water, the third row to Earth, and the fourth row to Fire. These attributions come directly from Dee's diaries. Therefore, the individual Lesser Angels and Cacodemons have elemental attributions above and beyond those of the quadrant in which their names appear.

Applying this schema to the figure above, the Lesser Angels of the sub-quadrant shown would be attributed thus. The letters of the shaded cross are not included in these names.

Air — CZNS (third row from top)
Water — TOTT (fourth row from top)
Earth — SIAS (fifth row from top)
Fire — FMND (bottom row)

These attributions have many practical applications – for example, if you wanted to cast a healing spell for mental illness, you might want to summon only those Angels of Medicine corresponding to Air (mental activity), Water (emotional activity), or perhaps both depending upon the nature of the illness. The many combinations of the Qabalistic worlds with these sub-elements are numerous and quite effective when employed to their full potential. It should be noted that it is not clear from the Dee diaries that the same sub-elemental relationship holds for the Kerubic Angels, but it is logical to think that it might. Those angels are also conjured in groups of four in a particular order, so if the arrangement holds the elemental attributions for the Kerubic angels of this sub-quadrant would be as shown here.

Air — RZLA
Water — ZLAR
Earth — LARZ
Fire — ARZL

The four Kerubic names are permutations of the four letters in the top row. As with the Lesser Angel names, the letter of the shaded cross is excluded.

Even though the terms "Kerubic" and "Lesser" imply some sort of hierarchical arrangement, it is not clear from the Dee diaries that a distinction is made within the Enochian spiritual hierarchy between these two classes of angels. Both have four-letter names, implying that they exhibit approximately the same degree of intelligence and coherence. The Cacodemons, on the other hand, have three-letter names, meaning that they are less complex beings with less innate intelligence. I have found this to be the case when working with them; while the more coherent angels are better at discerning the intent of a particular charge and more adept at navigating obstacles to the manifestation of a spell, the Cacodemons are fairly stupid. For the right sort of operations they can bring a great deal of power to bear, but they also are extremely literal-minded and have only a limited ability to navigate changing circumstances. For this reason, I generally recommend becoming familiar with the various classes of angels and how they work before moving on to conjuring the Cacodemons.

Very few authors work with the Cacodemons. This is in part because Dee left no conjurations for them, in part because the Golden Dawn magicians and Aleister Crowley ignored them, and in part because they represent the most negative, destructive aspect of a system that already has a reputation for being both powerful and dangerous. My suspicion is that Mathers and Wescott of the Golden Dawn, just like John Dee himself, most likely avoided the Cacodemons on the grounds of trying to distance themselves from anything resembling "black magick." Crowley was more adventurous in his magical practice, but as he received his training directly from Mathers he was likely taught little about this particular class of spirits. They merit only a brief mention in Crowley's Liber Chanokh and the full method for constructing their names is not even included in the text. I have personally found that while the Cacodemons are only suited for particular sorts of operations, working with them is no more dangerous than working with any other of the Enochian spirits.

Over the years various superstitions have circulated in the magical community regarding working with the Great Table and Enochian magick in general. Many of these are tales that I refer to as "Enochian Meltdown" stories. Supposedly working with Enochian magick is particularly dangerous to one's psyche, such that a higher percentage of people working Enochian magick encounter mental health issues than do individuals working with other systems of magick. I have posted on this subject several times now in various blog posts asking anyone who knew of a verifiable case in which this occurred to come forward and the response was underwhelming to say the least. It should be kept in mind that according to statistics compiled by psychology researchers nearly one person in four will encounter mental health issues and that about one person in twenty (~4.7%) will be diagnosed with either schizophrenia or bipolar disorder, considered the two most serious mental illnesses, at some point in their lives. With those numbers I expected my readers to produce a handful of stories that I could then compare to the overall incidence of mental illness in the population. However, only one case was ever brought to my attention and the person who reported it acknowledged that the individual in question was mentally ill before becoming involved with magick. This suggests that these stories are little more than urban myths, and that most people who work with the system never encounter anything of the sort.

A more bizarre idea along these same lines but on a global scale is the "Enochian Apocalypse" hypothesis put forth by Donald Tyson in the previously mentioned Tetragrammaton and Enochian Magic for Beginners. To some extent this idea originated with the Aurum Solis, whose Enochian system equates the four Great Table Kings with the Four Horsemen of the Apocalypse. However, Tyson elaborates on the idea much further, going so far as to state in Tetragrammaton that if any Enochian magician ever worked through all the Angelic Keys and conjurations it would set in motion the actual physical end of the world and that Aleister Crowley's working through the 30 Aethyrs as he describes in The Vision and the Voice may have caused the two great world wars of the twentieth century. Presumably Tyson received a lot of correspondence from magicians who pointed out that they had in fact gone through all the Keys and conjurations and the world still existed, because in Enochian Magic for Beginners he revised his hypothesis as relating to some mysterious "Apocalypse Working" that would include the Angelic Keys and conjurations along with certain other components that he does not describe. These omissions are highly convenient for Tyson, since it makes his claims impossible to falsify by any practical means.

The short take-away from this is that you will not destroy the world by working Enochian magick. The fact that Tyson's published speculations make such a disclaimer necessary is completely ridiculous. The dropping of two atomic bombs in 1945 did not destroy the world, and you certainly are not going to be able to do so by casting the wrong spell or conjuring the wrong class of spirits. The entire concept of a physical Apocalypse is questionable to begin with, as it depends upon a literal reading of the Book of Revelation as precise prophecy rather than history or literature. The text of the Revelation may be read in numerous ways, and while apocalyptic allusions can be found in the Angelic Keys, at no point do the angels ever explain to Dee and Kelley that Enochian magick would end the world. The angels do talk of a new golden age to come, which many Thelemites believe is a reference to the Aeon of Horus that arrived in 1904 with the reception of The Book of the Law, but this is a far cry from any sort of global cataclysm. Based on the quality of works such as his edition of Agrippa's Three Books of Occult Philosophy, Tyson should be a good enough researcher to realize this. All I can assume is that his claims are an attempt to cash in on the "scary" reputation that the Enochian system has among some magical practitioners. His most recent works have been on H.P. Lovecraft's Necronomicon and demonology, and those certainly sound sensationalistic to me.

These spirits have many powers and attributions not found among the Heptarchial Kings and Princes, and since there is little overlap between the two groups, familiarity with the Great Table will augment your magical arsenal substantially. In fact, between the Great Table and Mystical Heptarchy you will find the necessary spirits to accomplish just about any sort of magical operation that you desire. In addition, the elemental attributions of the Great Table allow for a high degree of precision in terms of setting those operations in motion.

Chapter 3
The Temple Arrangement

There is a current school of thought among some modern Enochian magicians that the detailed descriptions of apparel and temple furniture found in John Dee's Five Books of Mystical Exercises apply only to the rituals found in the Heptarchia Mystica. I disagree with this position for several reasons. First of all, Dee and Kelly continued to use the Holy Table and related equipment throughout their operations, not just during those that produced the Heptarchia Mystica. Second of all, the systems have many characteristics in common, notably the Angelic alphabet, which predates vast majority of the operations and is found on both the lamen and the Holy Table. Finally, and probably most importantly, using the temple furniture detailed in Mastering the Mystical Heptarchy for Great Table operations makes them a whole lot more effective in pure probability shift terms. The various pieces of apparel and temple furniture are described in greater detail in my first book, but for completeness this chapter will begin with a quick overview of how an Enochian temple should be set up and constructed.

The Enochian Ring:

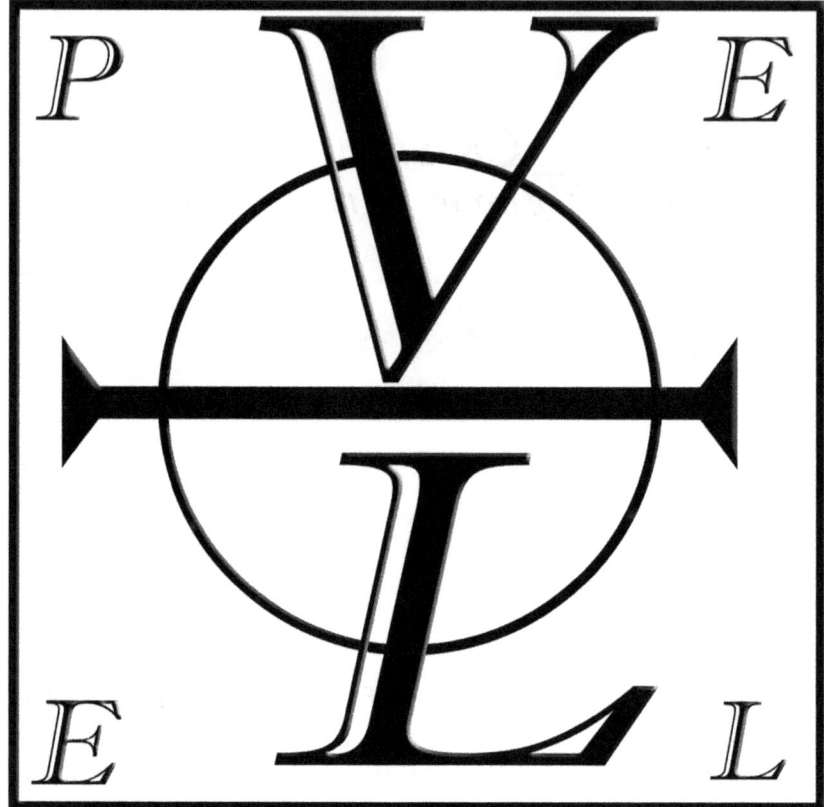

Figure 6. Face of the Enochian Ring

For the proper working of Enochian magick, the Magician must wear a ring made from pure gold inscribed with the specific arrangement of shapes and letters shown here.

The Angels told Dee and Kelly that without it they would "accomplish nothing." Therefore, some sort of ring bearing this design should be worn during all Enochian operations, even if it must be constructed from a less expensive material than gold. I have gotten good results with brass.

The Lamen:

Like the ring, the lamen should also be worn when performing Enochian rituals. It is made up of a grid of Angelic characters arranged as shown.

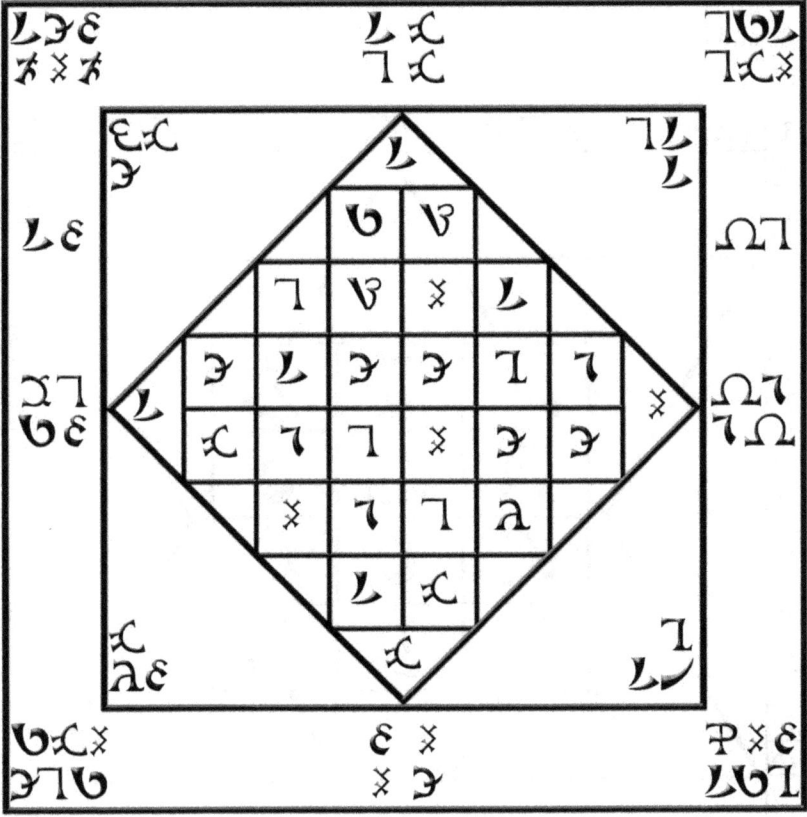

Figure 7. Enochian Lamen

The lamen was supposed to be drawn on parchment, which in those days referred to paper made from animal hide. The lamen I currently use is a brass plate with the Angelic characters engraved on one side, and is worn around the neck on a cord or chain such that it covers the anahata chakra or heart center.

The Robe:

According to the spirit diaries, the robe worn when working with the Enochian system should be white, unadorned, and, if possible, made from linen. I use a simple white linen tau-shaped robe, which conforms exactly to the text, but was expensive to make and is rather scratchy. I have also used robes made from other natural fibers such as cotton, which are easy to procure and less expensive, with good results.

The Holy Table:

Figure 8. Holy Table

The Holy Table is the centerpiece of an Enochian temple. The Angels specified that it should be approximately three feet square with legs of the same height, and made from "sweet wood." One writer, Geoffrey James, has suggested cedar,[1] which was sometimes referred to as "sweet" during the period in question. On the top of the Table is painted a set of lineal figures and Angelic characters in yellow.

---

1. Geoffrey James, *Enochian Evocation* (Berkeley Heights, NJ: Heptangle, 1984), 181.

A good inexpensive way to build a Holy Table is to pick up a 3 foot square card table. They are still often built to the exact dimensions recommended to Dee and Kelley, three feet square with four three-foot legs. Finding one with a wooden surface is ideal, but if that proves too difficult or costly you can go ahead and draw the appropriate figures onto the top with acrylic paint or even permanent marker. This may not work quite as effectively as a Table corresponding to the original specifications, but it should be sufficient.

The Sigillum Dei Aemeth:

The Sigillum Dei Aemeth ("True Seal of God") is a pantacle, or disk, that is placed in the center of the Holy Table. It should be nine inches in diameter and made from pure wax, though

Figure 9. Top of the Sigillum Dei Aemeth. The asterisk below the Y/14 square near the bottom of the diagram indicates that some experts believe the number in the square should be 15 rather than 14.

paraffin is an acceptable modern substitute. The top bears the design below, which may be easier to cast in some fashion than manually engrave into the wax due to its complexity.

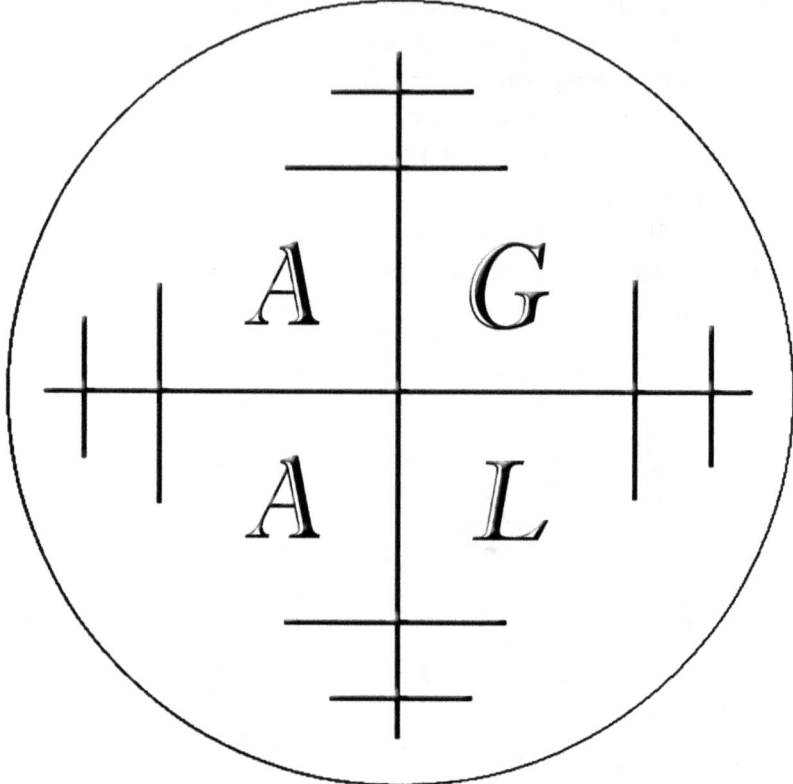

Figure 10. Bottom of Sigullum Dei Aemeth.

The bottom, on the other hand, bears the design shown in the next figure, which is much simpler and not at all difficult to engrave by hand.

In addition to the primary Sigillum that occupies the center of the Holy Table, smaller copies of it, four and a half inches in diameter, should be placed under each of the Table's four legs. As my Table lacks permanent legs I omit this portion of the temple setup, but my suspicion is that if your construction skills are superior to mine you will find that having them adds to the effectiveness of the overall setup.

The Ensigns of Creation:

The Ensigns of Creation are seven talismans that are placed on the Holy Table surrounding the Sigillum Dei Aemeth. They were originally supposed to be made from purified tin, but later Dee and Kelly were told to paint them onto the table itself using blue for the lines and red for the characters and letters. The seven Ensigns should be arranged or drawn evenly around the Sigillum as shown here.

Figure 11. Holy Table with Positions of Sigillum Dei Aemeth and Ensigns

The Ensigns are drawn or engraved as shown on the next page, and are attributed to the seven ancient planets.

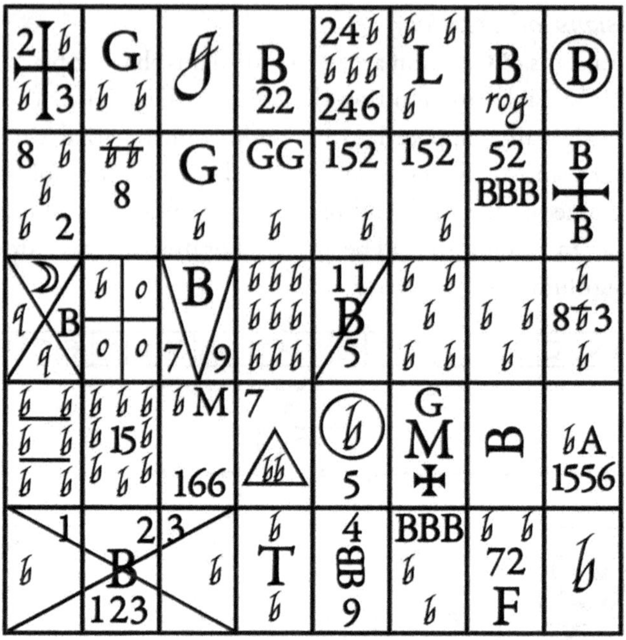

Figure 12. Ensign of Venus

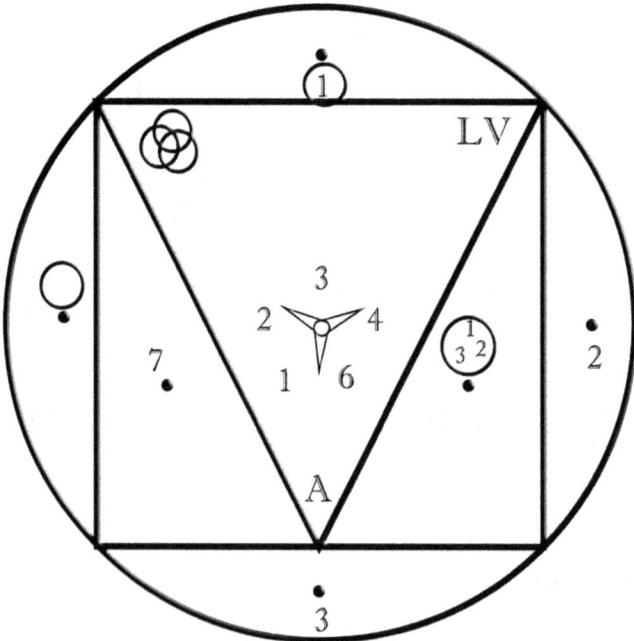

Figure 13. Ensign of the Sun

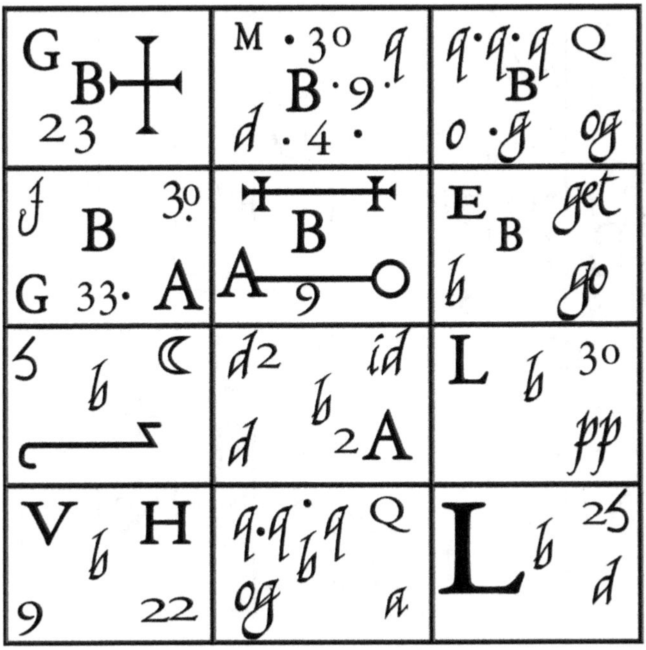

Figure 14. Ensign of Mars

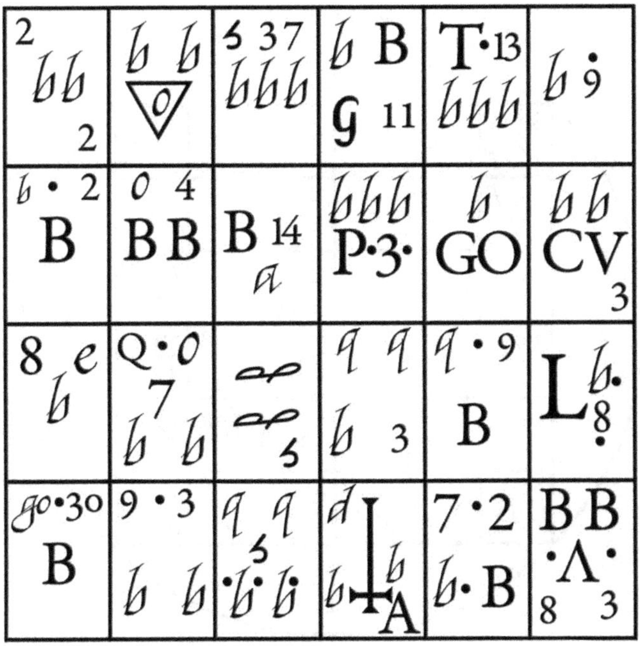

Figure 15. Ensign of Jupiter

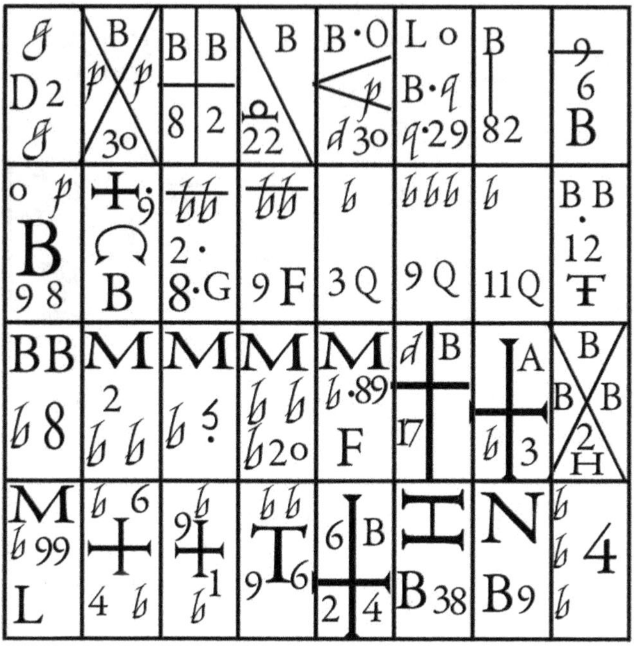

Figure 16. Ensign of Mercury

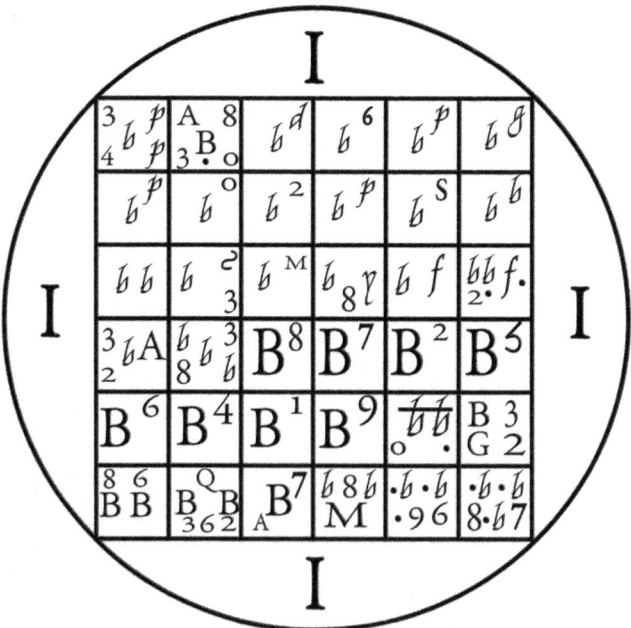

Figure 17. Ensign of Saturn

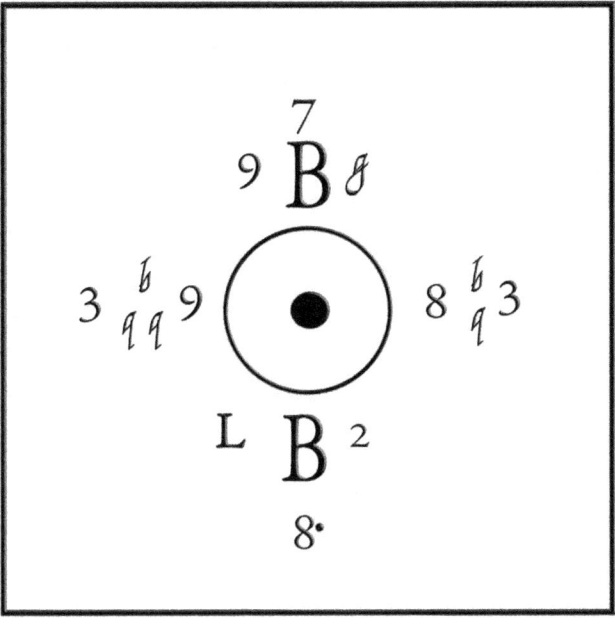

Figure 18. Ensign of the Moon

The Shewstone:

Dee and Kelley used a Shewstone, or scrying crystal much like the fairy-tale "crystal ball," to communicate with the Enochian angels. The stone should be placed in the center of the Holy Table, on top of the Sigillum Dei Aemeth and above the cloth so that it can be seen.

The Cloth:

The Sigillum, Ensigns, and Holy Table should be covered with a cloth of either red silk or "changeable red and green silk," presumably some sort of double-weave. Dee recommends both in different places in the diaries and as far as I can tell either will work. Silk, which Dee was directed to use, is best but natural fibers of whatever sort such as cotton will also work.

The Carpet:

The floor under the Holy Table should likewise be covered with a red carpet also made from silk. It is possible to find oriental-style rugs made from red silk, and though they are expensive they are just about the best solution to the problem. You can also use something like a sheet of red fabric or a red blanket, but make sure that you can walk comfortably around the Holy Table without disturbing the carpet too much or tripping over it.

The Book:

Dee was told to make a book containing all of the prayers, invocations, and conjurations that he and Kelley received so that he could read the various texts in ritual. In this, at least, your task is already done, at least for those involving the spirits of the Great Table — you are holding that book in your hands right now. The ritual template in the next chapter contains all of the necessary page references to flip back and forth between the appropriate texts for any sort of operation supported in the system.

The Banners:

The main addition to the Enochian temple for Great Table workings is that twelve fabric banners should be hung around the perimeter of the working space, forming a magical circle. The cloth of the banners should be silk, colored according to the four directions as seen in what is generally called the "golden talisman" vision because a golden talisman depicting the various elements of the Castles or Watchtowers seen in the vision is part of the Dee collection at the British Museum.

> East — Red ("Fresh Red Cullor")
> South — White ("Lilly White")
> West — Green ("Dark greene Cullor like garlicke blades")
> North — Black ("Blacke as of bilbery Juyce")

Each of these banners bears one of the twelve names of God formed by reading across the central row of each Great Table quadrant, drawn in the Angelic script. These should be written from left to right, just as the names appear on the Table itself. Many years ago it was contended by some authors that Angelic should be written right to left as is Hebrew, but there is no support for this idea in the Dee diaries except for the vague statement that Angelic was spoken in the Garden of Eden and after the expulsion of Adam and Eve they then began to speak Hebrew. In fact, the structure of the Angelic language has more in common with English and German, European languages that Dee spoke, than it does with Hebrew or any other Semitic tongue.

The color for the wording on the banners is not specified, but I have found the Golden Dawn "flashing color" method to be particularly effective in their construction. This consists of cutting the letters of the name from cloth that is of the background's complementary color and then sewing them onto the background. As red and green are complements, as are black and white, this method still only requires four colors of silk cloth, and if you are careful you can fashion the letters for the red banner our of leftover cloth from the green banner and so forth. With the sheen of the silk placing complementary colors next to each other produces a strong "flashing" effect, in which the letters of the banners seem to vibrate simply by virtue of their hue and placement.

Dee's diagram of the banners shows them hung like flags, but I have found that they work better hung vertically from dowels that are suspended on poles as shown here. This displays the cloths and lettering better and gives a real physical impression of being surrounded by a magical circle when you stand at the Holy Table in the center of your working space.

According to the Solomonic grimoire tradition, the most common diameter for a magical circle is nine feet. With a three-foot-square Holy Table, however,

Figure 19. Banner for ORO Displayed Vertically

this winds up being a bit cramped, especially if you are working with a group. As a Thelemite, I prefer an eleven-foot circle, as according to Aleister Crowley eleven is the number of magick. This allows more room for circumambulation while reciting the Angelic Keys and Great Table conjurations, particularly when passing the corners of the Holy Table. If your working space does not permit a full circle setup, the banners can also be hung on the four walls of your temple, with three to each of the four directions. The red banners should be hung on the east wall, the white banners on the south wall, and so forth.

While the colors on the banners are relatively easy to find in Dee's diaries, which name goes on which banner depends upon the version of the Great Table you decide to use. From the diaries it would appear that the upper left quadrant represents the east, the upper right the south, the lower right the west, and the lower left the north. Dee's conjurations in the British Museum collection were written prior to the reception of the Tabula Recensa and associate the directions with those particular quadrants based on the arrangement of the original Great Table. In 2010, Golden Hoard Press published The Practical Angel Magic of Dr. John Dee's Enochian Tables which seems to show a different arrangement, in which the lower left quadrant seems to correspond to south and the upper left quadrant seems to correspond to north.

The main problem I have with the Golden Hoard book is that while it claims to represent John Dee's lost book of Angelic conjurations written in Latin, reading through the text of those conjurations and comparing them to those found in the British Museum's Sloane collection rendered me somewhat dubious of that assertion. My reasoning is simple – the conjurations from Sloane show that Dee was an incredibly pious man, always inserting caveats and statements to the effect that he was a mere human being deigning to approach the divine in as respectful and to some extent as subservient a tone as he could manage. When I first started working with the Enochian system from a Solomonic perspective I reworked the

Great Table conjurations into what you will find in this book, removing most of those repetitive and redundant statements. I was surprised to find that the conjurations in the Golden Hoard book were remarkably similar to my own, with all the same statements taken out.

What this means is that at some point, probably in the seventeenth century, someone went through Dee's conjurations, made most of the same edits that I did, and assembled them into a working book of invocations. This person was almost certainly not John Dee, whose personal piety would most likely have lead him to consider the way in which both my conjurations and those found in the Golden Hoard book issue straightforward instructions to the angels to be presumptuous. After Dee, the next individual who we know worked with the Enochian material was Elias Ashmole, who in my opinion would have been much more willing to rework the conjurations along such lines than Dee ever would have been.

The other problem with relying on the Golden Hoard arrangement is that, in effect, when you lay out the Great Table along those lines you essentially get the Tyson arrangement, with MOR, DIAL, and HCTGA in the south and MPH, ARSL, and GAIOL in the north. As I mentioned in the previous chapter, in probability testing I found this arrangement to work surprisingly poorly. So even if the Golden Hoard texts really were written by Dee, it would seem that his understanding of the system was flawed when he put them together. Most scholars are of the opinion that Dee never made any practical use of the Great Table conjurations; he split with Kelley in 1588 and after that point no diaries indicating such thaumaturgic operations have survived – if they ever existed at all.

Circumambulations and Talismans:

Another difference between Heptarchial and Great Table operations is that with the Kings and Princes of the Heptarchia Mystica, the actual conjuration work is all done standing west of the Holy Table facing east. When working with the Great

Table, the angels are generally summoned in four groups, one from each direction. Dee's conjurations seem to include the assumption that rather than summoning individual angels, the magician instead should conjure all of the Angels of a particular class in order to accomplish a magical goal within their sphere of influence. So, for example, each quadrant of the Great Table has four Angels of medicine allocated to it, and in order to cast a healing spell you conjure all sixteen of them and then deliver your charge.

The most effective position in which to conjure one of these groups is to stand across the Holy Table from and facing the direction to which the group is attributed. So to conjure the Angels of medicine of the east you stand west of the Holy Table and face east, to conjure those of the south you stand north of the Holy Table and face south, and so forth. This sets up a line of magical attention that crosses the center of the Sigillum Dei Aemeth and then reaches out to the angels being summoned. By moving in a clockwise direction as you conjure each group, a magical vortex is set up in the center of the Sigillum that serves as a manifestation point for the angels.

This method of working requires some preparation as far as Great Table talismans go. Dee was told that all of the Angels of the Enochian system have corresponding talismans, and the instructions given regarding Heptarchial talismans were never rescinded or revised for the Great Table angels. As such, you should stand upon the appropriate talisman when reciting a particular conjuration, and since in a standard Great Table operation you need to summon angels from all four directions, you will need to have four talismans for each operation and they will need to be laid out on the floor of your temple such that you can step onto each of them in turn as you go around your Holy Table. This is another reason for an eleven-foot circle – if you plan on using opening and closing ritual forms, you will want room to move around your temple space performing them without stepping on any of your talismans until the proper time.

The Great Table:

Most Enochian magicians also outfit their temples with renderings of the Great Table itself. According to the Golden Dawn tradition, a tablet should be constructed for each of the quadrants and another bearing the four names that appear on the black cross. This fifth table is called the Tablet of Union, and according to the Golden Dawn system it represents the element of Akasha or Spirit, while the four quadrants represent the classical elements of Air, Fire, Earth, and Water. While even in Dee's arrangement these attributions are not entirely inaccurate, it is clear from his diaries that it is the directional attribution which is primary rather than the element.

As seen in the Lesser Rituals of the Pentagram and Hexagram, the Golden Dawn system uses two elemental arrangements. The first is called the "winds" order and corresponds to the elemental attributions of the archangels in the Lesser Ritual of the Pentagram.

>Raphael — Air — East
>Michael — Fire — South
>Gabriel — Water — West
>Auriel/Uriel — Earth — North

The other arrangement is based on the cardinal signs of the tropical zodiac, and is used in the Lesser Ritual of the Hexagram.

>Fire — East — Aries
>Earth — South — Capricorn
>Air — West — Libra
>Water — North — Cancer

From the rituals in which these elemental directions are used, it should be clear that the former represents the microcosmic elements while the latter represents the macrocosmic elements. This is all fine and good, and I use these same attributions in my own magical work. However, I part company with most Golden Dawn Enochian magicians when they assign the quadrants of the Great Table by element rather than direction.

In the Dee diaries and conjurations, the direction associated with each King never changes.

For example, the angel Bataivah is King of the East in every arrangement of the Great Table. In the Golden Dawn system, his attribution is Air because East = Air in the winds model. However, when switching from the winds model to the zodiacal model for a macrocosmic working, Bataivah's tablet (upper left) is taken from the east and placed in the west, because West = Air in the zodiacal model. But this is clearly wrong according to the original system; Bataivah should remain the King of the East regardless of the elemental model employed because his primary attribution is East rather than Air. So, in fact, if a Golden Dawn Enochian magician were really keeping this in mind, he or she would realize that the proper way to represent the shift from microcosm to macrocosm would be to switch Bataivah's attribution from Air to Fire and keep the Tablet of the East in the same place.

I will stress once more, as in my first book, that you do not need a full Enochian temple setup to get good magical results from these operations. I have heard of practitioners who apparently feel that they should not start doing any magical work until their temples are complete and incorporate all of the specified materials, an undertaking which takes a lot of time and involves significant expense. The lack of a temple full of equipment is a very poor reason to put off one's magical practice, and can even be invoked as a stalling tactic to avoid the work than any sort of technical concern. After twenty years of practicing the Enochian system my temple is still not complete by purist standards – the ring that I use is brass rather than gold, my Ensigns of Creation are made from tagboard, and my Holy Table lacks the four smaller Sigillums on which its legs are supposed to rest because it is a wooden tabletop that I usually set on top of a double-cube altar. Still, I have no trouble getting solid magical results.

I should also point out that most people trained in the Golden Dawn tradition do not generally use Holy Tables, Enochian rings, Enochian lamens, or anything similar. They usually have a set of tablets depicting the four quadrants of the Great Table and another depicting the Tablet of Union arrangement of the names from the Black Cross, but otherwise use standard double-cube altars and so forth for their operations – and the vast majority of them claim to get solid results with their methods. As far as I know, Aleister Crowley did not use any of the specified Enochian temple equipment and still managed to produce the best set of Enochian communications since Dee and Kelley's time, The Vision and the Voice. My advice to anyone interested in the Enochian system is always the same – get the equipment that you can easily obtain, make substitutions where necessary, and start in on the work as soon as possible.

Chapter 4
Great Table Ritual Template

As in Mastering the Mystical Heptarchy, this chapter breaks down the essential ritual structure for Great Table operations into its basic components. The template presented here is labeled in the same manner and includes some of the same elements, with steps derived from modern magical practices marked as optional so that they may be skipped by traditional Solomonic grimoire practitioners. The modern practices shown here are adapted from my own practice, and I have found them to be highly effective when performed in the manner shown.

II Great Table Ritual Template

0. Preparation

Set up the Enochian temple to the best of your ability as described in Chapter 3. Wear the Enochian ring, robe, and lamen. Stand to the west of the Holy Table facing east.

1A. Opening the Temple - Ceremonial (Optional)

A. Perform the Banishing AOEVEAE Pentagram Ritual (Appendix A page 220). Alternatively, you may open the temple with the Golden Dawn Lesser Banishing Ritual of the Pentagram page 211 or Aleister Crowley's Star Ruby.

B. If you intend your ritual to have a macrocosmic effect that extends beyond the psychological realm, perform the Invoking MADRIAX Hexagram Ritual (Appendix A page 224). Alternatively, if you opened with the LBRP you should perform the Lesser Invoking Ritual of the Hexagram (Appendix A page 215), or if you opened with the Star Ruby you should perform the Star Sapphire. The combination of a banishing pentagram ritual and an invoking hexagram ritual forms an operant field, as briefly explained above.

1B. Opening the Temple - Devotional

Perform the Prayer of Enoch (page 62-64). This prayer may be performed on its own to open the temple, or it may follow the ceremonial opening performed as step 1A.

2. The Preliminary Invocation

A. Perform the NAZ OLPIRT energy work exercise (Optional) (Appendix A page 230).

B. Perform the Original (page 72-73) or revised Fundamental Obeisance (page 73-74).

3. The Opening Keys

A. For an evocation, intone the First Key in Angelic followed by English (page 87-88).

B. For an invocation, intone the Second Key in Angelic followed by English (page 89).

C. For a ritual including both evocatory and invocatory elements, perform the First Key (page 87-88) followed by the Second Key (page 89). If you are working with another individual like Dee and Kelley did, with one person acting as magician and the other as scryer, the magician should read the First Key followed by the scryer reading the Second Key.

4. Tuning the Space

A. Your ritual may be scheduled so that it is being performed on the appropriate day, planetary hour, or phase of the Moon as explained in Chapter 9. This step is drawn from traditional grimoire practice, but it is nonetheless not required according to the original text as no timing methods for Great Table operations are described in Dee's diaries (Optional).

B. Perform the Greater Ritual of the Pentagram corresponding to the element appropriate to your operation or with all four elemental pentagrams drawn to the alchemical directions (East = Fire, South = Air, West = Water, North = Earth). For a ritual encompassing all four elements you may instead use the Revised Opening by Watchtower (page 126-132) (Optional).

Spirits	Angelic Keys
Angels of Natural Substances Angels of Medicine Cacodemons of Medicine	Third, Fourth, Fifth, Sixth
Angels of Transportation Angels of Gold and Precious Stones Cacodemons of Gold and Precious Stones	Seventh, Eighth, Ninth, Tenth
Angels of the Mechanical Arts Angels of Transformation Cacodemons of Transformation	Eleventh, Twelfth, Thirteenth, Fourteenth
Angels of Secret Discovery Angels of Living Creatures Cacodemons of Living Creatures	Fifteenth, Sixteenth, Seventeenth, Eighteenth

5. The Watchtower Keys

For rituals conjuring the Kings and Seniors, no additional Keys must be recited besides the First and/or Second. For the rest of the Great Table spirits, use the table above

The listed Keys should be recited to the four directions respectively following the order shown above, starting at the west of the Holy Table facing east and then moving clockwise to each direction in turn.

6. The Conjurations

A. Move around the Holy Table clockwise, placing the appropriate talismans on the floor to the four directions starting with the talisman for the spirits of the east to the west of the altar. Each talisman should be placed opposite the Holy Table from the direction appropriate to the corresponding spirits, as the magician must stand upon them and conjure across the Table.

Spirits	Conjurations	Talismans
Kings	Page 174	Page 145-147
Seniors	Page 175	Page 145-147
Angels of Natural Substances	Page 178	Page 147-149
Angels of Medicine	Page 184	Page 155-157
Cacodemons of Medicine	Page 193	Page 163-165
Angels of Transportation	Page 179	Page 149-151
Angels of Gold & Precious Stones	Page 185	Page 157-159
Cacodemons of Gold & Precious Stones	Page 194	Page 165-167
Angels of the Mechanical Arts	Page 180	Page 151-153
Angels of Transformation	Page 186	Page 159-161
Cacodemons of Transformation	Page 196	Page 167-169
Angels of Secret Discovery	Page 181	Page 153-155
Angels of Living Creatures	Page 188	Page 161-163
Cacodemons of Living Creatures	Page 197	Page 169-171

B. Move around the Holy Table clockwise once more, standing on each of the talismans in turn and reciting the corresponding conjuration to the spirits of each direction. Use the above table to locate the appropriate talisman and conjuration.

Once you arrive back at the west of the altar facing east, you need no longer stand upon the talisman as this is only necessary while reciting the conjurations.

7. *The Charge to the Spirit*

Deliver the Charge to the spirit or spirits that you have personally composed according the instructions given in Chapter 16.

8. *Closing the Temple*

A. Perform the License to Depart (page 205-206).

B. For rituals opened using the ceremonial method, conclude the MADRIAX (page 224) and AOEVEAE (page 220). Alternatively, if the ritual was opened with the Golden Dawn Lesser Rituals of the Pentagram and Hexagram, perform the Lesser Banishing Ritual of the Pentagram for a ritual that has only an external target or the Qabalistic Cross by itself for a ritual that is intended to affect the magician exclusively or both the magician and an external target. For the Star Ruby/Star Sapphire the same rules apply – close with either the Star Ruby or that ritual's form of the Qabalistic Cross depending upon the ritual's target.

C. Declare the temple closed. The ritual is now complete.

Chapter 5
Opening The Temple

As shown in the ritual template the temple may be opened for Great Table workings using devotional prayers, ceremonial forms, or both. Personally I prefer to use both and find my Enochian rituals to be at their most potent when incorporating the modern methods outlined in the ritual template, but I will add that the prayers are quite effective on their own for those practitioners who prefer to work with the original material on its own terms.

The Prayer of Enoch

This prayer was given to Dee and Kelley by the angel Ave on July 7th of 1584 in Krakow.[2] It is the essential initial devotional prayer used to open the Enochian temple.

Lord God the Fountain of true wisdom, thou that openest the secrets thy own self unto man, thou knowest mine imperfection and my inward darknesse:

How can I (therefore) speak unto them that speak not after the voice of man; or worthily call on thy name, considering that my imagination is variable and fruitlesse, and unknown to myself?

Shall the Sands seem to invite the Mountains: or can the small Rivers entertain the wonderful and unknown waves?

Can the vessel of fear, fragility, or that is of a determined proportion, lift up himself, heave up his hands, or gather the Sun into his bosom?

Lord it cannot be: Lord my imperfection is great: Lord I am lesse than sand: Lord, thy good Angels and Creatures excell me far: our proportion is not alike; our sense agreeth not:

Notwithstanding I am comforted; For that we have all one God, all one beginning from thee, that we respect thee a Creatour:

Therefore will I call upon thy name, and in thee, I will become mighty. Thou shalt light me, and I will become a Seer; I will see thy Creatures, and will magnifie thee amongst them.

---

2. Meric Casaubon, *True and Faithful Relation* (New York, NY: Magickal Childe, 1992), 196-197

*T*hose that come unto thee have the same gate, and through the same gate, descend, such as thou sendest. Behold, I offer my house, my labour, my heart and soul,

If it will please thy Angels to dwell with me, and I with them; To rejoyce with me, that I may rejoyce with them; To minister unto me, that I may magnifie thy name.

Then, lo the Tables (which I have provided, and according to thy will, prepared) I offer unto thee, and unto thy holy Angels, desiring them, in and through thy holy names:

That as thou art their light, and comfortest them, so they, in thee will be my light and comfort.

*L*ord they prescribe not laws unto thee, so it is not meet that I prescribe laws unto them:

What it pleaseth thee to offer, they receive; So what it pleaseth them to offer unto me, will I also receive.

Behold I say (O Lord) If I shall call upon them in thy name, Be it unto me in mercy, as unto the servant of the Highest.

Let them also manifest unto me, How, by what words, and at what time, I shall call them.

O Lord, Is there any that measure the heavens, that is mortal? How, therefore, can the heavens enter into man's imagination?

Thy creatures are the Glory of thy countenance: Hereby thou glorifiest all things, which Glory excelleth and (O Lord) is far above my understanding.

*I*t is great wisdom, to speak and talke according to understanding with Kings:

But to command Kings by a subjected commandment, is not wisdom, unlesse it come from thee. Behold Lord, How shall I therefore ascend into the heavens?

The air will not carry me, but resisteth my folly, I fall down, for I am of the earth.

Therefore, O thou very Light and true Comfort, that canst, and mayst, and dost command the heavens:

Behold I offer these Tables unto thee, Command them as it pleaseth thee:

And O you Ministers, and true lights of understanding, Governing this earthly frame, and the elements wherein we live.

Do for me as for the servant of the Lord: and unto whom it hath pleased the Lord to talk of you.

Behold, Lord, thou hast appointed me 50 times; Thrice 50 times will I lift my hands unto thee.

Be it unto me as it pleaseth thee, and thy holy Ministers. I require nothing but thee, and through thee, and for thy honour and glory:

But I hope I shall be satisfied, and shall not die, (as thou hast promised) until thou gather the clouds together, and judge all things: when in a moment I shall be changed and dwell with thee for ever.

Amen.

Ceremonial Forms

For those who are unfamiliar with the first book in this series, a few notes regarding my use of the Golden Dawn pentagram and hexagram rituals are in order. The Lesser Ritual of the Pentagram and Lesser Ritual of the Hexagram are presented here according to my operant method, in which the LBRP is followed by the LIRH to open what I call an operant field. This is different than how these rituals are generally taught in the Golden Dawn tradition, where students are instructed to follow the LBRP with the LBRH, banishing at both the microcosmic and macrocosmic levels. I have found, however, that much more potent magical results can be achieved by banishing at the microcosmic level followed by invocation at the macrocosmic level, which blends the two realms together into a unified field.

This allows the combinations of banishing and invoking forms of the Lesser Rituals to be grouped according to the following general schema. I refer to these combinations as Fields of four basic types.

Banishing Field (LBRP/LBRH):

This field in effect constitutes the "full shutdown" - it clears mental and spiritual forms from both the interior and exterior worlds. In can be used to completely cleanse a temple, banish spirits permanently, or neutralize a magical effect that is targeting the magician. What it also does, though, is shut down any ongoing spells that you have running unless they are bound to some anchor other than your personal consciousness. If, for example, you are casting a spell that you want to work over the next week, do not end the ritual with this combination unless you are convinced that you made a mistake and want to stop the spell from going into effect.

Invoking Field (LIRP/LIRH):

This combination energizes all ongoing magical effects, and can be used to begin a ritual that you want to operate in both the interior and exterior worlds. A good example of this is a spell to get a better job. You want the spell to affect your psyche in such a way that you seem more confident and capable, but you also want it to shift probabilities in the material world so that the right opportunity will come your way.

Centering Field (LIRP/LBRH):

This combination sets up a field in which the interior world is engaged while influences from the exterior world are neutralized. This field is ideal for exclusively psychological magical work of all sorts.

Operant Field (LBRP/LIRH):

This field clears the interior world and then merges it with the exterior world, setting up a space in which thought more easily becomes material reality. All of the energy of a spell cast within this field is targeted on the macrocosm, and the resulting probability shifts show that magick done this way influences the outside world significantly better.

Of these four the operant field is the primary field that you should be using when working with practical Enochian magick, and as a result this is the field that is set up when you follow the instructions in the template. You should always banish before you invoke, and thus the centering and invoking fields should be preceded by an initial LBRP. This makes their use somewhat more cumbersome, since the resulting sequences are LBRP/LIRP/LIRH and LBRP/LIRB/LBRH.

My original Enochian opening rituals, the AOEVEAE and MADRIAX, are also structured in this manner, based on my findings regarding the standard pentagram and hexagram rituals. Aleister Crowley's Star Ruby and Star Sapphire may also be substituted for the Lesser Pentagram and Lesser Hexagram rituals respectively, keeping in mind that the invoking form of the Star Sapphire should follow the banishing form of the Star Ruby for the same reasons as described above. The ritual forms for the Lesser Ritual of the Pentagram, the Lesser Ritual of the Hexagram, the AOEVEAE, and the MADRIAX can be found in Appendix A.

In April of 2011, shortly after Mastering the Mystical Heptarchy was submitted to my publisher, Donald Michael Kraig, author of Modern Magick,[3] weighed in on his blog addressing my description of the operant field method.[4] Kraig's book is the source from which most beginning magicians learn the LBRP/LBRH combination, though this is also the way that the various Golden Dawn orders have been teaching these rituals since before his book was published and he is not the inventor of the method. Kraig disagreed with my assessment of how these ritual combinations work, and recommended instead that following the LBRP/LBRH the magician should invoke using the Opening by Watchtower, a ritual written by Israel Regardie based on the Golden Dawn temple openings originally published in his book, The Golden Dawn.

---

3. Meric Casaubon, *True and Faithful Relation* (New York, NY: Magickal Childe, 1992), 196-197

4. Kraig, *The Map is not the Territory* (retrieved 5-17-2012 from http://www.llewellyn.com/blog/2011/04/the-map-is-not-the-territory/).

I have included a revised version of the Opening by Watchtower developed by my magical working group for Enochian operations in Chapter 8, as it is particularly suited for elemental operations such as those pertaining to the Great Table. I still recommend opening the temple using the LBRP/LIRH combination even if you plan on using it, but you should also feel free to experiment with the various ceremonial forms and find the method that works best for you. Not all magicians respond to ritual forms the same way, and it may be that, as Kraig comments in his blog post, "your map is not my map." In the end, the final measure of a magical technique is how well it works for you in practical, measurable ways, not how well it conforms to established methods that have become enshrined over time as dogma.

Chapter 6
Preliminary Invocations

When using the NAZ OLPIRT energy work exercise (Appendix A) as part of your opening procedure, it should precede the Fundamental Obeisance. This is because, as seen in the AOEVEAE pentagram ritual, the names from the Black Cross or Tablet of Union should precede the twelve names of God that reside at the top of the Great Table's spiritual hierarchy. While the process of conjuring a spirit involves the descent of the spiritual presence or divine light, the goal of the preliminary invocation phase is to align the magician's consciousness with that of the transcendent Godhead. This alignment facilitates communication with, and authority over, the conjured spirits.

The NAZ OLPIRT ritual activates the microcosmic elements within the subtle body of the magician, serving the same function as chakra meditations in the Taoist and Yogic schools. This process energizes the central nervous system, and thus correlates directly with the physical energy involved in increasing the firing rate of neurons throughout the body. If magick is viewed as a form of communication, that is, sending forth a particular signal that summons the spirit to appear, then this sort of energy work is like turning up the power on your transmitter. You can transmit the same information without it, but with it the signal you send will be much stronger.

As the preliminary invocation phase of ceremonial ritual work includes theurgic aspects even when the ritual proper has thaumaturgic goals, it is vitally important to the spiritual development of the magician. In fact, my usual recommendation is that the ritual opening up to this point be adopted as a daily practice. Most magical orders teach variations on this method; for example, in most of the Golden Dawn orders with which I am familiar the "standard" daily practice is generally the Lesser Banishing Ritual of the Pentagram followed by the Middle Pillar Exercise, in which the godnames of the spheres on the middle pillar of the Tree of Life are vibrated at the appropriate points on the body along with accompanying visualizations. Some of these groups add the Lesser Banishing Ritual of the Hexagram between the Lesser Ritual of the Pentagram and the Middle Pillar Exercise. As I mentioned in the chapter on Opening the Temple, my methods are similar except that I generally replace the banishing form of the hexagram ritual with the invoking form for operant workings.

The advantage of adopting the opening and preliminary invocation phases of ritual work as a daily practice is twofold. First of all, doing so will increase your skill with the preliminary invocation itself and it is no exaggeration to state that assumption of the Godhead is the central, most foundational practice of ritual magick. The better you become at it, the better your rituals will work. Second of all, it allows you to approach more complex rituals in a modular fashion, as any ritual you perform will open with the same set of actions that you practice every day. This means that in order to memorize a new ritual you have a lot less to learn. While some portions of ceremonial rituals like the Angelic Keys and Great Table Conjurations are designed to be read, it is much more effective to have the openings, closings, and basic ritual structure memorized so that you do not have to manage a script along with your book of conjurations when performing an operation.

The Fundamental Obeisance

For Great Table operations a new preliminary invocation replaces the Oration to God that is used in Heptarchial workings. Dee called this new invocation the "Fundamental Obeisance." It calls upon the twelve names of God that rule over the four quadrants of the Great Table. According to the Tabula Recensa they are arranged thus:

> East — ORO IBAH AOZPI
> South — MPH ARSL GAIOL
> West — OIP TEAA PDOCE
> North — MOR DIAL HCTGA

In the Fundamental Obeisance, alignment with the Godhead is accomplished by means of these twelve particular names of power that represent divinity in portions of the universe represented by their positions on the Great Table. The AOEVEAE and MADRIAX rituals can be combined with the Fundamental Obeisance as a highly effective daily practice regimen, as the Fundamental Obeisance calls upon the twelve names of God to transform the practitioner into a powerful and effective Enochian magician. Presumably this is a goal that magicians who plan on taking up the Enochian work all share.

As I discussed in Chapter 2, the four quadrants of the Holy Table may be related to the four Qabalistic worlds. These worlds in turn can be related to points on the human body. When reciting the Fundamental Obeisance it is a useful practice to vibrate each name slowly and fully while directing your attention to the corresponding point. A full vibration should completely fill your sphere of consciousness at least momentarily. This vibration may be accompanied by the visualization of a bright sphere of appropriately colored light centered on the point. As the three names are vibrated, you imagine this sphere becoming brighter, larger, and more coherent. The following table shows these associations.

Names	World	Point	Color
ORO IBAH AOZPI	Atziluth	Center of Forehead	Red
MPH ARSL GAIOL	Briah	Throat	White
OIP TEAA PDOCE	Yetzirah	Heart Center	Green
MOR DIAL HCTGA	Assiah	Feet	Black

Your hands may be used to direct and concentrate this light by touching the first three points for the first three sets of names respectively, and then standing with your arms at your sides for the final set as you cannot reach your feet and keep your spine straight at the same time (as is advisable for this sort of energy work).

John Dee's Fundamental Obeisance reads as follows, with the twelve names of God shifted to match the Tabula Recensa order:

> *O YHVH TzABAOTh, we invoke and implore most earnestly your Divine Power, Wisdom and Goodness, and most humbly and faithfully ask you to favor and assist us in all our works, words and cogitations, concerning, promoting or procuring your praise, honor and Glory.*
>
> *And by these your twelve mystical names. ORO, IBAH, AOZPI, MPH, ARSL, GAIOL, OIP, TEAA, PDOCE, MOR, DIAL, HCTGA, most ardently do we entreat and implore your Divine and Omnipotent Majesty: that all your faithful Angelic Spirits whose mystical names are expressed in this book and whose offices are briefly noted, in whatever part of the world they be and, in whatever time of our lives they are summoned by us by means of their peculiar powers or authority of your Holy Names (likewise contained in this book), that most swiftly they come to us visible, affable, and appear to us peacefully and remain with us visibly according to our wishes, and that they disappear at our request from us and from our sight.*
>
> *And through you and that reverence and obedience which they owe you in those twelve mystical names above*

mentioned, that they give satisfaction amicably to us also, at each and every moment in our lives, and in each and every deed or request to all, some or one of them, and to do this quickly, well, completely and perfectly to discharge, perfect and complete all this according to their virtues and power both general and individual and through the injunctions given them by you (O God) and their charged offices and ministry.

Amen.

The Revised Fundamental Obeisance

The following revised Fundamental Obeisance is what my magical working group and I use in our own ritual operations, modified to make it more generic in terms of theology. I have also added a reference to the Enochian name MAD (MAHD), which is given as the highest name of God by the Angel Madimi in one of the early portions of the True and Faithful Relation. The name MAD should be vibrated just as is recommended for the other twelve, except that it should be done with your hands at your sides, the sphere of light should encompass your entire body, and the light itself should be visualized as brightness composed of all the colors at once. This makes it appear for the most part like white light, but less a particular color and more an undifferentiated brilliance.

> *O Almighty and Omnipotent MAD, Lord and Creator of the universe, I, [Your Magical Name], devoted worshipper of the Highest, most earnestly invoke and call upon your divine power, wisdom, and goodness.*
>
> *I humbly and faithfully seek your favor and assistance to me in all my deeds, words, and thoughts, and in the promotion, procuring, and mingling of your praise, honour, and glory.*

Through these, your twelve mystical Names: ORO, IBAH, AOZPI, MPH, ARSL, GAIOL, OIP, TEAA, PDOCE, MOR, DIAL, HCTGA, I conjure and pray most zealously to your divine and omnipotent majesty, that all your Angelic* spirits might be called from any and all parts of the universe through the special domination and controlling power of your holy Names.

Let them come most quickly to me. Let them appear visibly, friendily, and peacefully to me.

Let them remain visible according to my will.

Let them vanish from me and from my sight when I so request.

Let them give reverence and obedience before you and your twelve mystical Names.

I command that they happily satisfy me in all things by accomplishing each and every one of my petitions, if not by one means, then by another, goodly, virtuously, and perfectly, with an excellent and thorough completeness, according to their virtues and powers, both general and unique, and by your united ministry and office, O God,

Amen.

So mote it be.

*Substitute Cacodemonic for Angelic when summoning Cacodemons.

This invocation acts as a counterpoint to the Prayer of Enoch, which precedes it in the Great Table ritual sequence. The self-deprecating portions of the Prayer of Enoch serve to purify the intent of the practitioner and prepare him or her to receive the majesty of God. The Fundamental Obeisance, on the other hand, invokes that majesty by means of the particular divine names of power that correspond to the Great Table. Success in this portion of the operation is unfortunately difficult to quantify, but it is nonetheless vitally important to any magical operation. The entire grimoire tradition is based upon the assumption of divine authority by the magician in order to summon, charge, and dismiss spirits. Aleister Crowley writes in Liber O vel Magus et Sagittae that:

> *Success in "banishing" is known by a "feeling of cleanliness" in the atmosphere; success in "invoking" by a "feeling of holiness." It is unfortunate that these terms are so vague.*[5]

I will add to this that when it comes to this feeling of holiness, few spirits can match the sense engendered by the strongest Enochian angels, though it should be noted that the most powerful Qabalistic archangels come close. Once you successfully evoke an Enochian entity, from that point onward you will always recognize the change in atmosphere that accompanies their arrival.

---

5. Aleister Crowley, *Magick: Book Four* (York Beach, ME: Samuel Weiser, 1997), 624.

Chapter 7
Angelic Pronunciation

The Angelic Keys, or Calls, make up what is probably the most famous portion of the Enochian system. It is from the Keys and their English translations that all "Enochian dictionaries" are created. In fact, the Keys make up the only portion of the system where the English and Angelic languages appear side by side.

Angelic Pronunciation: The pronunciation of the Angelic language is a matter of some debate among Enochian magicians. In Mastering the Mystical Heptarchy, I discussed some of my issues with the various pronunciation schemes that have been suggested over the years. In the Golden Dawn system, Hebrew vowels were originally inserted between consonants that were deemed too difficult to pronounce, and in fact I have heard the rumor that Wynn Wescott once held the position that each individual Angelic letter should be pronounced as a syllable in full. Keep that in mind as you read through the Keys; it should be clear how incredibly unwieldy this method would be in practice.

Most modern Enochian magicians have now reached the consensus that Dee's pronunciation notes, vague in spots as they are, offer the best window into how the language is supposed to be pronounced. Still, disagreements remain over how to read those pronunciation notes. Aaron Leitch has recently published a quite comprehensive book on the Angelic language (The Angelical Language, Volume II) in which he recommends a method first proposed by Leo Vinci in his Gmicalzoma Enochian dictionary, now out of print, in which single letters can be read as the full name of the English letter that the Angelic character represents. As I mentioned in my previous book, this strikes me as profoundly incorrect. A similar disagreement revolves around the use of hard versus soft sounds for the various Angelic consonants that have multiple sounds in English. Leitch prefers reading Dee's notes with soft sounds in many places whereas most of my pronunciations are hard. My guess is that if both of us were to read Angelic side by side, his would sound more like English and mine more like German. In fact, the structure of Angelic words shows influences from both of these languages.

My rationale is that if possible, Dee's notes should be read with a single vowel or consonant sound per letter. There are a few Angelic letters that can apparently have multiple sounds, but Dee makes note of this in the few places in which it occurs. It makes little sense to me that Dee would write a G meaning it to sound like a J when he could have just written J. He certainly does that with the letter I, which apparently can have both an I-vowel and a J-consonant sound in Angelic (IAD is pronounced as written, while the J is explicitly noted for IAIDA, which in the pronunciation notes is written as starting with J rather than I). Similarly, Angelic has a letter for S but none for K, so it makes the most sense to me that the letter C should be pronounced as K. It also seems strange to me that if Dee really was trying to communicate the pronunciation of the language to future generations he would nonetheless vary the pronunciation of consonants as they appear in his pronunciation notes without any notations to that effect. This implies to me that the notes should consist of a more standardized phonetic scheme than the one Leitch recommends.

It should be added that, according to the pronunciation scheme I use, Angelic vowel sounds do not combine, whereas consonant sounds do. Whether or not this was how Dee intended his notes to be read is impossible to determine from the surviving diaries, but I have found that in practice it works well. For example, the word QAA which is part of my magical motto Ananael Qaa is pronounced QUAH-ah rather than QUAH, but the name OMEBB is pronounced OH-meb rather than OH-meh-beb or some similar rendering in which the two B's are kept as separate sounds.

This table shows the twenty-one Angelic letters along with their names, English equivalents, and sounds.

Angelic	Name	English	Sound
	Un	A	Short A
	Pa	B	B
	Veh	C	K
	Gal	D	D
	Gaph	E	Short E
	Or	F	F
	Ged	G	Hard G
	Na	H	H
	Gon	I	Long E or Y
	Ur	L	L
	Tal	M	M
	Drux	N	N
	Med	O	Long O
	Mals	P	P
	Ger	Q	Q (KW)
	Don	R	R
	Fam	S	S
	Gisg	T	T
	Van	V	Short U or V
	Pal	X	X
	Ceph	Z	Z or Zod

The use of the syllable "Zod" in place of the letter Z is more significant when working with the Great Table angels than it is with the Heptarchial Kings and Princes. In the Golden Dawn system Z is always pronounced as the syllable "Zod" but in fact what was communicated to Dee was that this is only done some of the time and that it changes the meaning of words. In effect, the use of "Zod" rather than the Z consonant sound marks the word as more strongly associated with God. As such, "Zod" should only be used in Great Table names that are referred to as names of God. So, for example, for the angels of the sub-quadrants the Z sound would be used, but for the names on the controlling cross "Zod" would be spoken instead. Similarly, the twelve names of God for each quadrant and names of the Kings incorporate "Zod," while the names of the Seniors do not.

While the Golden Dawn pronunciation system of inserting the vowel from the corresponding Hebrew letter between consonants is awkward, it is also true that sometimes vowel insertion is necessary. Generally I insert vowel sounds according to the Golden Dawn method simply because it sounds better than inserting schwa sounds[6] between every difficult consonant set. This is done according to the vowel sound found in the name of the corresponding Hebrew consonant, as shown here.

Hebrew Consonant	Hebrew Letter Name	Angelic Letter	Vowel Sound
B	Beth	ꝟ	e
G	Gimel	ʊ	i
D	Daleth	ɔ	a
H	Heh	ෆ	e
V	Vav	ꜣ	A
Z	Zain	ꝓ	A
Ch	Cheth	℟ෆ	E
T	Teth	✔	E
Y	Yod	ꝫ	O

---

6. The schwa is a shortened "uh" sound, as pronounced between consonants in the second syllable of the English word "rhythm."

Hebrew Consonant	Hebrew Letter Name	Angelic Letter	Vowel Sound
K	Kaph	ß	A
L	Lamed	ᒼ	A
M	Mem	ᛖ	E
N	Nun	ᔓ	U
S	Samekh	ᒡ	A
P	Peh	Ω	E
Tz	Tzaddi	Γ	A
Q	Qoph	ᚒ	O
R	Resh	ε	E
Sh	Shin	ᒡᏇ	I
Th	Tau	╱Ꮗ	A

    This vowel insertion system is highly syncretic and has no real basis in the original Dee material so I use it sparingly. For example, I pronounce the word VORSG pretty much as written so that it sounds a lot like "VORSK" with the last letter a hard G rather than a K. However, according to the traditional Golden Dawn pronunciation it would be "VaOReSaJi," inserting the a from Vav, the e from Resh, the a from Samekh, and the i from Gimel, in addition to using a soft G that I believe Dee would have written as a J in his pronunciation notes if that was how he intended the word to be vocalized. In fact, once you practice the unfamiliar "SG" sound for a bit you will find that you do not need any of the additional vowels in order to say it properly.

    In some cases, though, vowel insertion is the best option. The first of the three names of God corresponding to the south on the Tabula Recensa, MPH ARSL GAIOL, consists of three consonants and no vowel sounds. In the modern Golden Dawn Tradition, MPH is generally pronounced as "EM-peh," which does not conform to even the standard Golden Dawn rules. This may have been where the idea that the names of English letters could be used as part of Angelic words came from. This pronunciation is not found in Aleister Crowley's Liber Chanokh but does appear in Israel Regardie's The Golden Dawn, so it most likely was adopted by the later Stella Matutina lineage at some point between around 1900 and 1934 and was not part of the original Golden Dawn system. While some sort of vowel sound has to be inserted into MPH and other words like it, I prefer to conform to the more standard Golden Dawn pronunciation of inserting the appropriate vowel sound after the consonant. MPH is thus pronounced "MEH-peh" inserting the short e vowel sounds from Mem and Peh. Since I only use this rule as necessary to allow pronunciation of the word, I would not add an extra short e from Heh after the H and pronounce the name "MEH-peh-heh" as the full Golden Dawn pronunciation method would dictate.

An interesting counterpoint to MPH is the first of the three names of God corresponding to the north on the Tabula Recensa, MOR DIAL HCTGA. In the modern Golden Dawn Tradition, the first word of this name is generally pronounced as "E-mor," which is much more inexplicable than applying the same rule to MPH. Even advocates of stating English letter names, such as Aaron Leitch and before him Leo Vinci, pronounce Angelic words as written if they consist of reasonable vowel and consonant combinations. In that light, it should be obvious that this name can simply be pronounced as "MOR" without any additional consonant insertions. Like "EM-peh," "E-mor" is not found in Crowley's Liber Chanokh but first appears in Regardie's The Golden Dawn. As Regardie is known to have referred to the leaders of the Hermes Temple into which he was initiated as "inepti," one wonders how unclear their understanding of the Angelic language might have been. Perhaps the leading e sound on these two words has no esoteric significance at all but rather resulted from a misunderstanding of the declared Golden Dawn pronunciation rules, and due to Regardie's book was subsequently adopted as correct.

The Leaves of Liber Loagaeth

While I have criticized some aspects of Aaron Leitch's pronunciation method in both this book and Mastering the Mystical Heptarchy, his

The Angelical Language: Volume I includes an extremely well put-together schema for using the leaves of Liber Loagaeth in conjunction with the Angelic Keys. Liber Loagaeth is a collection of 49 "leaves" or utterances similar to, but not identical with, the Angelic language of the Keys that were received by Dee and Kelley following the Heptarchial material, but before the Watchtower arrangement and the Angelic Keys. The leaves follow a simple base-49 layout like the Keys and can be related to them by number, keeping in mind that Leaf 1 corresponds to the silent true first key, Leaf 2 corresponds to Key 1, and so forth. When used in this manner, the Leaf should directly precede the corresponding Key. As I have not personally experimented with this method to any significant degree, instead of including the leaves in my ritual template and reproducing them here, I recommend that you pick up a copy of Leitch's Angelical Language: Volume I and try it out for yourself. The only caveat I will add is that Leitch contends in the book that rather than the Keys corresponding to the Great Table quadrants and sub-quadrants, they instead correspond only to the leaves of Liber Loagaeth. I disagree with that particular statement and do use the Keys as part of my Great Table operations, but I imagine that incorporating the Leaves into those operations as well could open up many new possibilities.

One idea that is definitely not true regarding the leaves is that in some mysterious manner they encode the Necronomicon found in the short stories of H.P. Lovecraft. At one point Lovecraft wrote up a brief history of this mysterious and wholly fictional tome, and in it mentioned that it had been translated at one point by none other than Dr. John Dee. From that small tidbit, George Hay went on to publish a version of the Necronomicon through Skoob Esoterica in 1993, claiming that it was in fact extracted from the text of Dee's Liber Loagaeth. Even though Lovecraft himself wrote that his dreaded grimoire was merely a literary device that he invented, the idea that the book really does, or did, exist and is somehow connected to John Dee, is an idea that simply refuses to fade away. The Leaves actually have no apparent English translation, at least not anywhere in the spirit diaries.

Chapter 8
The Angelic Keys

There are forty-nine actual Keys — eighteen attributed to the Great Table, thirty attributed to the Aires (which differ from one another by only the name of the Aire), and the true "First Key" that precedes the other forty-eight. I have divided the Keys into three groups: the Opening Keys, used to open and close the Temple, the Watchtower Keys, which correspond to the various regions of the Great Table, and the Aethyr Keys, which correspond to the thirty Aires. In Mastering the Mystical Heptarchy, I discussed the use of the first two Keys in the context of Heptarchial operations, which is not a method made use of by many other Enochian magicians. For Great Table operations, though, it is clear that these two Keys should be employed. According to the general consensus among most modern Enochian magicians, the first two Angelic Keys correspond to the Black Cross or Tablet of Union, and the subsequent sixteen correspond to the sixteen sub-quadrants of the Great Table.

The Opening Keys

Silence – the True "First Key":

As I first mentioned in Mastering the Mystical Heptarchy, the true "First Key" is "not to be sounded," that is, it is silent. Generally speaking, I implement this Key by performing a brief meditation that serves to quiet my wandering thoughts and separate my ritual thoughts from those of my normal life prior to the start any magical ritual, as well as by inserting a brief pause prior to reading the so-called First and/or Second Keys. If you decide to experiment with the Leaves of Liber Loagaeth, keep in mind that the numbering of the 49 Leaves is offset by one from the traditional numbering of the 48 spoken Keys. The First Leaf thus corresponds to the brief pause, the Second Leaf to the First Angelic Key, the Third Leaf to the Second Angelic Key, and so forth.

The First Key:

While this "First Key" is actually the second, I have not labeled it as such in order to maintain consistency with other writings on Enochian Magick. The First Key is used to activate the Enochian Temple when performing rituals involving evocation – that is, the calling of the Enochian angels into the Holy Table. As an Opening Key, it precedes the use of all Watchtower Keys for Great Table operations.

When working with cacodemons, the text of this Key is slightly changed. The asterisk following the word VAOAN, meaning "truth," is to note that the word should be VOOAN, pronounced "VO-o-an" as written. This Key should always be used when working with the cacodemons, as invoking them directly is not advised. They should always be evoked into the Holy Table and commanded from there like the demons from other goetic traditions are summoned into triangles. The entropic and destructive natures of the various classes of cacodemons do not render them particularly suitable for inhabiting your sphere of consciousness.

The Second Key:

The Second Key is used to open the Enochian temple for rituals involving invocation – that is, the calling of the Enochian angels into oneself. Invocation and evocation are not necessarily contradictory; I have performed rituals in which I invoked the form of a particular angel in order to call a second angel into the Holy Table that was under the authority of the first. In the case of such a ritual, both Keys are read beginning with the First. Otherwise, for a ritual involving invocation only, the Second Key replaces the First.

The First Angelic Key

OL SONF VORSG, GOHO IAD BALT LANSH CALZ VONPHO, SOBRA Z-OL ROR I TA NAZPSAD GRAA TA MALPRG. DS HOL-Q QAA NOTHOA ZIMZ OD COMMAH TA NOBLOH ZIEN: SOBA THIL GNONP PRGE ALDI DS VRBS OBOLEH GRSAM: CASARM OHORELA CABA PIR DS ZONRENSG CAB ERM JADNAH: PILAH FARZM ZURZA ADNA GONO IADPIL DS HOM TOH SOBA IPAM LU IPAMIS DS LOHOLO VEP ZOMD POAMAL OD BOGPA AAI TA PIAP PIAMOL OD VAOAN*. ZACARE CA OD ZAMRAN ODO CICLE QAA ZORGE, LAP ZIRDO NOCO MAD HOATH JAIDA.

* Use VOOAN here when working with cacodemons.

Phonetic:

OL SONF VORSG go-HO i-AD BALT LANSH KALZ VON-pho, SO-bra zod-OL ROR I TA NAZ-psad GRA-a TA MAL-perg. DES HOL-quo QUA-a not-HO-a ZIMZ, OD KO-mah TA NO-bloh zi-EN: SO-ba THIL gi-NONP per-GE AL-di

DES VURBS O-bu-leh gir-SAM: ka-SARM o-ho-RE-la ka-BA PIR DES zon-RENSG KAB ERM JAHD-na: PE-lah FARZM OD ZUR-za ad-NA GO-no i-AHD-pil DES HOM TOH SO-ba i-PAM LU i-PAHM-is, DES LO-huh-lo VEP ZOMD po-A-mal OD BOG-pa ah-uh-I TA pi-AP pi-A-mol OD VA-o-an*. za-ka-REH KA OD ZAM-ran: O-do kik-LEH QUA-a zor-GEH, LAP ZIR-do NO-ko MAD ho-ATH ja-I-da.

* Pronunciation of VOOAN is VO-o-an.

English:

I reign over you, sayeth the God of Justice in power exalted above the firmaments of wrath, in whose hands the Sun is as a sword, and the Moon as a through-thrusting fire which measureth your garments in the midst of my vestures, and trussed you together as the palms of my hands: whose seats I garnished with the fire of gathering, and beautified your garments with admiration to whom I made a law to govern the Holy Ones and delivered you a rod with the Ark of Knowledge.

Moreover you lifted up your voices and swore obedience and faith to him that liveth and triumpheth whose beginning is not, nor end cannot be which shineth as a flame in the midst of your palace and reigneth among you as the balance of righteousness, and truth: move, therefore, and show yourselves: open the mysteries of your creation: be friendly unto me: for I am the servant of the same your God: the true worshipper of the highest.

The Second Angelic Key

ADGT VPAAH ZONGOM FAAIP SALD VIIV L SOBAM IALPRG IZAZAZ PIADPH CASARMA ABRAMG TA TALHO PARACLEDA Q-TA LORS-L-Q TURBS OOGE BALTOH GIUI CHIS LUSD ORRI OD MICALP CHIS BIA OZONGON. LAP NOAN TROF CORS TAGE O-Q MANIN JAIDON. TORZU GOHEL ZACAR CA CNOQUOD, ZAMRAN MICALZO OD OZAZM VRELP LAP ZIR IOIAD.

Phonetic:

AD-git VEH-puh-a ZONG-om fa-uh-IP SALD VI-iv LA so-BAM i-AL-perg i-zuh-ZAZ pi-AD-peh, kas-AR-ma ab-RAMG TA TAL-ho pa-ruh-KLEH-da QUO-ta LORS-el-quo TURBS O-uh-ge BAL-toh gi-u-I CHIS OR-ri OD mi-KALP CHIS bi-A O-zun-gon. LAP no-AN TROF KORS ta-GE O-quo ma-NIN JA-i-don tor-ZU GO-hel za-KAR KA KNO-quod, ZAM-ran mi-KAL-zo OD o-ZA-zam VRELP LAP ZIR i-O-i-ad.

English:

Can the wings of the winds understand your voices of wonder, O you the second of the first, whom the burning flames have framed within the depths of my jaws, whom I have prepared as cups for a wedding, or as the flowers in their beauty for the chamber of righteousness.

Stronger are your feet than the barren stone: and mightier are your voices than the manifold winds.

For, you are become a building such as is not but in the mind of the all-powerful.

Arise, sayeth the first, move therefore unto his servants: show yourselves in power.

And make me a strong seething: for I am of him that liveth forever.

The Watchtower Keys

Most magicians working with the Enochian system agree that the sixteen Keys ranging from the third to the eighteenth are related to the sixteen sub-quadrants of the Great Table. This is also how I use these Keys, but I do not make use of the popular Golden Dawn Key Order to relate them to the sub-quadrants. In Liber Chanokh, Aleister Crowley describes this order thus, with the numbers given representing particular Keys.

1: Governs generally as a whole the tablet of Union. Use it first in all invocations of Angels of that tablet, but not at all with other 4 tables.

2: Used as an invocation of Angels E H N B representing governance of Spirit in the Tablet of Union: also proceeds, in the second place, all invocations of Key tablet Angels. Not used in invocations of 4 other tables.

3, 4, 5, 6: Used in invocations of Angels of Tablet of Union, also of angels of 4 terrestrial tablets, thus —

3: Used to invoke Angels of the letters of the line E X A R P

For those of Tablet ORO as a whole and for the lesser angle of this tablet, which is that of the element itself, viz. I D O I G O. So for others—

The remaining 12 Keys refer to the remaining lesser angles of the tables, the order of the elements being Air, Water, Earth, Fire.[7]

Using this arrangement, you would open your ritual with the First or Second Key depending on the particular angels you will be conjuring. Second, you would follow this with Key 3, 4, 5, or 6 depending on which of the four quadrants those angels reside within. Third, you would employ Key 7, 8, or 9 for an Airy sub-quadrant, 10, 11, or 12 for a Watery sub-quadrant, 13, 14, or 15 for an Earthy sub-quadrant, or 16, 17, or 18 for a Fiery sub-quadrant.

---

7. Aleister Crowley, Lon Milo Duquette, Christopher Hyatt, *Enochian World of Aleister Crowley* (Phoenix, AZ: New Falcon, 1991), 81.

For a sub-quadrant with the same elemental attribution of the quadrant (Air of Air, Water of Water, Earth of Earth, Fire of Fire) this third step is not necessary, as the elemental attribution does not shift. While many magicians working this order claim to get good results, in my opinion there are several significant problems with this widely-used but awkward arrangement.

First of all, it is clear to me from their content that the first four Keys in this section, Keys three through six, are a group, and that the last four, Keys fifteen through eighteen, are also a group. The Golden Dawn arrangement groups the first four together but then subdivides the remaining twelve into groups of three. To my way of thinking, it is not consistent or logical to put the Keys that begin "O, thou governor of the first flame" and "O, thou governor of the second flame" in different groups. Second of all, with the Golden Dawn arrangement the directions mentioned in the Keys get confusing if you actually are using them with a physical Holy Table. Rather than an orderly east-south-north-west progression, to open sections of the Great Table you must move around the Holy Table several times to face the proper directions as they are read. Finally, the simplest solution, dividing the Keys up into four groups of four Keys and assigning them using a simple east-south-west-north progression corresponding to the different classes of spirits for the most part works just fine.

I have found that when working with a full Enochian temple arrangement, it is best to stand opposite the direction to which you are addressing the Key – that is, you stand in the west facing the east when you are reading a call addressed to the east, so that you are looking across the table. This maintains the focus of the ritual, which is really the center of the Holy Table or any object placed there, such as a crystal. The Watchtower Keys are normally read in groups of four in a pattern akin to the arrangement of Dee's invocations, beginning with the east and proceeding clockwise around the temple. This arrangement is reflected in my arrangement of these Keys – for most rituals, they should be read in numerical order beginning with the Key addressing the east for the class of spirits with which you are working. Each of these classes has its own attributions and powers, as you will see in the chapter dealing with the Great Table conjurations. Also, it should be noted that the Kings and Seniors do not seem to need any further Keys read beyond the First and/or Second and can be conjured in a straightforward manner once the mode of working has been set.

The Third Angelic Key

The Third Key begins the first group, composed of Keys three through six. These Keys are attributed to the Angels of Natural Substances, the Angels of Medicine, and the Cacodemons of Medicine, with the Third Key related to the east and to Fire. In these four keys the directions are referred to as the four angles. This reference alludes to the location of these spirits in the upper left sub-quadrant of each Great Table quadrant. Just as in going around the Great Table you begin with the upper left quadrant, each angle begins with the upper left sub-quadrant.

> MICMA, GOHO PIAD, ZIR COMSELH AZIEN BIAB OS LONDOH. NORZ CHIS OTHIL GIGIPAH, VNDL CHIS TA PUIM: Q MOSPLEH TELOCH QUIIN TOLTORG CHIS, I CHIS GE, M OZIEN, DST BRGDA OD TORZUL. ILI EOL BALZARG OD AALA THILN OS NETAAB, DLUGA VOMSARG LONSA CAPMIALI VORS CLA, HOMIL COCASB, FAFEN, IZIZOP OD MIINOAG DE GNETAAB, VAUN NA NAEEL: PANPIR MALPIRGI, CAOSG PILD NOAN VNALAH BALT OD VOOAN. DO OAIP MAD GOHOLOR, GOHUS, AMIRAN. MICMA, IEHUSOZ CACACOM OD DOOAIN NOAR MICAOLZ AAIOM CASARMG GOHIA ZACAR, VNIGLAG OD IMUAMAR PUGO PLAPLI ANANAEL QAAN.

Phonetic:

> mik-MA, go-HO pi-AD, ZIR KOM-se-lah az-i-EN bi-AB OS LON-doh. NORZ KHIS O-thil gi-GI-pa, VAND-la KHIS TA PU-im: QUO MOS-pleh TE-loch quo-i-IN TOL-torg CHIS, I CHIS GEH, ME o-ZI-en, DAST BERG-dah OD TOR-zul. I-li i-OL BAL-zarg OD a-a-LA THILN OS NE-ta-ab, DLU-ga VOM-sarg LON-sah kap-mi-A-li VORS KLA, ho-MIL KO-ka-sab, FA-fen, I-zi-zop OD mi-I-no-ag DE gne-TA-ab, va-UN na-

NA-e-el: PAN-pir mal-PIR-gi, ka-OSG PILD NO-an VNA-la BALT OD vo-O-an. DO O-i-ap MAD go-HO-lor, go-HUS, A-mi-ran. mik-MA, i-e-HU-soz ka-KA-kom OD do-o-a-IN no-AR mi-KA-olz a-a-I-om ka-SARMG go-HI-a ZOD-a-kar, VA-ni-glag OD IM-ua-mar PU-go PLA-pli a-NA-na-el QUA-an.

English:

Behold, sayeth your God, I am a circle on whose hands stand 12 kingdoms.

Six are the seats of living breath, the rest are as sharp sickles: or the horns of death wherein the creatures of the earth are, to are not, except mine own hand, which sleeps and shall rise.

In the first I made you stewards and placed you in seats 12 of government, giving unto every one of you power successively over 456, the true ages of time, to the intent that, from your highest vessels and the corners of your governments, you might work my power: pouring down the fires of life and increase, continually on the earth, thus you are become the skirts of justice and truth.

In the name of the same, your God, lift up, I say, yourselves.

Behold, his mercies flourish and name is become mighty amongst us in whom we say move, descend and apply yourselves unto us as unto partakers of the secret wisdom of your creation.

The Fourth Angelic Key

The Fourth Key is attributed to the Angels of Natural Substances, the Angels of Medicine, and the Cacodemons of Medicine of the south and of Air.

OTHIL LASDI BABAGE OD DORPHA GOHOL, GCHISGE AUAUAGO CORMP PD, DSONF VI VDIV, CASARMI OALI MAPM SOBAM AG CORMPO, CRPL, CASARMG CROODZI CHIS OD VGEG DST CAPIMALI CHIS CAPIMAON: OD LONSHIN CHIS TA LO CLA: TORGU, NOR QUASAHI, OD F CAOSGA: BAGLE ZIRENAIAD, DSI, OD APILA. DOOAIP QAAL ZACAR OD ZAMRAN OBELISONG RESTEL AAF NOR MOLAP.

Phonetic:

o-THIL LAS-di BA-ba-ge OD DOR-pha go-HOL, gi-KHIS-ge a-UA-ua-go KORMP PED, da-SONF VI VDIV, ka-SAR-mi O-a-li MA-pem so-BAM AG korm-PO, ka-rep-LA, ka-SARMG kro-OD-zi KHIS OD VA-geg DAST ka-pi-MA-li KHIS ka-pi-ma-ON: OD LON-shin KHIS TA LO KLA: tor-GU, NOR qua-SA-hi, OD FA ka-OS-ga: BAG-le zi-re-NA-i-ad, da-SI, OD a-PI-la. do-o-a-IP QUA-al za-KAR OD ZAM-ran o-BE-li-song rest-EL a-AF NOR MO-lap.

English:

I have set my feet in the south and have looked about me saying, are not the thunders of increase numbered 33, which reign in the second angle, under whom I have placed 9639 whom none hath yet numbered, but one, in whom the second beginning of things are and wax strong which also successively are the number of time: and their powers are as the first 456: arise, you sons of pleasure, and visit the earth: for I am the Lord your God, which is, and liveth.

In the name of the Creator move, and show yourselves as pleasant deliverers that you may praise him amongst the sons of men.

The Fifth Angelic Key

The Fifth Key is attributed to the Angels of Natural Substances, the Angels of Medicine, and the Cacodemons of Medicine of the west and of Water.

SAPAH ZIMII DUIB, OD NOAS TAQUANIS ADROCH DORPHAL CAOSG OD FAONTS PERIPSOL TABLIOR, CASARM AMIPZI NA ZARTH AF OD DLUGAR ZIZOP ZLIDA CAOSGI TOLTORGI, OD ZCHIS ESIASCH L TAVIU OD IAOD THILD DS PERAL HUBAR PEOAL SOBA CORMFA CHIS TA LA VLS OD QCOCASB. CA NIIS OD DARBS QAAS, FETH ARZI OD BLIORA IAIAL EDNAS CICLES: BAGLE? GEIAD I L.

Phonetic:

sa-PAH ZI-mi-i du-IB, OD no-AS ta-qu-A-nis AD-roch DOR-phal ka-OSG OD fa-ONTS PE-rip-sol ta-bli-OR, ka-SARM a-MIP-zi NA ZARTH AF OD DLU-gar ZI-zop zod-LI-da ka-OS-gi tol-TOR-gi, OD zod-KHIS e-SI-asch LA ta-vi-U OD i-A-od THILD DAS pe-RAL HU-bar pe-O-al SO-ba KORM-fa KHIS TA LA VALS OD quo-KO-kasb. KA ni-IS OD DARBS quo-A-as, feth-AR-zi OD bli-O-ra i-A-i-al ED-nas KIK-les: BA-gle? ge-i-AD I LA.

English:

The mighty sounds have entered into the third angle, and are become as olives in the olive mount looking with gladness upon the earth and dwelling in the brightness of the heavens as continual comforters, unto whom I fastened pillars of gladness 19 and gave them vessels to water the earth with her creatures, and they are the brothers of the first and second and the beginning of their own seats which are garnished with continually burning lamps 69636 whose numbers are as the first, the ends, and the contents of time.

Therefore come you and obey your creation, visit us in peace and comfort.

Conclude us as receivers of your mysteries. For why? Our Lord and Master is all one.

The Sixth Angelic Key

The Sixth Key is attributed to the Angels of Natural Substances, the Angels of Medicine, and the Cacodemons of Medicine of the north and of Earth.

GAH S DIU CHIS EM, MICALZO PILZIN, SOBAM EL HARG MIR BABALON OD OBLOC SAMVELG DLUGAR MALPRG ARCAOSGI OD ACAM CANAL SOBOLZAR FBLIARD CAOSGI OD CHIS ANETAB OD MIAM TAVIV OD D DARSAR SOLPETH BIEN BRITA OD ZACAM GMICALZO SOB HAATH TRIAN LUIAHE ODECRIN MAD QAAON.

Phonetic:

GAH SA DI-u KHIS EM, mi-KAL-zo PIL-zin, SO-bam EL HARG MIR ba-BA-lon OD O-blok SAM-velg DLU-gar MAL-perg ar-ka-OS-gi OD a-KAM ka-NAL so-BOL-zar fa-bli-ARD ka-OS-gi OD KHIS a-NE-tab OD mi-AM ta-VIV OD DA DAR-sar SOL-peth bi-EN BRI-ta OD ZA-kam gi-mi-KAL-zo sob-HA-ath TRI-an lu-i-A-he o-de-KRIN MAD quo-a-a-ON.

English:

The spirits of ye fourth angle are nine, mighty in the firmaments of waters, whom the first hath planted a torment to the wicked and a garland to the righteous *giving unto them fiery darts to vane the earth and 7699 continual workmen whose courses visit with comfort the earth and are in government and continuance as the second and the third wherefore hearken unto my voice, I have talked of you and I move you in power and presence, whose works shall be a song of honor and the praise of your God in your creation.*

The Seventh Angelic Key

The Seventh Key refers back to the East and is the first Key of the second group, attributed to the Angels of Transportation, the Angels of Gold and Precious Stones, and the Cacodemons of Gold and Precious Stones. The Seventh Key is attributed to the spirits of this group pertaining to the east and to Fire.

RAAS I SALMAN PARADIZ OECRIMI AAO IALPIRGAH, QUIIN ENAY BUTMON OD INOAS NI PARADIAL CASARMG VGEAR CHIRLAN OD ZONAC LUCIFTIAN CORS TA VAUL ZIRN TOLHAMI SOBA LONDOH OD MUAM CHIS TAD ODES VMADEA OD PIBLIAR OTHIL RIT OD MIAM. CNOQUOL RIT, ZACAR, ZAMRAN, OECRIMI QADAH: OD OMICAOLZ AAIOM BAGLE PAPBOR IDLUGAM LONSHI OD VMPLIF VGEGI BIGLIAND.

Phonetic:

RA-as I-sal-man pa-ra-DI-zod o-E-kri-mi a-a-O i-al-PIR-gah, qui-IN e-NAY BUT-mon OD i-NO-as NI pa-RA-di-al ka-SARMG va-GE-ar KHIR-lan OD ZO-nac lu-KIF-ti-an KORS TA va-UL ZIRN tol-HA-mi SO-ba lon-DOH OD mu-AM KHIS TAD o-DES va-MA-de-a OD PI-bli-ar o-THIL RIT OD MI-am. KNO-quol RIT, za-KAR, ZAM-ran, o-e-KRI-mi QUA-dah: OD o-MI-ka-ol-zod a-a-I-om BA-gle PAP-bor i-DLU-gam LON-shi OD vam-PLIF va-Ge-gi big-LI-and.

English:

The east is a house of virgins singing praises amongst the flames of the first glory, wherein the Lord hath opened his mouth and they are become 28 living dwellings in whom the strength of men rejoiceth and they are appareled with ornaments of brightness such as work wonders on all creatures whose kingdoms and continuance are as the third and fourth strong towers and places of comfort, the seats of mercy and continuance.

O you servants of mercy, move, appear, sing praises unto the Creator: and be mighty amongst us for to this remembrance is given power and our strength waxeth strong in our comforter.

The Eighth Angelic Key

The Eighth Key is attributed to the Angels of Transportation, the Angels of Gold and Precious Stones, and the Cacodemons of Gold and Precious Stones of the south and of Air. While the Key does not directly mention the South directly, it does refer to midday when the Sun is in the south, at least in the Northern Hemisphere.

BAZMELO ITA PIRIPSON OLN NAZAVABH OX CASARMG URAN CHIS UGEG DSA BRAMG BALTOHA GOHO IAD SOLAMIAN TRIAN TALOLCIS ABAIUOVIN OD AZIAGIER RIOR. IRGIL CHIS DA DSPAAOX BUFD CAOSGO DSCHIS ODIPURAN TELOAH CACRG O ISALMAN LONCHO OD VOUINA CARBAF. NIISO, BAGLE AUAUAGO GOHON: NIISO, BAGLE MOMAO SIAION OD

MABZA IADOIASMOMAR POILP NIIS ZAMRAN CIAOFI CAOSGO OD BLIORS OD CORSI TA ABRAMIG.

Phonetic:

BAZ-me-lo I-ta pi-RIP-son OLN na-za-VABH OX ka-SARMG u-RAN KHIS va-GEG dsa-BRAMG bal-TO-ha go-HO-i-ad so-LA-mi-an tri-AN ta-LOL-kis a-ba-I-u-o-nin OD a-zi-A-gi-er ri-OR. IR-gil KHIS DA das-PA-a-OX BUFD ka-OS-go das-KHIS o-di-PU-ran TE-lo-ah ka-KURG O i-SAL-man LON-cho OD vo-u-I-na KAR-baf. ni-I-so, BA-gle a-u-A-u-a-go go-HON: ni-I-so, BA-gle MO-ma-o si-A-i-on OD MAB-za i-a-do-i-AS-mo-mar po-ILP ni-IS ZAM-ran ki-A-o-fi ka-OS-go OD bli-ORS OD KOR-si TA a-BRA-mig.

English:

The midday the first is as the third heaven made of hyacinth pillars 26 in whom the elders are become strong which I have prepared for my own righteousness, sayeth the Lord, whose long continuance shall be as bucklers to the stooping dragon and like unto the harvest of a widow.

How many are there which remain in the glory of the earth which are and shall not see death until this house fall and the dragon sink.

Come away, for the thunders have spoken: come away, for the crowns of the temple and the coat of him that is, was, and shall be crowned are divided.

Come, appear to the terror of the earth and to our comfort and of such as are prepared.

The Ninth Angelic Key

The Ninth Key is attributed to the Angels of Transportation, the Angels of Gold and Precious Stones, and the Cacodemons of Gold and Precious Stones of the west and of Water.

MICAOLI BRANSG PRGEL NAPTA IALPOR (DS BRIN EFAFAFE P VONPHO OLANI OD OBZA: SOBA VPAAH CHIS TATAN OD TRANAN BALYE), ALAR LUSDA SOBOLN, OD CHIS HOLQ CNOQUODI CIAL. VNAL ALDON MOM CAOSGO TA LASOLLOR GNAY LIMLAL: AMMA CHIIS SOBCA MADRID ZCHIS, OOANOAN CHIS AUINY DRILPI CAOSGIN, OD BUTMONI PARM ZUMVI CNILA: DAZIZ ETHAMZ ACHILDAO: OD MIRC OZOL CHIS PIDIAI COLLAL. ULCININ, A SOBAM UCIM. BAGLE? IADBALTOH CHIRLAN PAR. NIISO OD IP EFAFAFE BAGLE ACOCASB ICORSKA VNIG BLIOR.

Phonetic:

mi-ka-O-li BRANSG PER-gel NAP-ta YAL-por (DAS BRIN e-FA-fa-fe PE VON-pho o-LA-ni OD OB-za: SOB-ka va-PA-ah KHIS ta-TAN OD TRA-nan bal-YE), a-LAR LUS-da so-BOLN, OD KHIS HOL-quo kno-QUO-di ki-AL. va-NAL AL-don MOM ka-OS-go TA LAS OL-lor GNAY LIM-lal: am-MA khi-IS SOB-ka ma-DRID zod-KHIS, o-o-A-no-an KHIS a-u-I-ny DRIL-pi ka-OS-gi, OD but-MO-ni PARM ZUM-vi KNI-la: da-ZIZ e-THAMZ a-KHIL-da-o: OD MIRK o-ZOL KHIS pi-di-A-i kol-LAL. val-KI-nin, A SO-bam U-kim. BA-gle? i-ad-BAL-toh KHIR-lan PAR. ni-I-so OD IP e-FA-fa-fe BA-gle a-KO-casb i-KORS-ka va-NIG bli-OR.

English:

A mighty guard of fire with two-edged swords flaming (which have vials 8 of wrath for two times and a half:

whose wings are of wormwood, and the marrow of salt,) have settled their feet in the west, and are measured with their ministers 9996.

These gather up the moss of the earth as the rich man doth his treasure: cursed are they whose iniquities they are, in their eyes are millstones greater than the earth and from their mouths run seas of blood: their heads are covered with diamond: and upon their heads are marble sleeves.

Happy is he, on whom they frown not. For why?

The God of righteousness rejoiceth in them.

Come away and not your viols for the time is such as requireth comfort.

The Tenth Angelic Key

The Tenth Key is attributed to the Angels of Transportation, the Angels of Gold and Precious Stones, and the Cacodemons of Gold and Precious Stones of the north and of Earth.

CORAXO CHIS CORMP OD BLANS LUCAL AZIAZOR PAEB SOBA LILONON CHIS VIRQ OP EOPHAN OD RACLIR MAASI BAGLE CAOSGI DS IALPON DOSIG OD BASGIM: OD OXEX DAZIZ SIATRIS OD SALBROX CYNXIR FABOAN UNALCHIS CONST DS DAOX COCASG OL OANIO YOR VOHIM OL GIZYAX OD EORS COCASB PLOSI MOLUI DS PAGEIP LARAG OM DROLN MATORB COCASB EMNA L PATRALX YOLCI MATB NOMIG MONONS OLORA GNAY ANGELARD OHIO OHIO OHIO OHIO OHIO OHIO OHIO NOIB OHIO CAOSGON BAGLE MADRID I ZIROP CHISO DRILPA. NIISO CRIP IP NIDALI.

Phonetic:

ko-RAX-o KHIS CORMP OD BLANS LU-kal a-ZI-a-zor pa-EB SO-ba li-LO-non KHIS VIR-quo OP e-O-phan OD RA-klir ma-A-si BA-gle ka-OS-gi DAS YAL-pon DO-sig OD BAS-gim: OD OX-ex da-ZIZ si-A-tris OD SAL-brox KINX-ir fa-BO-an u-NAL-khis KONST DAS DA-ox ko-KASG OL o-A-ni-o YOR VOH-im OL GIZ-yax OD E-ors ko-KASG PLO-si mo-lu-I DAS pa-GE-ip LA-rag OM DROLN ma-TORB ko-KASB EM-na LA PA-tralx YOL-ki MA-tab NO-mig MO-nons o-LO-ra GNAY an-GE-lard o-HI-o o-HI-o o-HI-o o-HI-o o-HI-o o-HI-o no-IB o-HI-o ka-OS-gon BA-gle ma-DRID I zi-ROP KHI-so DRIL-pa. ni-i-SO KRIP IP ni-DA-li.

English:

The thunders of judgment and wrath are numbered and are harbored in the north in the likeness of an oak whose branches are nests 22 of lamentation and weeping, laid up for the earth which burn night and day: and vomit out the heads of scorpions and live sulfur mingled with poison.

These be the thunders that 5678 times in the 24th part of a moment roar with a hundred mighty earthquakes and a thousand times as many surges which rest not neither know any time here.

One rock bringeth forth 1000 even as the heart of man doth his thoughts.

Woe, woe, woe, woe, woe, woe, yea, woe be to the earth for her iniquity is, was, and shall be great.

Come away, but not your noises.

The Eleventh Angelic Key

The Eleventh Key refers back to the East, and begins the third group of Keys, attributed to the Angels of the Mechanical Arts, the Angels of Transformation, and the Cacodemons of Transformation. The Eleventh Key is attributed to the spirits of this group pertaining to the east and to Fire.

> OXIAYAL HOLDO OD ZIROM O CORAXO DS ZILDAR RAASY OD VABZIR CAMLIAX OD BAHAL NIISO SALMAN TELOCH CASARMAN HOLQ OD TI TA ZCHIS SOBA CORMF I GA. NIISA BAGLE ABRAMG NONCP. ZACAR CA OD ZAMRAN: ODO CICLE QAA: ZORGE: LAP ZIRDO NOCO MAD: HOATH IAIDA.

Phonetic:
> ox-i-AY-al HOL-do OD ZI-rom O ko-RAX-o DAS ZIL-dar ra-A-sy OD VAB-zir kam-LI-ax OD ba-HAL ni-I-so SAL-man te-LOCH ka-SAR-man HOL-quo OD TI TA zod-KHIS SO-ba KORMF I GA. ni-I-sa BA-gle ab-RAMG NON-kap. za-KA-re KA OD ZAM-ran: O-do KIK-le qua-A: ZOR-ge: LAP ZIR-do NO-ko MAD: ho-ATH i-A-i-da.

English:
> The mighty seat groaned and they were 5 thunders which flew into the east and the eagle spoke and cried with a loud voice, come away, and they gathered them together and became the house of death of whom it is measured and it is as they are whose number is 31.
>
> Come away, for I have prepared for you.
>
> Move, therefore, and show yourselves: open the mysteries of your creation: be friendly unto me: for I the servant of the same your God: the true worshiper of the highest.

The Twelfth Angelic Key

The Twelfth Key is attributed to the Angels of the Mechanical Arts, the Angels of Transformation, and the Cacodemons of Transformation of the south and of Air.

NONCI DSONF BABAGE OD CHIS OB HUBAIO TIBIBP ALLAR ATRAAH OD EF DRIX FAFEN MIAN AR ENAY OVOF SOBA DOOAIN AAI IVONPH. ZACAR, GOHUS, OD ZAMRAN: ODO CICLE QAA: ZORGE: LAP ZIRDO NOCO MAD: HOATH IAIDA.

Phonetic:

NON-ki DSONF BA-ba-ge OD KHIS OB hu-BA-i-o TI-bi-bep AL-lar at-RA-ah OD EF DRIX FA-fen ma-IN AR E-nay o-VOF SO-ba do-O-a-in a-A-i i-VONPH. za-KAR, go-HUS, OD ZAM-ran: O-do KIK-le qua-A: ZOR-ge: LAP ZIR-do NO-ko MAD: ho-ATH i-A-i-da.

English:

O you that reign in the south and are 28 the lanterns of sorrow, bind up your girdles and visit us.

Bring down your train 3663 that the Lord may be magnified whose name amongst you is wrath.

Move, I say, and show yourselves: open the mysteries of your creation: be friendly unto me: for I am the servant of the same your God: the true worshipper of the highest.

The Thirteenth Angelic Key

Contained within the Thirteenth Key is the most difficult decision I have ever made regarding the Angelic Keys. The Thirteenth Key is the only Key of the sixteen Watchtower Keys that gives an inconsistent direction — as is the case with the Twelfth Key, the direction given in the Thirteenth Key is also south, instead of west. While a critic might point out that this shows my Key arrangement has inconsistencies just like the Golden Dawn Key order, I would counter that the system presented here has a single inconsistency whereas the Golden Dawn system contains many of them.

I made several attempts to resolve this problem over the years. The first "solution" was to ignore the problem and read the Thirteenth Key, as written, to the West, but this felt incorrect in ritual work. There are really only two possibilities in terms of copying or transcribing errors: that the Keys were numbered incorrectly, or that the word for South was erroneously used instead of West. I experimented with swapping Keys Thirteen and Eight, since the Eighth Key does not explicitly name a direction, but "midday" is really the wrong association for the west. I finally decided to replace BABAGEN, South, with SOBOLN, West. However, if you find yourself disagreeing with that decision, I have also clearly noted where the substitution was done in the text of the Key, in both Angelic and English.

The Thirteenth Key is attributed to Angels of the Mechanical Arts, the Angels of Transformation, and the Cacodemons of Transformation of the west and of Water.

>NAPEAI SOBOLN* DSBRIN VX OOAONA LRING VONPH DOALIM EOLIS OLLOG ORSBA DSCHIS AFFA: MICMA ISRO MAD OD LONSHITOX DS IVMD AAI GROSB. ZACAR OD ZAMRAN: ODO CICLE QAA: ZORGE: LAP ZIRDO NOCO MAD: HOATH IAIDA.

* *This word is BABAGEN in the original text of the Key.*

Phonetic:

>na-PE-a-i SO-boln* das-BRIN VAX o-o-A-o-na la-RING VONPH do-A-lim e-O-lis OL-log ORS-ba das-KHIS AF-fa: mik-MA IS-ro MAD OD lon-shi-TOX DAS IV-med a-A-i

GROSB. za-KAR KA OD ZAM-ran: O-do KIK-le qua-A: ZOR-ge: LAP ZIR-do NO-ko MAD: ho-ATH i-A-i-da.

* Pronunciation of BABAGEN is ba-BA-gen.

English:

Oh you swords of the west* which have 42 eyes to stir up wrath of sin, making men drunken which are empty: behold the promise of God and his power which is called amongst you a bitter sting.

Move and show yourselves: open the mysteries of your creation: be friendly unto me: for I am a servant of the same your God: the true worshipper of the highest.

* This word is "of the south" in the original text of the Key.

The Fourteenth Angelic Key

The Fourteenth Key is attributed to the Angels of the Mechanical Arts, the Angels of Transformation, and the Cacodemons of Transformation of the north and of Earth.

NOROMI BAGIE PASBS OIAD DS TRINT MIRC OL THIL DODS TOLHAM CAOSGO HOMIN DS BRIN OROCH QUAR: MICMA BIAL OIAD AISRO TOX DSIVM AAI BALTIM. ZACAR OD ZAMRAN: ODO CICLE QAA: ZORGE: LAP ZIRDO NOCO MAD: HOATH IAIDA.

Phonetic:

no-RO-mi ba-GI-e PAS-bes o-I-ad DAS TRINT MIRK OL THIL DODS TOL HA-mi ka-OS-go HO-min DAS BRIN O-roch QUAR: mik-MA bi-AL o-I-ad a-IS-ro TOX DSI-vam a-A-i BAL-tim. za-KAR OD ZAM-ran: O-do KIK-le qua-A: ZOR-ge: LAP ZIR-do NO-ko MAD: ho-ATH i-A-i-da.

English:

O you sons of fury, the daughters of the just, which sit upon 24 seats vexing all creatures of the earth with age which have under you 1636: behold the voice of God, the promise of him which is called amongst you Fury, or Extreme Justice.

Move and show yourselves: open the mysteries of your creation: be friendly unto me: for I am the servant of the same your God: the true worshipper of the highest.

The Fifteenth Angelic Key

The Fifteenth Key is the first of the final group of Watchtower Keys, attributed to the Angels of Secret Discovery, the Angels of Living Creatures, and the Cacodemons of Living Creatures. The Fifteenth Key is attributed to the spirits of this group pertaining to the east and to Fire.

ILS TABAAN LIALPRT CASARMAN VPAAHI CHIS DARG DSOADO CAOSGI ORSCOR DS OMAX MONASCI BAEOUIB OD EMETGIS IAIADIX: ZACAR OD ZAMRAN, ODO CICLE QAA: ZORGE, LAP ZIRDO NOCO MAD, HOATH IAIDA.

Phonetic:

ILS ta-BA-am li-AL-pert ka-SAR-man va-pa-A-hi KHIS DARG das-o-A-do ka-OS-gi ORS-kor DAS O-max mo-NAS-ki ba-E-o-u-ib OD e-MET-gis i-a-I-a-dix: za-KAR OD ZAM-ran: O-do KIK-le qua-A: ZOR-ge: LAP ZIR-do NO-ko MAD: ho-ATH i-A-i-da.

English:

> *O thou the governor of the first flame, under whose wings are 6739 that weave the earth with dryness which knoweth the great name righteousness and the seal of honor: move and show yourselves, open the mysteries of your creation, be friendly unto me, for I am the servant of the same your God: the true worshipper of the highest.*

The Sixteenth Angelic Key

The Sixteenth Key is attributed to the Angels of Secret Discovery, the Angels of Living Creatures, and the Cacodemons of Living Creatures of the south and of Air.

ILS VIUIALPRT SALMAN BALT DS ACROODZI BUSD: OD BLIORAX BALIT: DSINSI CAOSG LUSDAN EMOD DSOM OD TLIOB DRILPA GEH YLS MADZILODARP. ZACAR OD ZAMRAN: ODO CICLE QAA: ZORGE: LAP ZIRDO NOCE MAD: HOATH IAIDA.

Phonetic:

ILS vi-u-I-al-pert SAL-man BALT DAS BRIN ac-ro-OD-zi BUSD: OD bli-OR-ax ba-LIT: da-SIN-si ka-OSG LUS-dan E-mod da-SAM OD tli-OB DRIL-pa GEH YILS mad-ZI-lo-darp. za-KAR OD ZAM-ran: O-do KIK-le quo-A-A: ZOR-ge: LAP ZIR-do NO-ko MAD: ho-ATH i-A-i-da.

English:

> *O thou second flame, the house of justice which hast thy beginning in glory: and shalt comfort the just: which walkest on the earth with feet 8763 that understand and*

separate creatures: great art thou in the God of stretch-forth-and-conquer.

Move, therefore, and show yourselves: open the mysteries of your creation: be friendly unto me: for I am the servant of the same your God: the true worshipper of the highest.

The Seventeenth Angelic Key

The Seventeenth Key is attributed to the Angels of Secret Discovery, the Angels of Living Creatures, and the Cacodemons of Living Creatures of the west and of Water.

ILS DIALPRT SOBA VPAAH CHIS NANBA ZIXLAY DODSIH ODBRINT FAXS HUBARO TASTAX YLSI SOBAIAD IVONPOVNPH ALDON DAXIL OD TOATAR: ZACAR OD ZAMRAN, ODO CICLE QAA, ZORGE, LAP ZIRDO NOCE MAD, HOATH IAIDA.

Phonetic:
ILS di-AL-pert SO-ba va-PA-ah KHIS NAN-ba ZIX-lay DOD-sih od-BRINT FAXS hu-BA-ro TAS-tax YL-si so-ba-I-ad i-VON-po-vanph AL-don DAX-il OD to-A-tar: za-KAR OD ZAM-ran: O-do KIK-le qua-A: ZOR-ge: LAP ZIR-do NO-ko MAD: ho-ATH i-A-i-da.

English:
O thou third flame, whose wings are thorns to stir up vexation: and hast 7336 lamps living going before them whose God is wrath in anger: gird up thy loins and hearken.

Move and show yourselves, open the mysteries of your creation, be friendly unto me, for I am the servant of the same your God: the true worshipper of the highest.

The Eighteenth Angelic Key

The Eighteenth Key is attributed to the Angels of Secret Discovery, the Angels of Living Creatures, and the Cacodemons of Living Creatures Fire of the north and of Earth.

ILS MICAOLZ OLPIRT IALPRG BLIORS DS ODO BUSDIR OIAD OUOARS CAOSGO CASARMG LAIAD ERAN BRINTS CAFAFAM DS IVMD AQLO ADOHI MOZ OD MAOFFAS BOLP COMOBLIORT PAMBT: ZACAR OD ZAMRAN, ODO CICLE QAA, ZORGE, LAP ZIRDO NOCO MAD, HOATH IAIDA.

Phonetic:

ILS mi-ka-OLZ OL-pirt i-AL-perg bli-ORS DAS O-do BUS-dir o-I-ad o-u-O-ars ka-OS-go ka-SARMG la-I-ad e-RAN BRINTS ka-FA-fam DAS IV-med a-QUO-lo a-DO-hi MOZ OD ma-OF-fas BOLP ko-MO-bli-ort PAM-bet: za-KAR OD ZAM-ran, O-do KIK-le qua-A, ZOR-ge, LAP ZIR-do NO-ko MAD, ho-ATH i-A-i-da.

English:

O thou mighty light and burning flame of comfort, which openest the glory of God to the center of the earth, in whom the secrets of truth 6332 have their abiding which is called in thy kingdom IOYE and not to be measured: be thou a window of comfort unto me.

Move and show yourselves, open the mysteries of your creation, be friendly unto me, for I am the servant of the same your God: the true worshipper of the highest.

Chapter 9
Tuning the Space

Once the general preliminary invocation and Opening Keys have been performed, the next step in the ritual is to tune the working space to match the attribution of the spirit that is to be conjured. The function of this step is to create a magical environment that will be favorable to both the spirit being conjured and the desired outcome of the ritual. Note that as shown in the template the Tuning step is preceded by the Opening Keys but followed by the Watchtower Keys. This makes the order of the book slightly irregular, but grouping the Angelic Keys together in one chapter is more consistent overall.

Planetary Days and Hours:

For planetary rituals, Renaissance magicians generally tuned their working space using the appropriate planetary days and hours as explained in Mastering the Mystical Heptarchy. The planetary days follow the standard Western attributions for the days of the week:

Sunday = Sun
Monday = Moon
Tuesday = Mars
Wednesday = Mercury
Thursday = Jupiter
Friday = Venus
Saturday = Saturn

Figuring out the planetary hour is somewhat more involved. Each day begins at sunrise with the first hour of the day. The time from sunrise to sunset is then divided into twelve equal parts, which are the hours of the day. The time from sunset to sunrise is then likewise divided into twelve equal parts, which are the twelve hours of the night. This means that the amount of time allotted to the hours of the day and hours of the night will only be equal on the equinoxes — the hours of the day will be longer in summer and the hours of the night will be longer in winter.

These tables show the arrangement of the planetary hours for the day and night. The most efficacious time to perform a standard planetary ritual is on the day and hour of the planet. For example, a solar ritual would be most effective when performed on a Sunday during the first or eighth hour of the day, or the third or tenth hour of the night, since those hours are attributed to the Sun on every Sunday.

No such system exists for working with elemental entities, though the elements may loosely be related to the planets as follows:

Fire — Mars or Sun	Water — Jupiter or Moon
Air — Mercury or Moon	Earth — Venus or Saturn
Active Spirit — Sun	Passive Spirit — Moon

One fundamental difference between the Great Table and Heptarchial angels is that the Great Table angels are summoned in groups. While they have particular elemental aspects individually, it seems that the general method Dee proposed involved summoning them in such a way that their particular powers spanned the entire elemental realm. As such, in many cases such timing will not be particularly relevant to Great Table workings whereas it is extremely important for Heptarchial ones.

Table 6: Planetary Hours of the Day – Sunrise to Sunset

	Sunday	Monday	Tuesday	Wednesday	Thursday	Friday	Saturday
1	Sun	Moon	Mars	Mercury	Jupiter	Venus	Saturn
2	Venus	Saturn	Sun	Moon	Mars	Mercury	Jupiter
3	Mercury	Jupiter	Venus	Saturn	Sun	Moon	Mars
4	Moon	Mars	Mercury	Jupiter	Venus	Saturn	Sun
5	Saturn	Sun	Moon	Mars	Mercury	Jupiter	Venus
6	Jupiter	Venus	Saturn	Sun	Moon	Mars	Mercury
7	Mars	Mercury	Jupiter	Venus	Saturn	Sun	Moon
8	Sun	Moon	Mars	Mercury	Jupiter	Venus	Saturn
9	Venus	Saturn	Sun	Moon	Mars	Mercury	Jupiter
10	Mercury	Jupiter	Venus	Saturn	Sun	Moon	Mars
11	Moon	Mars	Mercury	Jupiter	Venus	Saturn	Sun
12	Saturn	Sun	Moon	Mars	Mercury	Jupiter	Venus

Table 7: Planetary Hours of the Night – Sunset to Sunrise

	Sunday	Monday	Tuesday	Wednesday	Thursday	Friday	Saturday
1	Jupiter	Venus	Saturn	Sun	Moon	Mars	Mercury
2	Mars	Mercury	Jupiter	Venus	Saturn	Sun	Moon
3	Sun	Moon	Mars	Mercury	Jupiter	Venus	Saturn
4	Venus	Saturn	Sun	Moon	Mars	Mercury	Jupiter
5	Mercury	Jupiter	Venus	Saturn	Sun	Moon	Mars
6	Moon	Mars	Mercury	Jupiter	Venus	Saturn	Sun
7	Saturn	Sun	Moon	Mars	Mercury	Jupiter	Venus
8	Jupiter	Venus	Saturn	Sun	Moon	Mars	Mercury
9	Mars	Mercury	Jupiter	Venus	Saturn	Sun	Moon
10	Sun	Moon	Mars	Mercury	Jupiter	Venus	Saturn
11	Venus	Saturn	Sun	Moon	Mars	Mercury	Jupiter
12	Mercury	Jupiter	Venus	Saturn	Sun	Moon	Mars

Phases of the Moon:

In some traditions the phases of the Moon correspond to the four classical elements. This provides another possible method for timing operations that are associated with a particular element, though as is the case with planetary days and hours such timing will not be relevant to an operation that calls upon spirits of more than one element. The phases of the moon are associated as follows:

>New Moon — Earth
>First Quarter — Air
>Full Moon— Fire
>Last Quarter — Water[8]

At each of these phases, the Moon enters into the corresponding element and remains there until it reaches the next phase and moves on to the next one in the sequence, so an operation attributed to Earth would be performed between the New Moon and the First Quarter, one attributed to Air would be performed between the First Quarter and Full Moon, and so forth.

Incense:

Many systems of evocation involve the use of incense that the conjured spirit uses to shape a rudimentary form for the magician to observe. There are no explicit references in the Dee diaries to the use of any particular incense, and it is not clear that any was ever used. Kelley viewed the spirits in a scrying stone rather than seeing them appear in patterns of smoke. Some incenses corresponding to the four classical elements according to Aleister Crowley's Liber 777 (column XLII) are as follows:

> Fire: Olibanum, all Fiery Odors.
> Air: Galbanum.
> Water: Onycha, Myrrh.
> Earth: Storax, all Dull and Heavy Odors.

As with the planetary incenses listed in Mastering the Mystical Heptarchy, the italicized descriptions for Fire and Earth do not

---

8. Frater Barrabbas, Lunar Mysteries and the Art of Moon Magick - Part 2 (Retrieved 5/25/2012 from http://fraterbarrabbas.blogspot.com/2012/04/lunar-mysteries-and-art-of-moon-magick_13.html

necessarily follow any standard pattern, but rather are subjective and should be determined by the magician for him or herself. Also, since the spirits of the Great Table are normally summoned in groups, most operations generally correspond to more than one element. A good inclusive elemental incense is Dittany of Crete, which Liber 777 relates to the Qabalistic sphere of Malkuth, the Kingdom. Malkuth is the tenth sphere on the Tree of Life and represents the entire elemental realm.

The Greater Ritual of the Pentagram

Modern magicians tune their working spaces using elemental rites such as the Greater Ritual of the Pentagram found in the Thelemic and Golden Dawn traditions, which is used to invoke or banish the force of a particular element. In the Lesser Ritual of the Pentagram, the Pentagram of Earth is traced to all four directions with a different name of God at each quarter. In the Greater ritual, two pentagrams are traced at each quarter instead of one. The first is either the Pentagram of Active or Passive Spirit depending upon which element is being invoked or banished. Fire and Air are active elements so you use the Pentagram of Active Spirit, and Water and Earth are passive so you use the Pentagram of Passive Spirit. The second is the pentagram of the element being summoned. Each pentagram is traced in the color corresponding to the element, and each is followed by the Sign attributed to that element as described in Aleister Crowley's Liber O vel Manus et Sagittae.

The basic sequence performed at each of the four quarters, starting in the east and moving clockwise, is as follows:

(A) Trace appropriate Spirit Pentagram in the corresponding color.

(B) Vibrate godname associated with (A).

(C) Give the sign corresponding to (A).

(D) Trace pentagram of the element being summoned in the corresponding color.

(E) Vibrate godname associated with (D).

(F) Give sign corresponding to (D).

Steps A and B, and steps D and E, may be combined, provided they are performed as part of one single, smooth motion. When using the ritual in this manner you should be intoning and projecting the name as you trace the lines of the pentagram in order to imbue the figure with the energy of the breath. When using this ritual with the Enochian temple setup, my general practice is to perform the tracings and vibrations across the Holy Table, such that when drawing the pentagram in the eastern quarter I stand to the west of the altar facing east, when tracing the pentagram in the south I stand to the north of the altar facing south, and so forth.

Figure 20. The Pentagrams of Active Spirit

The Pentagrams of Active Spirit are traced in bright electric purple, like lavender but more intense. The corresponding name of God is AHIH (Eheieh), attributed to Kether (the crown), the most spiritual point on the Qabalistic Tree of Life, and the corresponding signs are the Rending and Closing of the Veil. The Sign of Rending the Veil is given by extending the hands in front of you, palms facing outwards, and then moving the hands apart as though opening a heavy curtain. The Sign of Closing the Veil is given by extending the hands in front of you and to both sides of the body, palms facing inwards. The hands are then brought together, as though closing a heavy curtain. Rending the Veil corresponds to the invoking form of both pentagrams, and Closing the Veil corresponds to the banishing form. The signs represent the opening and closing of the Veil of Paroketh, which allows entry into Tiphareth, beauty, the Qabalistic sphere of the Sun.

There is some variation among magical traditions in how the Rending and Closing of the Veil is taught. Another version that I have seen associates Rending of the Veil with Active Spirit and Closing of the Veil with Passive Spirit, and to be fair this is one possible reading of the description for these signs given in Crowley's Liber O. However, it makes little sense to me that when invoking Passive Spirit one would give the Closing of the Veil, or when banishing Active Spirit one would give the Rending of the Veil. According to my own experimentation, the version given here is both the most logical and the most effective.

Figure 21. The Pentagrams of Passive Spirit

The Pentagrams of Passive Spirit are traced in dark violet. The corresponding name of God is AGLA. As is the case with the Pentagrams of Active Spirit, the corresponding signs are the Rending and Closing of the Veil, and they are used in the same manner. AGLA represents the phrase Ateh Gibor le-Olahm Adonai, meaning "Thou art mighty forever, Lord." It contains the name Adonai, which corresponds to Malkuth (the kingdom), the most material point on the Qabalistic Tree of Life.

Figure 22. The Pentagrams of Fire

The Pentagrams of Fire are traced in red. The corresponding name of God is ALIM (Elohim). The Sign of Fire is given by forming a triangle with the thumbs and forefingers of both hands and holding it up so that the backs of the hands face the forehead. The center of the forehead should be in the center of the triangle. The sign alludes to the upright triangle, which is the traditional alchemical symbol of Fire, and the Ajna chakra or third eye.

Figure 23. The Pentagrams of Water

The Pentagrams of Water are traced in blue. The corresponding name of God is AL or EL. The Sign of Water is given by making a triangle with the thumbs and forefingers of both hands, as in the Sign of Fire, but then placing the triangle at the base of the torso point downwards, with the palms facing the body. The sign alludes to the downward-pointing triangle, which is the traditional symbol of Water, and the Svadasthana chakra.

Figure 24. The Pentagrams of Air

The Pentagrams of Air are traced in yellow. The corresponding name of God is YHVH (Yahweh). The Sign of Air is given by extending the arms to the sides with both elbows bent upwards to form right angles. The wrists are then bent so that the palms face upwards. The sign alludes to the position of the Egyptian god Shu, who was believed to hold up the sky.

Figure 25. The Pentagrams of Earth

The Pentagrams of Earth are traced in green. The corresponding name of God is ADNI (Adonai). The Sign of Earth is given by taking a step forward with the right foot and holding the arms so that the right is up and forward, 45 degrees from vertical, and the left is down and back, also 45 degrees from vertical. The arms should form a straight line. The sign alludes to the position of the Egyptian god Set, who was represented fighting Horus, the son of his brother Osiris, and holding the arms with one pointing up and the other pointing down alludes to the Hermetic maxim "As above, so below."

Finally, once pentagrams have been traced to all four quarters, the ritual is concluded by turning back to face the east and raising your wand or finger to the heavens. You then exclaim "let the divine light descend!" and bring your ritual tool or finger down in a vertical line until reaches the working space on the altar. When working with the Angels of the Great Table this will be the center of the Sigillum Dei Aemeth. For the invoking form, the accompanying visualization is a column of light matching the color used for the pentagram descending from the heavens and coming to rest in the center of the working space. For the banishing form, rather than the light coming to rest it should instead be visualized as filling the temple space and then fading as it purifies the working area of the specified elemental influence. Generally speaking, you will be using the invoking form when working with the Angels of the Great Table, as they are dismissed using the License to Depart rather than the banishing form of this ritual.

In order to facilitate workings that span the elemental realm, the Greater Ritual of the Pentagram may be performed with the pentagram of each element traced to the appropriate direction. When utilized in this manner, the pentagrams should be placed matching the alchemical directional order of the Great Table, with Fire in the East, Air in the South, Water in the West, and Earth in the North.

The Revised Opening by Watchtower

A more elaborate elemental opening ritual that incorporates elements of the Greater Ritual of the Pentagram is the Opening by Watchtower, written by Israel Regardie based on the temple openings used in the Golden Dawn tradition. The original version of the ritual has some rough points, but my magical working group and I spent some time a few years back reworking it into a more appropriate rite for Enochian operations employing the Dee system rather than that of the Golden Dawn. It should be used in place of the Greater Ritual of the Pentagram for operations that incorporate all four elements. The script here includes notations for group workings, though it can be performed by a single individual taking the Officiant role.

One of the elements of Regardie's ritual that I have retained in this script is the use of the standard Golden Dawn elemental magical tools — the Wand for Fire, the Dagger for Air, the Cup for Water, and the Pantacle for Earth. To these I generally add two, the Invoking Wand and Banishing Dagger, both attributed to Spirit. The Banishing Dagger is used to trace banishing pentagrams and hexagrams such as are found in the banishing forms of the Lesser Rituals of the Pentagram and Hexagram. The Invoking Wand is used to trace Invoking pentagrams and hexagrams such as are found in the invoking forms of those same rituals. These weapons are also used when performing the Greater Ritual of the Hexagram and can be used for the Greater Ritual of the Pentagram as well, though if you also have the four standard ritual tools I find that you get a slightly more coherent field if you perform the latter rite using the appropriate elemental tool instead. For Enochian workings, you should always hold whatever tool you are using in the hand that wears the Enochian ring.

As none of these tools are part of the Enochian temple setup, you may also use a system of mudras or hand positions that I have developed to represent each element if you would like to incorporate the Opening by Watchtower into your Enochian rituals. These gestures should be made with the hand that wears the Enochian ring.

> Fire — Hold your hand vertical, with palm facing inward. Close your fist such that your thumb points forward between your index and middle finger. This gesture is called "the fig" and dates back to the ancient Middle East as a means of warding off the "evil eye." It represents the Wand. This gesture may be used for the Invoking Wand as well as the Fire Wand.
>
> Air — Hold your hand vertical, with palm facing inward. Then point straight ahead with your index and middle

finger held together. This gesture is called "sword fingers" and is used in Chinese Qigong and Tai Chi Chuan. It represents the Dagger. This gesture may be used for the Banishing Dagger as well as the Air Dagger.

Water — Hold your palm flat, facing the ground. Then bend your wrist so that your open palm faces forward. This gesture represents the Cup.

Earth — Hold your palm flat, facing the ground. Then make a fist. This gesture represents the Pantacle.

The Revised Opening by Watchtower is performed as follows. It invokes all of the elements including Active and Passive Spirit together rather than a single elemental force. As this ritual has been adapted for Enochian workings, it assumes a temple setup consisting of the Holy Table, Sigillum Dei Aemeth, Ensigns of Creation, Banners, and so forth. It should be noted that while the previous ritual forms are cast across the Holy Table, in the Opening by Watchtower the Officiant or some other participant should instead stand at the appropriate quarter and face outwards when tracing the pentagrams and performing the corresponding vibrations. This ritual works well for a group, particularly one with four or more participants. With that many people, each participant can invoke one of the elements, with the Officiant performing the final invocation of Spirit and the opening of the Veil of Paroketh.

Even though they are not part of the standard Enochian temple setup, the various elemental tools may be placed on the Holy Table without impairing its function so long as they are not placed on or touching the Sigillum Dei Aemeth itself.

The Revised Opening by Watchtower Ritual

I. The Four Elements

Officiant begins at the west of the Holy Table facing east. He or she takes the Banishing Dagger, inhales deeply, and presses the dagger to the lips. As the breath is expelled, the dagger is swept down and back until it points downward and behind the Officiant at about a 45-degree angle.

Officiant:

    ADRPAN VOVINA OD CORS TA DOBIX!
    (adr-PAN vo-VEE-nah OD KORS TA doh-BEEX)

The Banishing Dagger is then returned to the altar.

The original Opening by Watchtower begins with the statement *"Hekas, hekas, este bebeloi!"* This phrase means *"Afar, afar, o ye profane!"* and is a general exordium intended to expel any remaining negative magical influences from the temple used in many Golden Dawn rituals. The phrase above translates from Angelic into English as *"Cast down the Dragon and such that fall."* In the Angelic Keys, the word VOVIN (Dragon) and its several variations allude to the devil and/or demonic forces, while ADRPAN, *"cast down,"* is the best Angelic translation for *"banish."*

Officiant goes to the east, takes the Fire wand, and makes the supernal triangle facing east.

The Supernal triangle is made by using the weapon to tap the corners of an equilateral triangle. You start with the top point, then tap the lower right point, then tap the lower left point.

He or she then holds the wand above head level and circumambulates once clockwise.

All participants rotate accordingly, visualizing a wall of fiery red light surrounding the temple. Attention should be directed across the altar.

Each person should visualize the fiery red light on the side of the temple opposite from where they are standing. Their gaze should be directed across the altar even while circumambulating along with the Officiant.

Officiant:

> *And when, after all the phantoms have vanished,*
> *thou shalt see that holy and formless Fire,*
> *that Fire which darts and flashes*
> *through the hidden depths of the Universe!*
> *Hear thou the Voice of Fire!*

Ideally, the Officiant should make this statement in the time it takes him or her to perform one full circumambulation, so that he or she arrives back in the east on the last word.

Officiant completes the circumambulation and then traces the Invoking Pentagram of Fire in red to the east with the wand while vibrating:

ORO IBAH AOZPI
(OH-ro EE-bah ah-oh-ZOD-pee).

The wand is then returned to the altar.

Officiant next proceeds to the south, takes the Air dagger, and makes the supernal triangle facing south. He or she then holds the dagger above head level and circumambulates once clockwise.

All participants rotate accordingly, visualizing a wall of bright white light surrounding the temple just inside the wall of red light. Attention should be directed across the altar.

Officiant:

> *Such a Fire existeth,*
> *extending through the rushing of Air.*
> *Or even a Fire formless,*
> *whence cometh the image of a voice.*
> *Or even a flashing light, abounding, revolving,*
> *whirling forth, crying aloud!*

Officiant completes the circumambulation and then traces the Invoking Pentagram of Air in white to the south with the dagger while vibrating

MPH ARSL GAIOL
(MEH-peh AR-sal gah-ee-OL).

The dagger is then returned to the altar.

Officiant goes to the west, takes the Water cup, and makes the supernal triangle facing west. He or she then holds the cup above head level and circumambulates once clockwise.

All participants rotate accordingly, visualizing a wall of green light surrounding the temple just inside the wall of white light. Attention should be directed across the altar.

Officiant:
> *So therefore first,*
> *the priest who governeth the works of Fire*
> *must sprinkle with the lustral Water*
> *of the loud and resounding sea!*

Officiant completes the circumambulation and then traces the Invoking Pentagram of Water in green to the west with the cup while vibrating:

OIP TEAA PDOCE
(oh-EEP TEH-ah-ah PDO-keh).

The cup is then returned to the altar.

Officiant goes to the north, takes the Earth pantacle, and makes the supernal triangle facing south. He or she then holds the pantacle above head level and circumambulates once clockwise.

All participants rotate accordingly, visualizing a wall of black light surrounding the temple just inside the wall of green light. Attention should be directed across the altar.

Officiant:
> *This Fire descendeth into that darkly splendid world,*
> *wherein continually ariseth Nature,*
> *delighting in myriad forms —*
> *precipitous, nurturing, winding, and welcoming,*
> *ever revealing a body infused with the light of the Spirit.*

In the original Opening by Watchtower ritual, the four statements related to the elements are taken from the Chaldean Oracles of Zoroaster. The first three are rendered pretty much as they appear in the text, with the order of the second and third switched to accommodate the alchemical order of the directions. This last one, though, my group completely rewrote, on the grounds that it seemed to reify the "spirit good/matter bad" dichotomy that has poisoned far too many spiritual systems.

Officiant completes the circumambulation and then then traces the Invoking Pentagram of Earth in black to the south with the earth pentacle while vibrating:

MOR DIAL HCTGA
(MOR dee-AHL hek-TGAH).

The pantacle is then returned to the altar.

II. The Vortex

Officiant circumambulates clockwise back to the west of the altar and faces east. All participants rotate accordingly. He or she then takes the Fire or Invoking wand, traces the Invoking Pentagram of Active Spirit in bright violet above the altar, and then sweeps the wand straight down and traces the Invoking Pentagram of Passive Spirit below the altar, holding the visualization of both figures while vibrating:

EHNB
(EH-nub).

The Angelic word EHNB is formed by taking the first letters of the names of each of the four elements as they appear on the Black Cross or Tablet of Union (Exarp = Air, Hcoma = Water, Nanta = Earth, and Bitom = Fire). This formula signifies both aspects of the Spirit element, and as such it is vibrated here once following the tracing of both Spirit pentagrams.

The pentagram above the Holy Table should be traced as though it is set into the ceiling. This requires more skill at visualization than tracing to the directions, since the wand has to be held upward at about a 45 degree angle and the image should be slightly distorted by perspective. The Officiant may need to step back slightly to trace below the Holy Table. The pentagram will be partially obscured by the altar cloth, but it should nonetheless be visualized in full set into the floor.

Officiant sets down the wand.

All make and hold the Sign of Apophis and Typhon, with arms held up and outwards at an angle of approximately 60 degrees with the palms turned inwards.

All:

> Thee we invoke, who art universe.
> Thee we invoke, who art in nature formed.
> Thee we invoke, the vast and the mighty.
> Source of darkness, source of light.

This invocation is adapted from the rituals of the Open Source Order of the Golden Dawn.

All make the Sign of Silence, bringing the finger of the right hand or thumb to the lips. The four walls of light are now visualized melting together into grayish light and forming into a cube that surrounds the temple. Pentagrams in the appropriate colors appear on all six faces – red in the east, white in the south, green in the west, black in the north, bright violet above, and dark purple below. There is a short pause to allow for as much detail as possible.

Officiant:

> The visible Sun is the dispenser of light unto the Earth.
> Let us therefore form a vortex in this chamber that the invisible Sun of Spirit may shine herein.

All circumambulate four times, focusing on the center of the Holy Table and visualize the entire Temple rising on the planes through the four elements. On the first circumambulation, a wall of black surrounding the temple is visualized for Earth, on the second green for Water, on the third white for Air, and on the fourth red for Fire. At the conclusion of this all arrive back at their original places, with Officiant to the west of the altar. The cube surrounding the temple is then visualized as melting into a sphere of golden light encompassing the entire space.

III. Opening the Veil

This final gesture alludes to the entry into Tiphareth, the sphere of the Sun on the Tree of Life. The four circumambulations that make up the vortex represent the four spheres below Tiphareth, which are generally attributed to the four elements in Hermetic Qabalah. By passing through those spheres the Officiant and his or her working group find themselves on the threshold of the solar realm. The gesture of Rending the Veil, made by placing the advancing the hands together and then moving them apart as though opening a curtain, represents the opening of the portal that allows access to this sphere.

Officiant:

> Peh Resh Kaph Tau.
> The word is PAROKETH,
> which is the veil of the sanctuary.
> In and by that word
> (makes the Sign of Rending the Veil),
> I open the veil.

All make the Sign of the Enterer directed at the center of the altar.

The Sign of the Enterer, given by advancing the hands at shoulder width, palms down, at the level of the eyes as you take a short step forward with the left foot, represents stepping through the portal, an action that all participants must perform for themselves.

All:

ABRAHADABRA

All then make the Sign of Osiris Risen.

This word and sign signify arrival at the sphere of Tiphareth. The Sign of Osiris Risen is performed by crossing the arms over the chest, like the typical posture of an Egyptian mummy, with the left arm crossed over the right. The figure thus formed by the elbows, hands, and head alludes to the pentagram or blazing star.

The microcosm and macrocosm are now aligned and fully engaged for the Great Table working to follow. As this version of the Opening by Watchtower was developed by me and my magical working group, the Thelemic formula of ABRAHADABRA is employed at this point.

Non-Thelemites may wish to substitute some other formula from their tradition with similar attributions.

A Christian magician may wish to repeat the Keyword Analysis from the Lesser Ritual of the Hexagram, or vibrate the formula YHShVH (Jesus, YHVH infused with the letter Shin, representing the four elements merged with Spirit).

Great Table Conjurations

Chapter 10
Great Table Conjurations

Once the ritual space has been properly tuned using ritual forms, planetary hours, phases of the Moon, or some other method, the magician then may proceed to conjuring the angels appropriate to his or her operation. One of the most significant differences between Dee's system and the conventional modern approach to working with the angels of the Great Table is that their powers differ substantially from those given in the Golden Dawn Enochian system. When the Golden Dawn founders assembled their version of the Great Table, it seems that they mostly ignored the powers communicated to Dee and Kelley and assigned their own based on nineteenth-century Hermetic Qabalah. The exception to this is the Kings, who according to the spirit diaries were never allocated particular powers. In the Golden Dawn system, the four Kings are attributed to the four elements, which I have found to be mostly correct. However, given the Tabula Recensa arrangement of the Great Table and the alchemical order of the directions from the "round house" vision, aside from Iczhihal in the north, the elements and directions that correspond to the Kings in the Dee system are different than those used by Golden Dawn magicians.

King	Direction	Element	Traditional Powers (Liber 777)
Bataivah	East	Fire	Evocation, Pyromancy
Raagiosl	South	Air	Divination
Edlrprnaa	West	Water	The Great Work, Talismans, Crystal-gazing
Iczhihal	North	Earth	Alchemy, Geomancy, Making of Pantacles, Travels on the Astral Plane

For reference, in the Golden Dawn system, Bataivah is related to the East and to Air, Raagiosl to the West and to Water, and Edlprnaa to the South and to Fire, all with corresponding powers allocated by element. Iczhihal's attributions of North and Earth are the same in both systems. It should be noted that with the Kings in the Dee system, their individual attributions are less important because they are generally summoned as a group. All four of the Kings evoked together span the entire elemental realm and I have yet to come across a phenomenon that they are unable to influence to some degree when conjured in this manner.

All of the other Great Table angels are more specialized, and their powers do not break down along the lines set forth in Liber 777. The twenty-four Seniors govern "Knowledge and Judgment in Human Affairs" and are useful for both obtaining any sort of information related to the human sphere as well as influencing the minds of other individuals and groups of people. The letters found in the four sub-quadrants of each direction encode the names of two classes of angels and one class of demons, referred to as Cacodemons by Dee. Their powers are allocated as shown here.

The Golden Dawn Enochian system ascribes secondary elemental attributions to each sub-quadrant based on its arrangement. For example, it considers the upper left sub-quadrant of the upper left quadrant to represent Air of Air, the upper right sub-quadrant of the upper left quadrant to represent Fire of Air, and so forth. This idea

Sub-quadrant	Location	Description
Upper Left	Four names formed from the letters above the controlling cross	Angels of Natural Substances. These angels seem to be primarily of use in alchemical operations, and are capable of determining or influencing the properties of particular chemicals or materials.
Upper Left	Four names formed from the letters below the controlling cross	Angels of Medicine, conjured for healing operations.
Upper Left	Eight names formed from the letters below the controlling cross in conjunction with letters from the black cross	Cacodemons of Medicine, conjured to cause diseases.
Upper Right	Four names formed from the letters above the controlling cross	Angels of Transportation. From the text of the conjuration, it is unclear whether the function of these angels is to physically move objects or to keep travelers safe on long journeys, such as sailing voyages.
Upper Right	Four names formed from the letters below the controlling cross	Angels of Metals and Precious Stones. These angels are essentially treasure-finding spirits like those found in many other Solomonic grimoires, with the additional ability to locate suitable sites for mining and so forth.
Upper Right	Eight names formed from the letters below the controlling cross in conjunction with letters from the black cross	Cacodemons of Metals and Precious Stones. Dee was told that while the angels associated with this Quadrant can be conjured to find veins of metallic ore, the Cacodemons can be conjured to acquire "the money, coined."
Lower Right	Four names formed from the letters above the controlling cross	Angels of the Mechanical Arts, conjured to influence or obtain knowledge of engineering and technology in general.

Sub-quadrant	Location	Description
Lower Right	Four names formed from the letters below the controlling cross	Angels of Transformation, conjured to transform one thing into another. These are good general angels for creating changes of various sorts in the material world.
Lower Right	Eight names formed from the letters below the controlling cross in conjunction with letters from the black cross	Cacodemons of Transformation. It is unclear from the diaries what the distinction is between these Cacodemons and the corresponding angels. The sense I get from working with them is that the angels are most appropriate to "creative" change and the Cacodemons most appropriate to "destructive" change.
Lower Left	Four names formed from the letters above the controlling cross	Angels of Secret Discovery, conjured to allow the magician to learn the secrets of others. This is a similar power to that ascribed to Bnapsen, the King of Saturday, in the Heptarchial system.
Lower Left	Four names formed from the letters below the controlling cross	Angels of Living Creatures of the Four Elements. These angels are conjured in order to obtain information about or influence creatures other than humans. This includes "elementals," spirits that inhabit the various elements.
Lower Left	Eight names formed from the letters below the controlling cross in conjunction with letters from the black cross	Cacodemons of Living Creatures of the Four Elements. As with the Angels of Transformation, it is unclear how these Cacodemons differ from the corresponding angels and the sense I have is that they represent a more destructive aspect of the angels' power. I would imagine that you would summon the Cacodemons rather than the angels to kill or injure a creature, for example.

is drawn from an early seventeenth-century text called the Treatise on Angel Magic that relates the sub-quadrants to the sixteen signs of geomancy.

In the Dee system, elements are ascribed to the angels and Cacodemons of the sub-quadrants according to the arrangement discussed in the chapter on the Great Table. Reading down the four angel names from a particular sub-quadrant, the first is attributed to Air, the second to Water, the third to Earth, and the fourth to Fire. What this means is that if you want to summon, for example, only the Angels of Medicine related to Air to heal some sort of thought disorder, you would conjure only the first name of the four from each direction. You can also combine elements, so that to heal a thought disorder with emotional components you might want to summon only the first two Angels of Medicine from each of the four directions, those being attributed to the elements of Air and Water.

Physical Manifestations

Like the Kings and Princes of the Heptarchia Mystica, the Angels of the Great Table do not generally physically appear over the Sigillum Dei Aemeth but rather may be scried using a crystal or dark mirror placed there. The strongest physical effects I generally experience when the angels arrive are temperature changes and shifts in candle flames. Even so, there is a discernable shift in the atmosphere of the temple when the angels are present and after a few operations you should become familiar with it. This sense of presence is unsurprisingly similar to that generated by the Heptarchial Kings and Princes.

In the course of my magical experiments I have found that Enochian spirits of whatever sort can often raise the needle on an electromagnetic field (EMF) detector on command once they are present, so long as the detector's probe is placed over the Sigillum. In order to test this out for yourself, the best sort of detector is one with a detachable probe that can be positioned a short distance from the detector. Otherwise, the entire device would need to be placed on the Sigillum and this can be difficult with larger instruments. Ghost hunters sometimes use a device called a K2 meter to ask simple yes/no questions of spirits, and while I have yet to experiment with such a meter myself, based on the EMF fluctuations I have measured, I expect that it would probably work.

Using a device as simple as an EMF or K2 meter is helpful in that it can provide an objective sign that the spirit is present without requiring the spirit to exert nearly as much physical energy as some grimoire magicians like to demand. While it may be possible for a spirit to produce poltergeist phenomena, commanding it to do so before taking it seriously strikes me as wasteful and even silly. The overall power of a spirit may be sufficient to produce a probability shift of a particular degree, but if you command the spirit to exert most of that influence to perform tricks there will be little left over to accomplish the magical intent for which you summoned the spirit in the first place.

Chapter 11
Great Table Talismans

Unlike the Kings and Princes of the Heptarchia Mystica, the Angels of the Great Table quadrants have no obvious talismans or sigils detailed in the Dee diaries. In order to construct such talismans, I have once more adapted an idea first published in Geoffrey James' *Enochian Evocation*. James simply proposes that the talisman for a particular group of angels could consist of the portion of the Great Table grid in which the group of angels resides. So, for example, a talisman for the Angels of Medicine of the east would consist of the 5x6 grid of Angelic letters found in the upper left sub-quadrant of the upper left quadrant.

This is a relatively elegant solution with one problem – for each sub-quadrant there are two groups of angels and one group of Cacodemons who would then be summoned using the same talisman. Whether or not the two groups of angels could share a talisman, the idea of sharing one between angels and Cacodemons strikes me as problematic at best. In order to deal with this issue, the talismans here incorporate a 5x6, 6x6, or 6x7 grid along with sigil marks showing which group of angels the talisman represents. This means each group of angels and Cacodemons have their own unique talisman designs.

The sigil marks follow the standard practice dating back at least as far as Agrippa's Three Books of Occult Philosophy of starting each individual line with a small circle and ending with a small line perpendicular to the direction in which the names are being read. The names sigilized on the talismans include those of the angels or cacodemons to which the talisman belongs along with the controlling names used to conjure them.

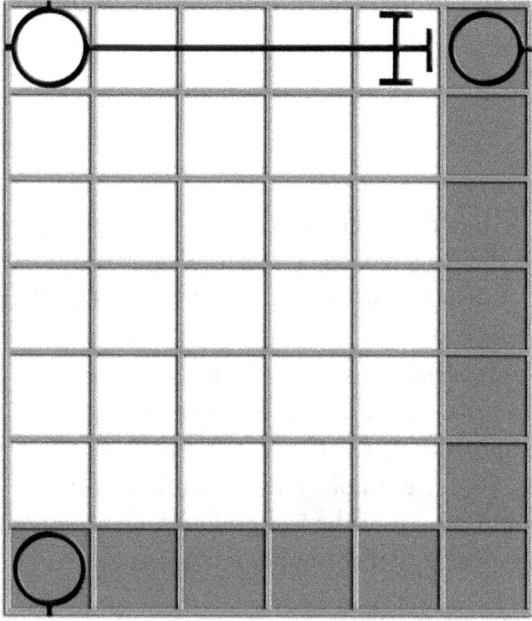

Figure 26. Sigil Marks for Angels above the Controlling Cross

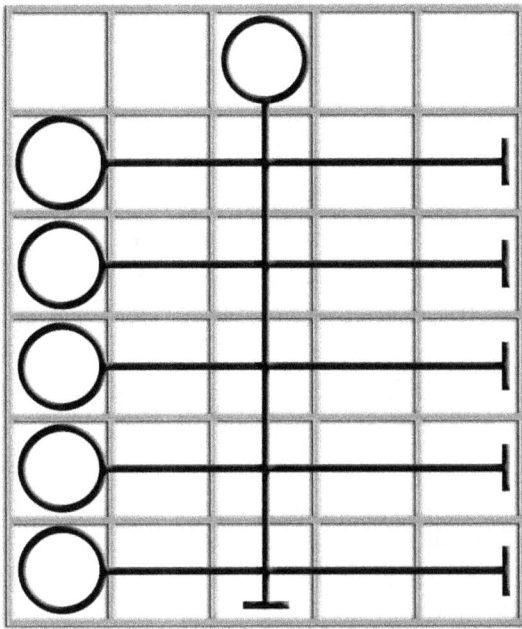

Figure 27. Sigil Marks for Angels below the Controlling Cross

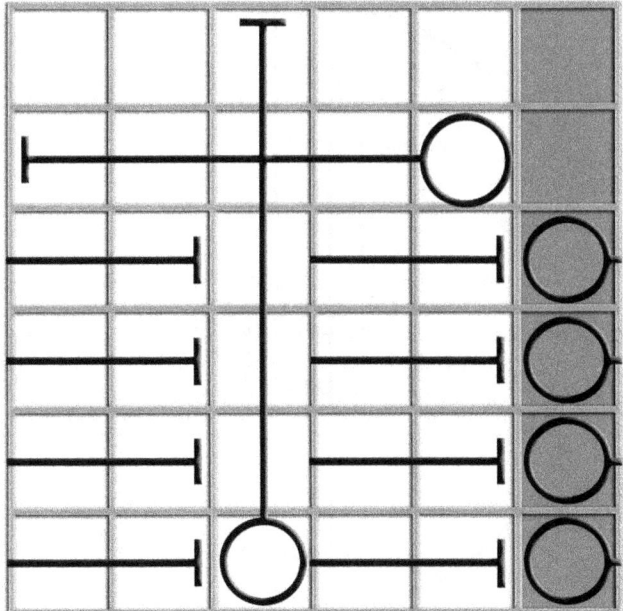

Figure 28. Sigil Marks for Cacodemons

The grid with sigil marks is then filled in with the appropriate letters in Angelic script to mark the quadrant to which the talisman corresponds. This creates a unique sigil for each group of angels within the quadrants. The shaded sections represent letters from the Black Cross, which are incorporated into the controlling names of the angels above the controlling cross and the names of the individual cacodemons.

Talismans for the Kings and Seniors are not quite as straightforward to assemble. The King occupies the center of the quadrant and the Seniors form a cross extending outward to the edges of the quadrant grid. One could, therefore, create a talisman that reproduces the entire quadrant with the King and Seniors marked. This is essentially how James recommends constructing talismans for the Seniors, and it also bears some similarity to the method practiced by the Aurum Solis, in which a small reproduction of each quadrant is constructed as a metal talisman and held during operations. However, I have simplified the design shown here as a cross bearing only the letters of the names for the King and Seniors of the quadrant along with the appropriate sigil marks for the Kings, Seniors, and three names of God.

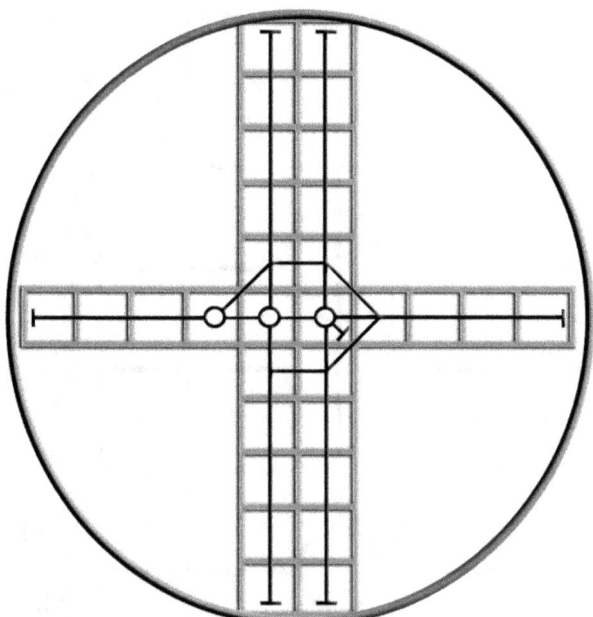

Figure 29. Sigil Marks for the Kings and Seniors

Much as the same talisman is used in the Heptarchial system for both the King and Prince, the Kings and Seniors share the same talisman design. In effect, rather than a corresponding Prince, each King has six associated Seniors that act as Ministers. In fact, Dee did not write conjurations for the Kings, but rather stopped at the level of the Seniors. However, I have personally had great success evoking the Kings with my own conjuration based on the one Dee wrote for the Seniors. The hierarchy is relatively obvious, with the Kings summoned by the three names of God.

It should be noted that these talismanic designs for the Watchtower angels are rectangular figures whereas those for the Heptarchial angels are circular. As modern readers of Dee's diaries are left guessing at the designs for the Great Table talismans, none of us can ever be sure, but rectangular tablets are the most obvious solution given the manner in which the names are derived from the quadrants and sub-quadrants. There may also be some deeper symbolism related to the alchemical concept of "squaring the circle" involved in the transition from the planetary spheres to the elemental realm.

Figure 30. Talisman for the Kings and Seniors of the East

Figure 31. Talisman for the Kings and Seniors of the South

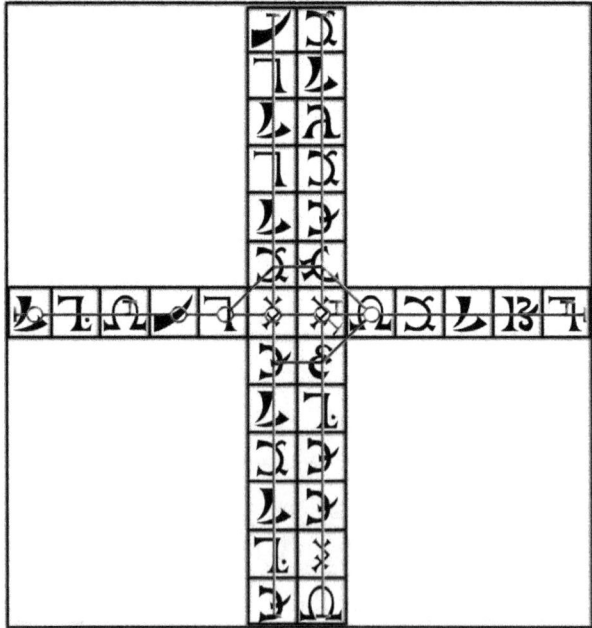

Figure 32. Talisman for the Kings and Seniors of the West

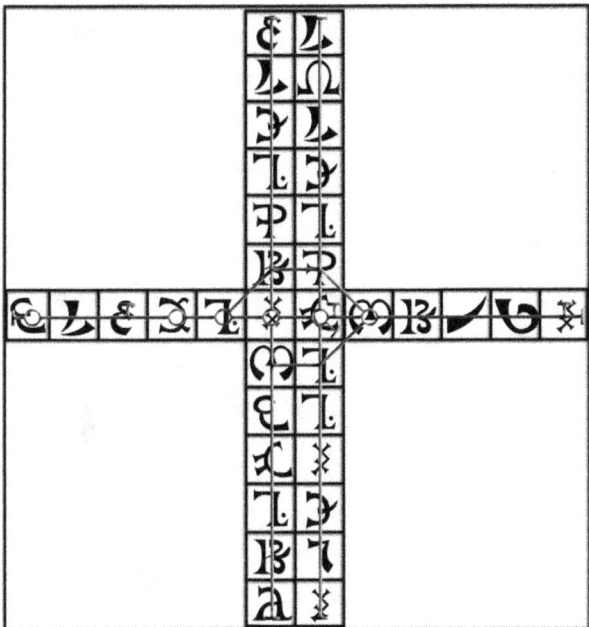

Figure 33. Talisman for the Kings and Seniors of the North

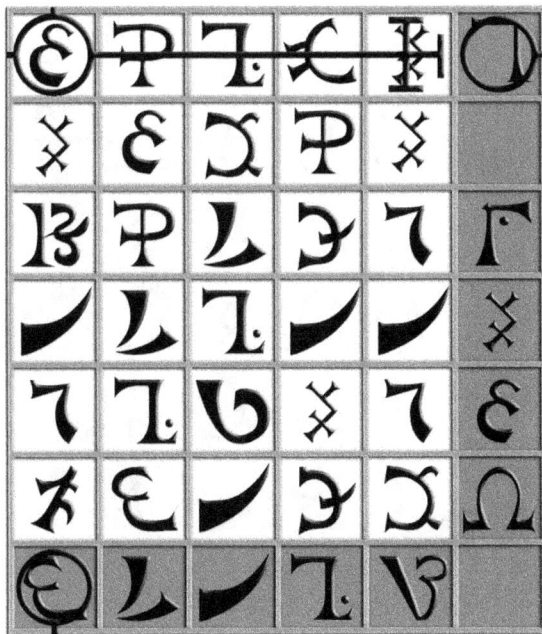

Figure 34. Talisman for the Angels of Natural Substances of the East

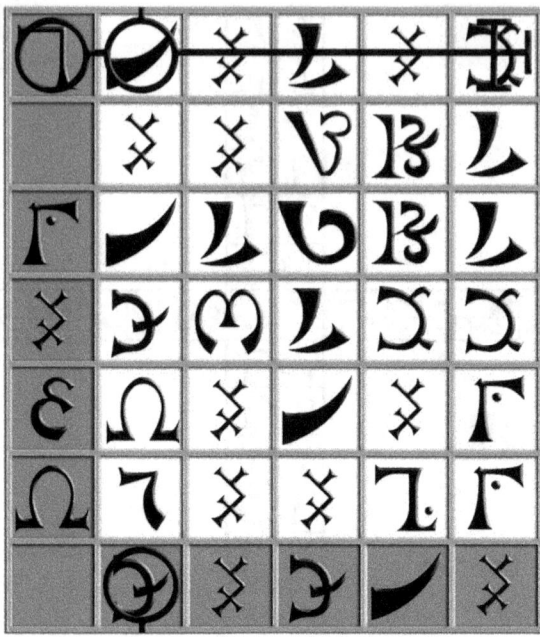

Figure 35. Talisman for the Angels of Natural Substances of the South

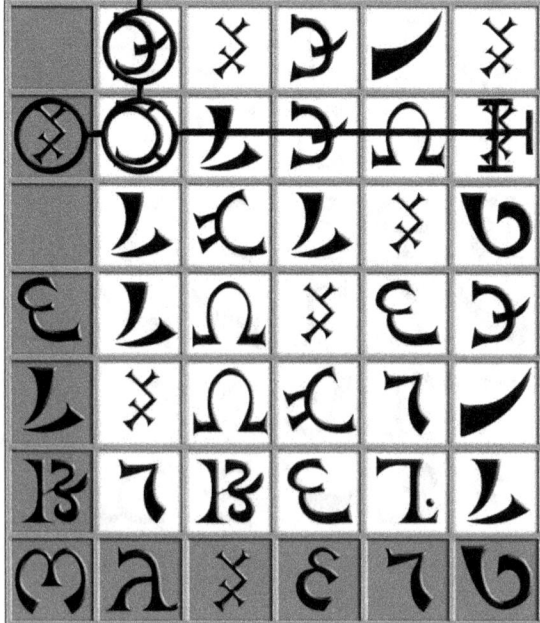

Figure 36. Talisman for the Angels of Natural Substances of the West

Figure 37. Talisman for the Angels of Natural Substances of the North

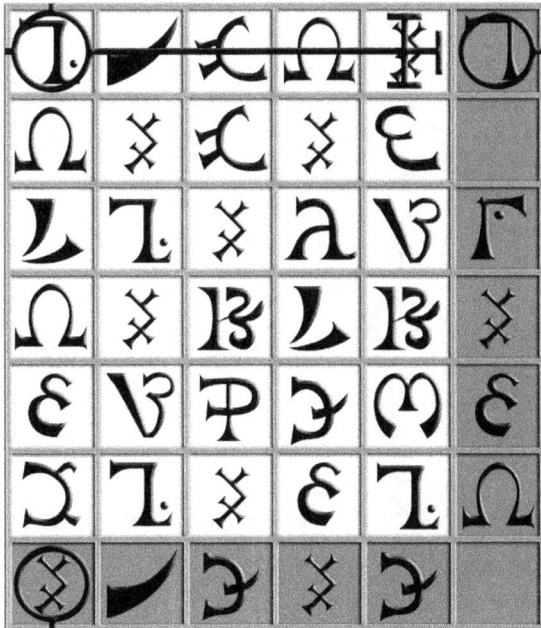

Figure 38. Talisman for the Angels of Transportation of the East

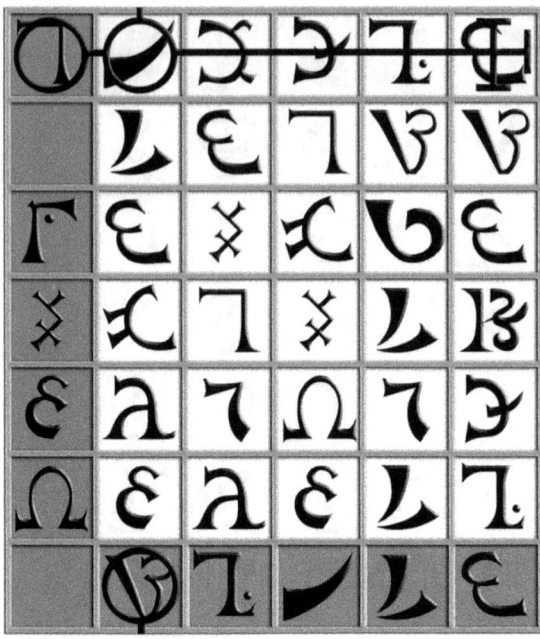

Figure 39. Talisman for the Angels of Transportation of the South

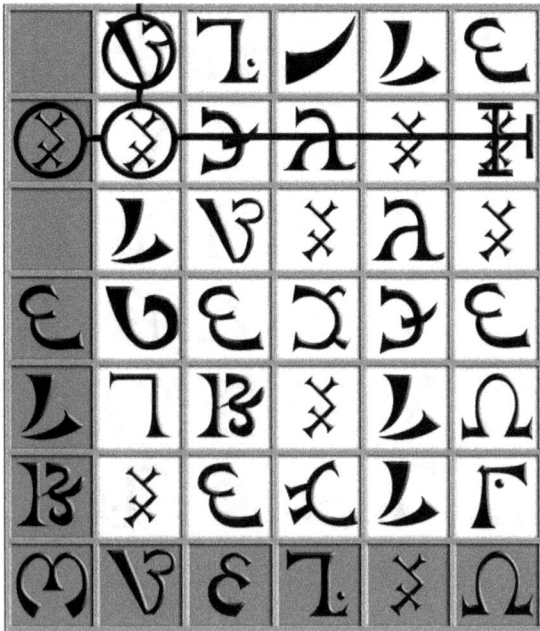

Figure 40. Talisman for the Angels of Transportation of the West

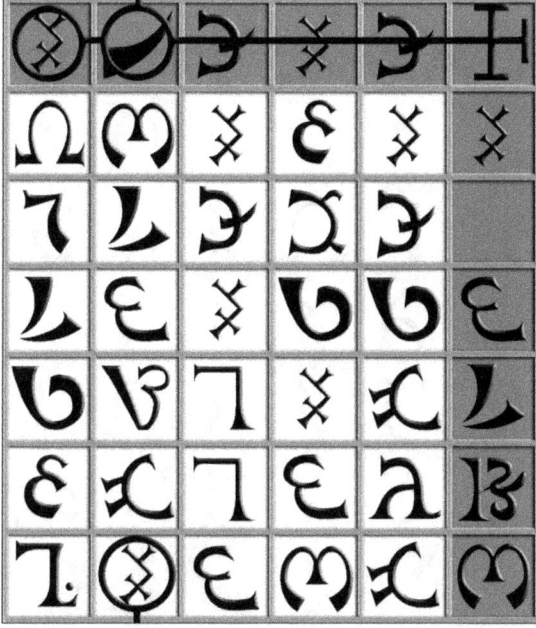

Figure 41. Talisman for the Angels of Transportation of the North

Figure 42. Talisman for the Angels of the Mechanical Arts of the East

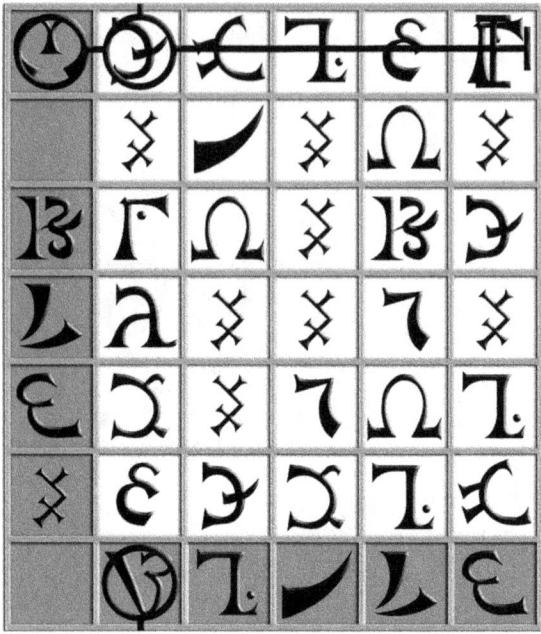

Figure 43. Talisman for the Angels of the Mechanical Arts of the South

Figure 44. Talisman for the Angels of the Mechanical Arts of the West

Figure 45. Talisman for the Angels of the Mechanical Arts of the North

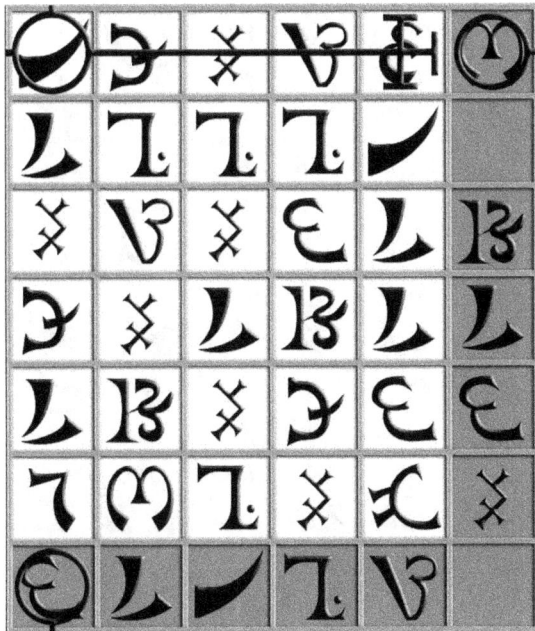

Figure 46. Talisman for the Angels of Secret Discovery of the East

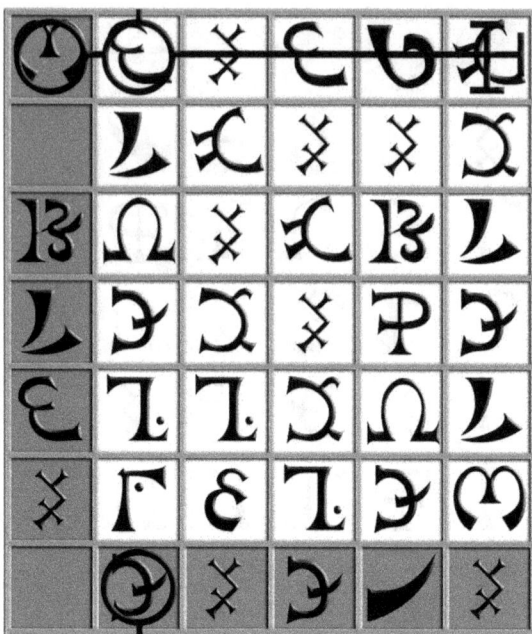

Figure 47. Talisman for the Angels of Secret Discovery of the South

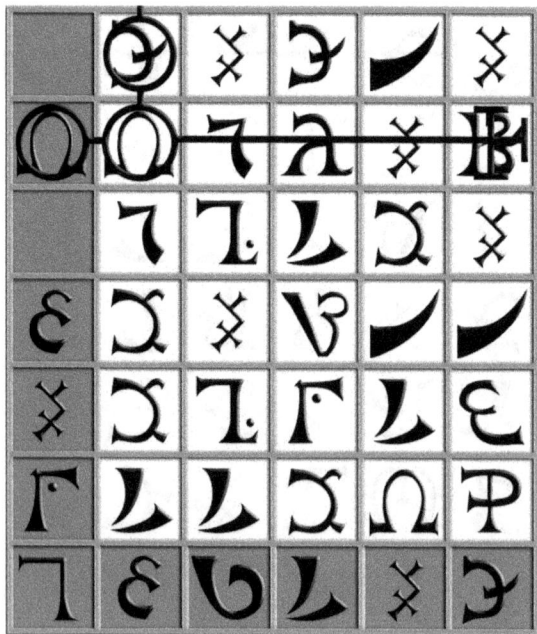

Figure 48. Talisman for the Angels of Secret Discovery of the West

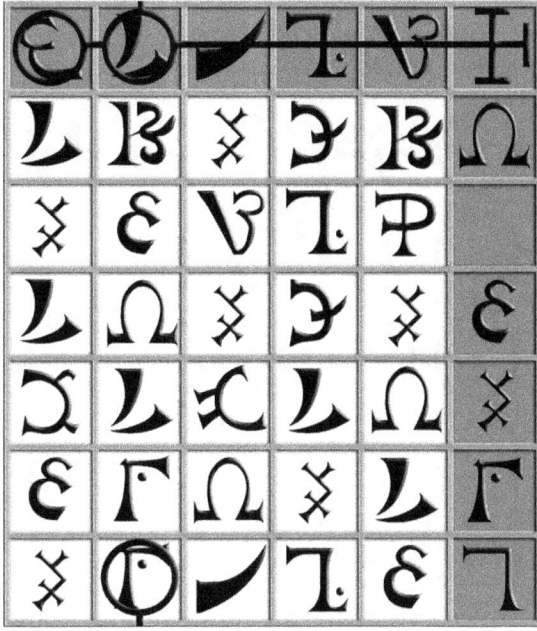

Figure 49. Talisman for the Angels of Secret Discovery of the North

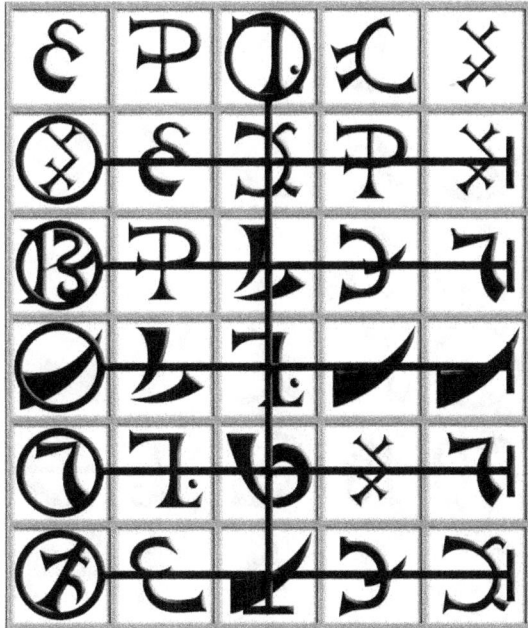

Figure 50. Talisman for the Angels of Medicine of the East

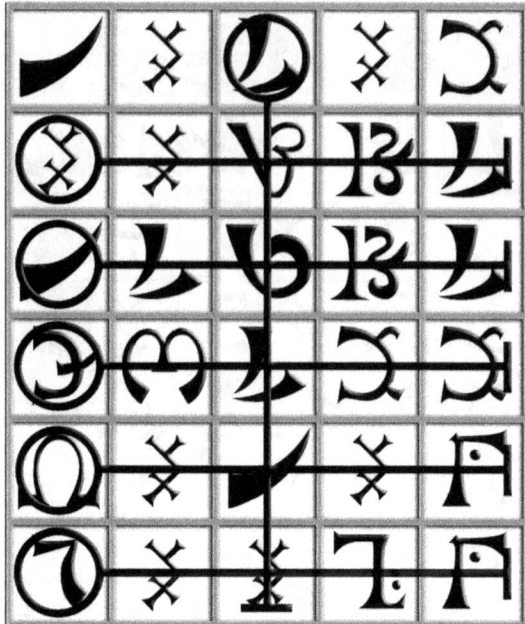

Figure 51. Talisman for the Angels of Medicine of the South

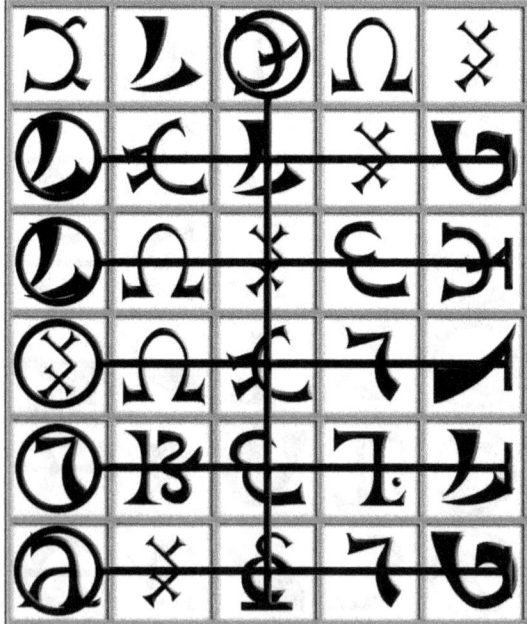

Figure 52. Talisman for the Angels of Medicine of the West

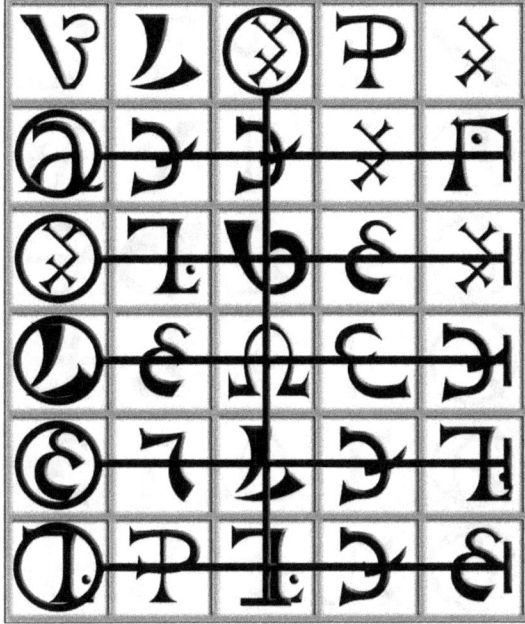

Figure 53. Talisman for the Angels of Medicine of the North

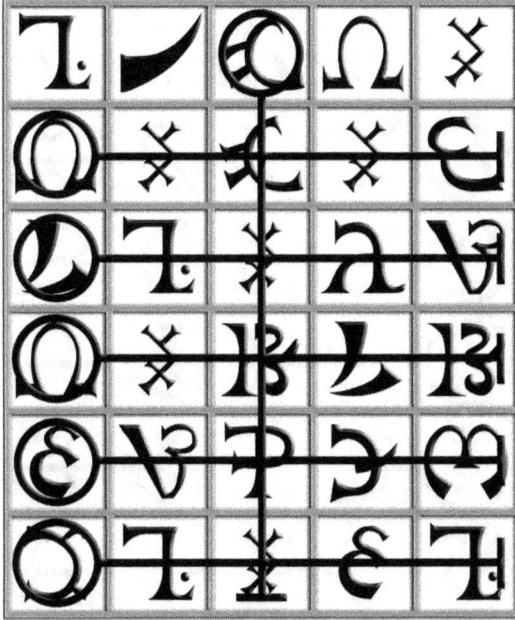

Figure 54. Talisman for the Angels of Metals and Precious Stones of the East

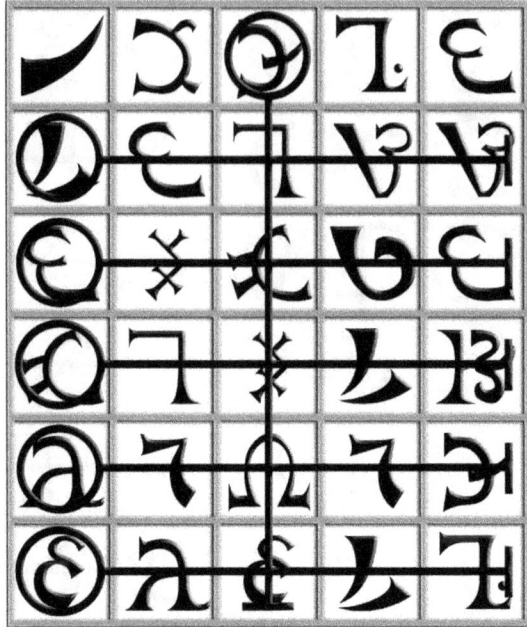

Figure 55. Talisman for the Angels of Metals and Precious Stones of the South

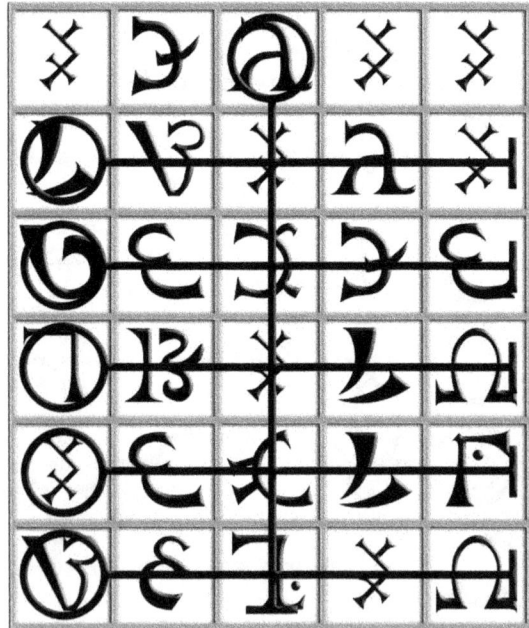

Figure 56. Talisman for the Angels of Metals and Precious Stones of the West

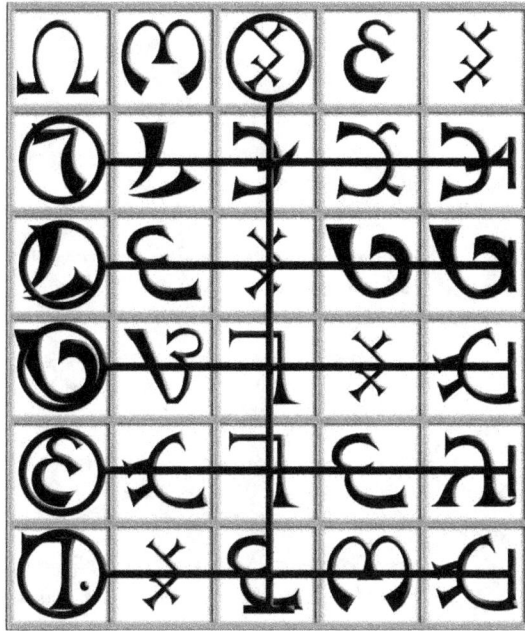

Figure 57. Talisman for the Angels of Metals and Precious Stones of the North

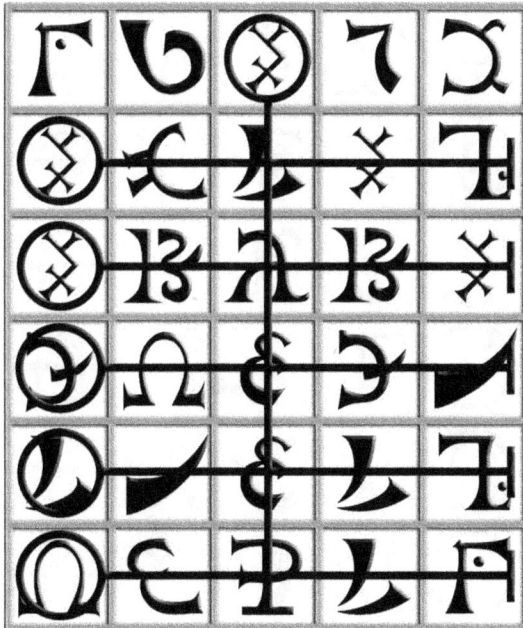

Figure 58. Talisman for the Angels of Transformation of the East

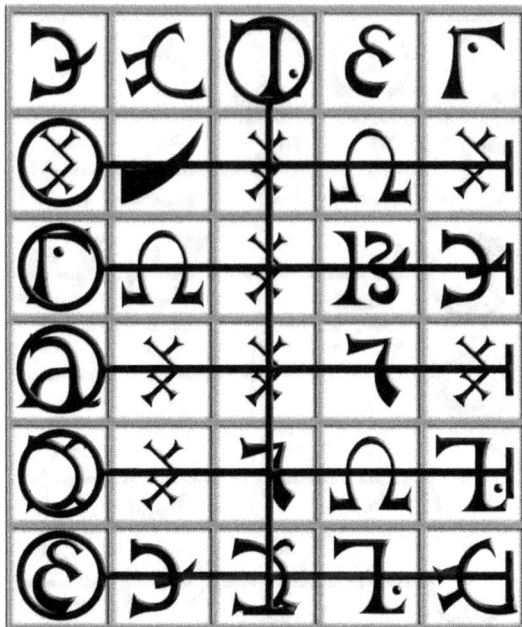

Figure 59. Talisman for the Angels of Transformation of the South

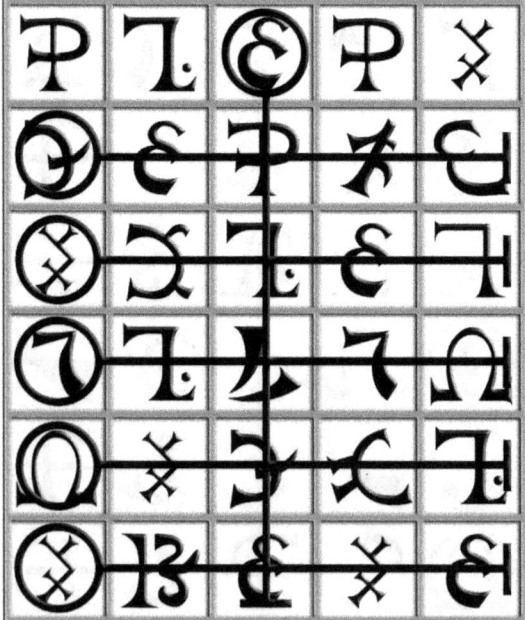

Figure 60. Talisman for the Angels of Transformation of the West

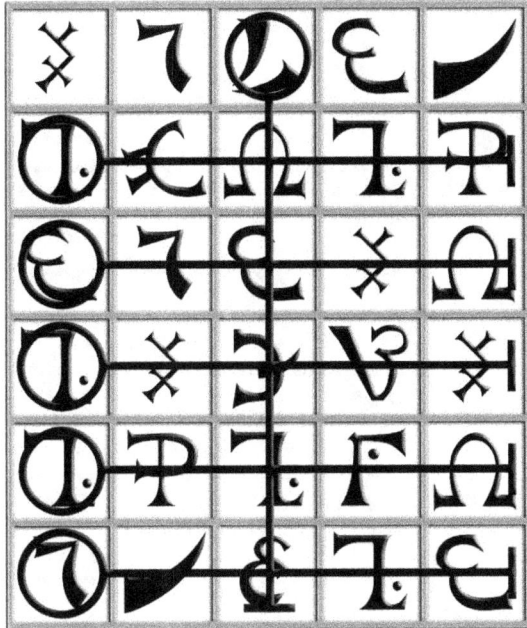

Figure 61. Talisman for the Angels of Transformation of the North

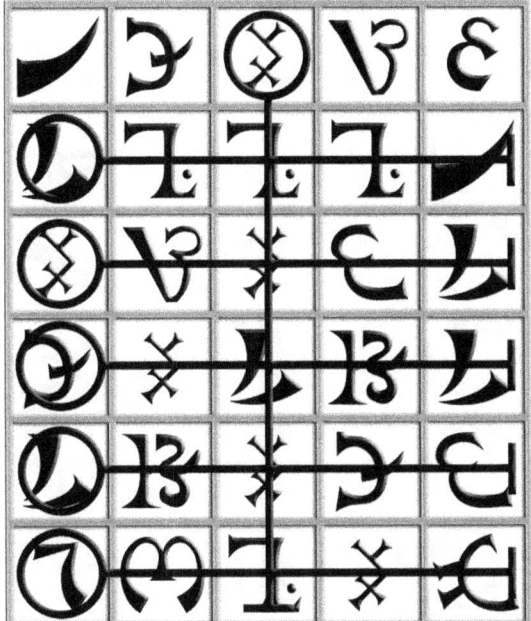

Figure 62. Talisman for the Angels of Living Creatures and the Four Elements of the East

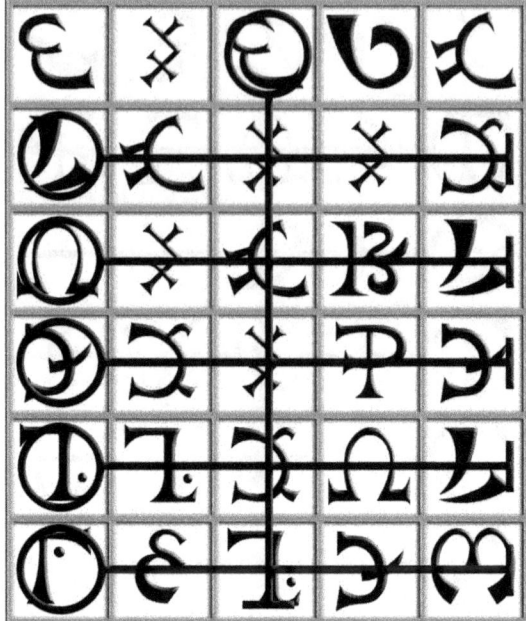

Figure 63. Talisman for the Angels of Living Creatures and the Four Elements of the South

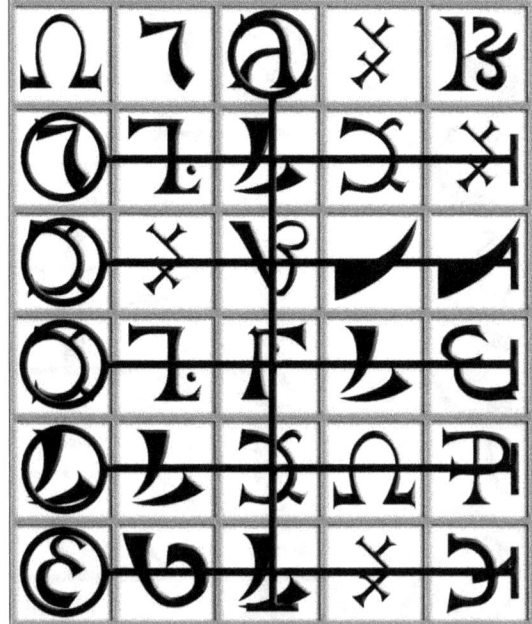

Figure 64. Talisman for the Angels of Living Creatures and the Four Elements of the West

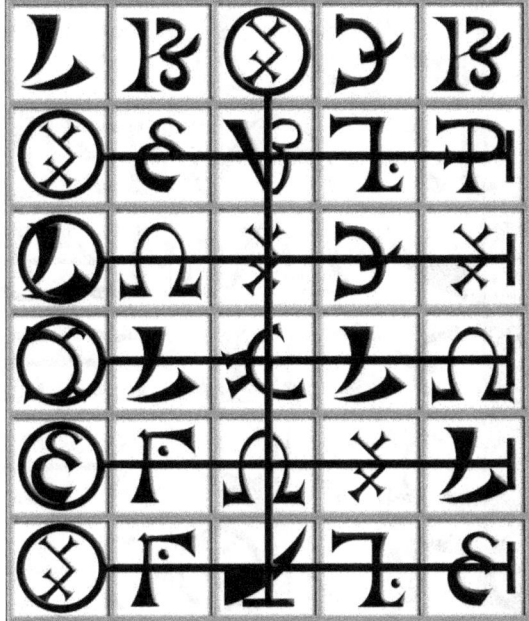

Figure 65. Talisman for the Angels of Living Creatures and the Four Elements of the North

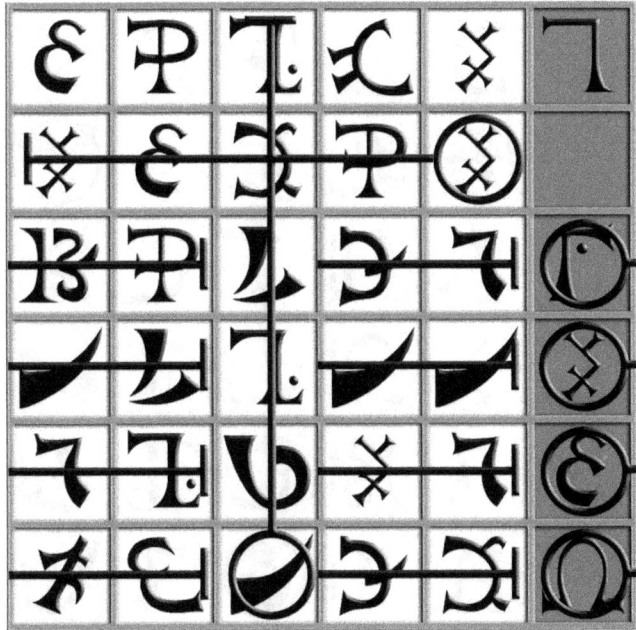

Figure 66. Talisman for the Cacodemons of Medicine of the East

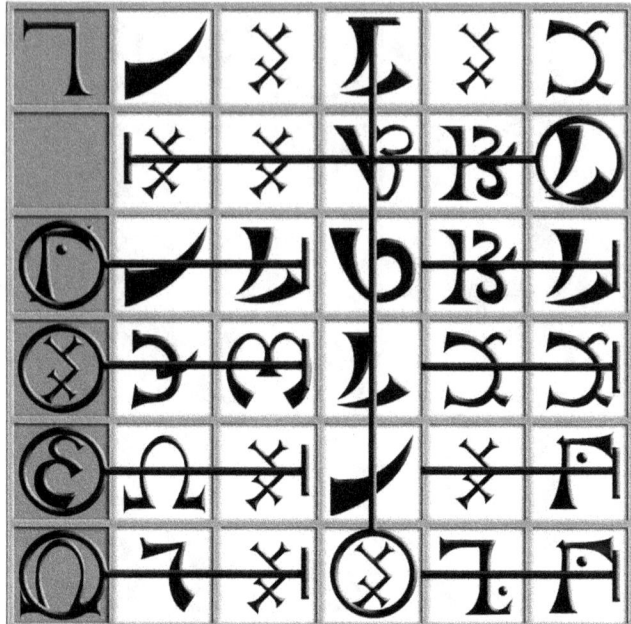

Figure 67. Talisman for the Cacodemons of Medicine of the South

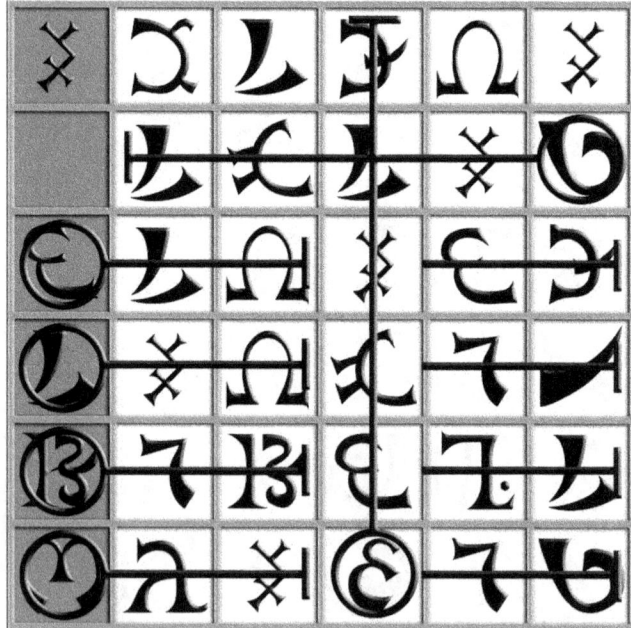

Figure 68. Talisman for the Cacodemons of Medicine of the West

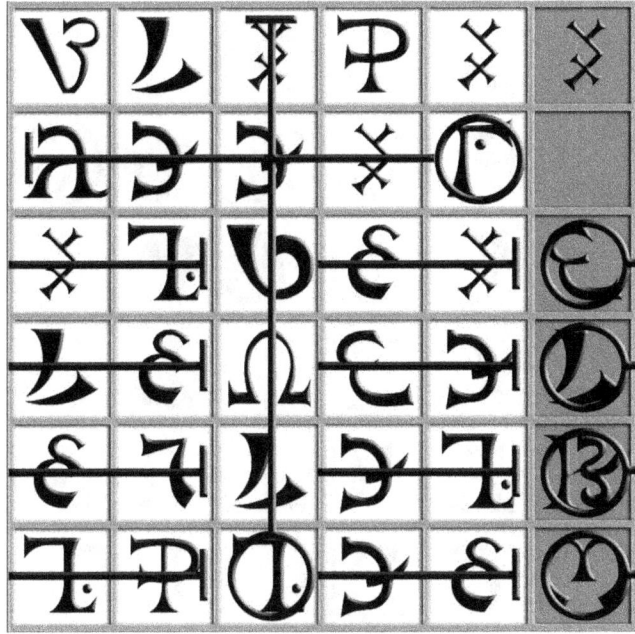

Figure 69. Talisman for the Cacodemons of Medicine of the North

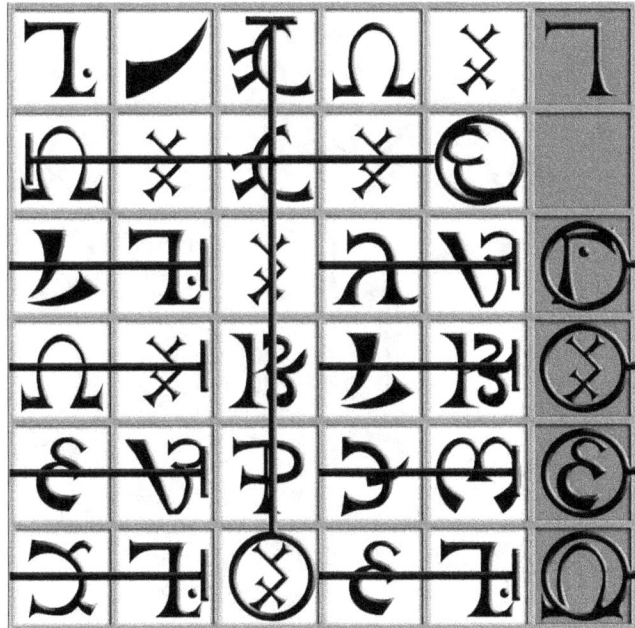

Figure 70. Talisman for the Cacodemons of Metals and Precious Stones of the East

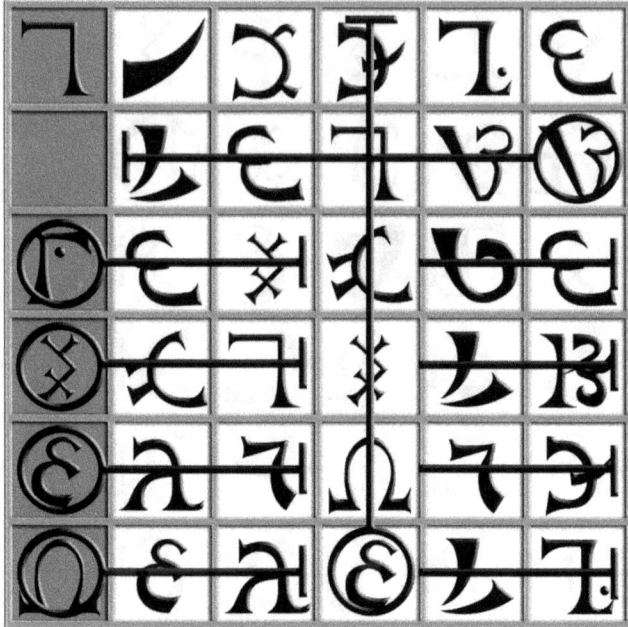

Figure 71. Talisman for the Cacodemons of Metals and Precious Stones of the South

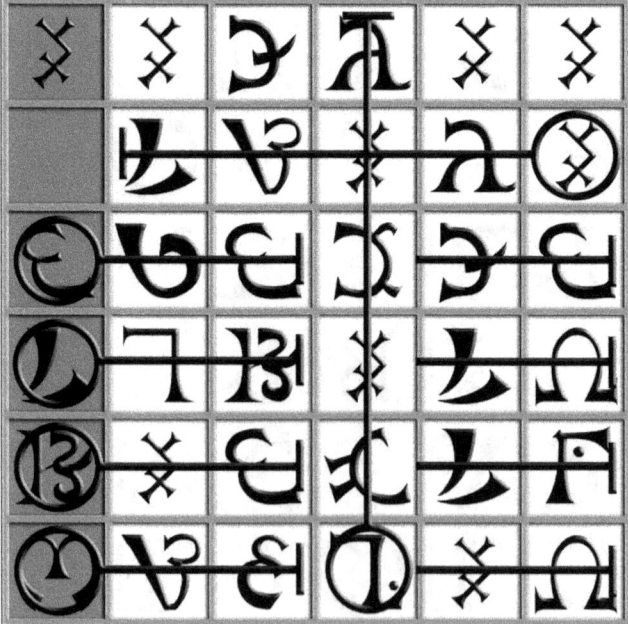

Figure 72. Talisman for the Cacodemons of Metals and Precious Stones of the West

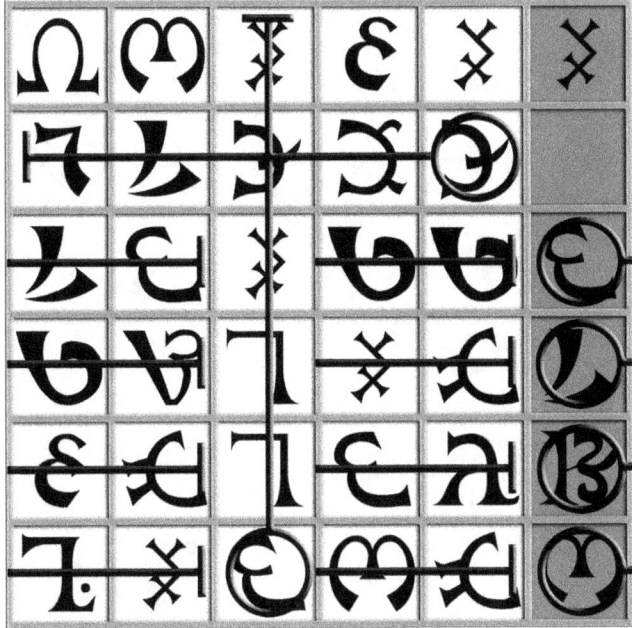

Figure 73. Talisman for the Cacodemons of Metals and Precious Stones of the North

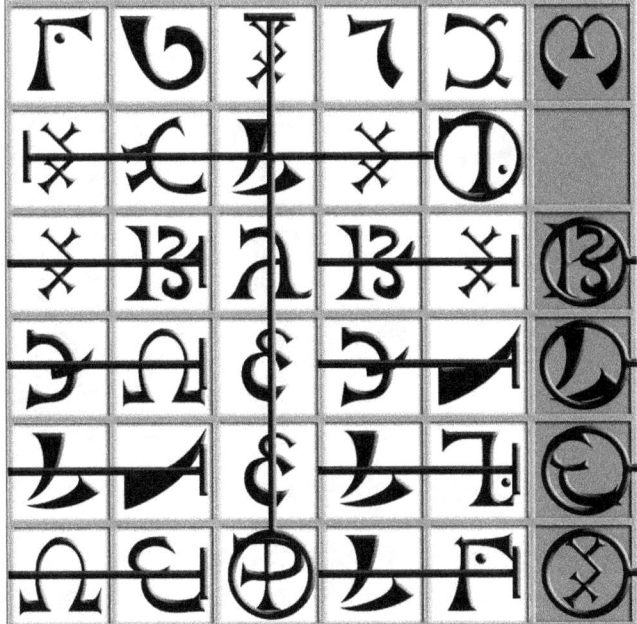

Figure 74. Talisman for the Cacodemons of Transformation of the East

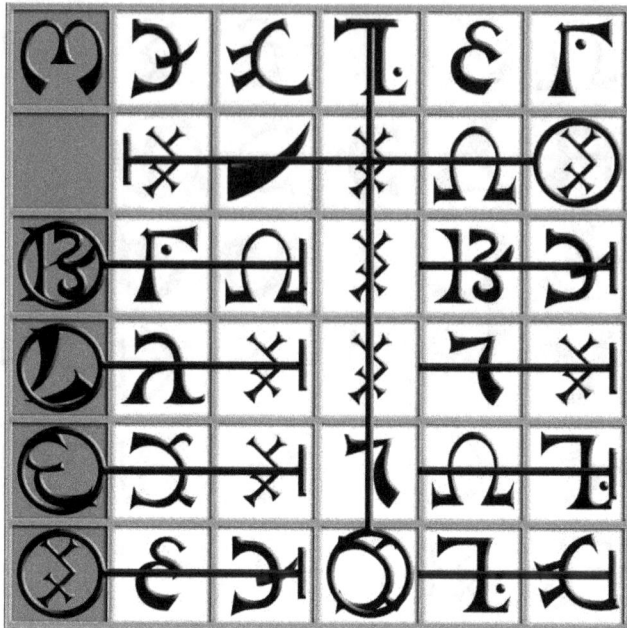

Figure 75. Talisman for the Cacodemons of Transformation of the South

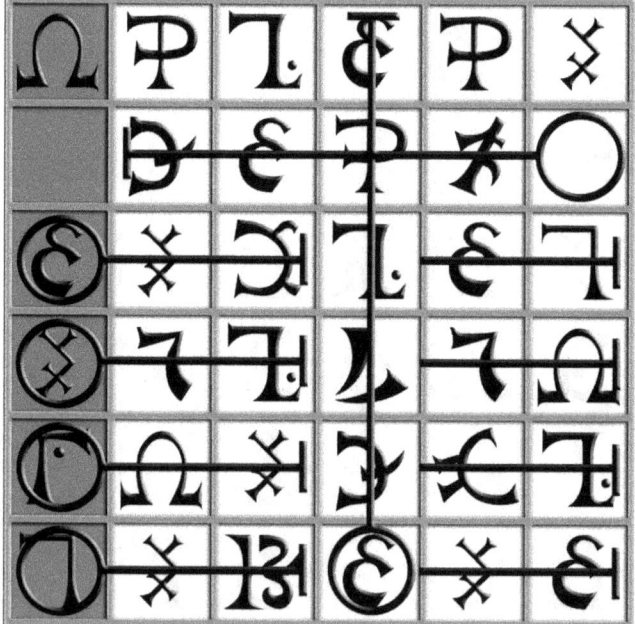

Figure 76. Talisman for the Cacodemons of Transformation of the West

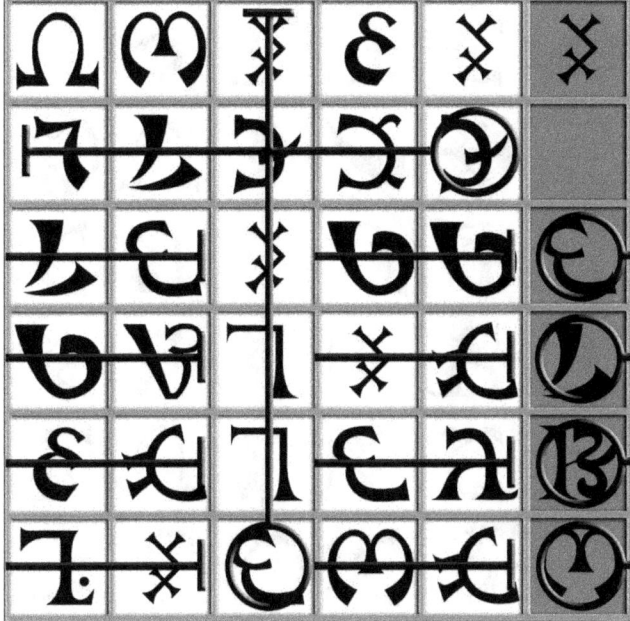

Figure 77. Talisman for the Cacodemons of Transformation of the North

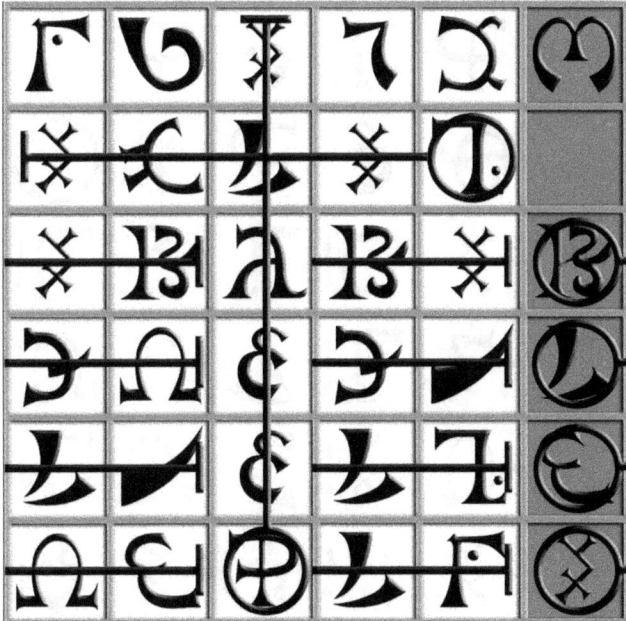

Figure 78. Talisman for the Cacodemons of Living Creatures and the Four Elements of the East

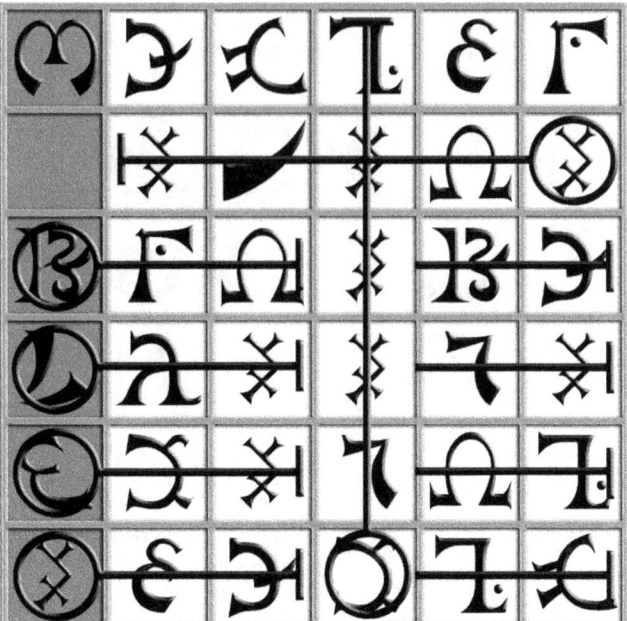

Figure 79. Talisman for the Cacodemons of Living Creatures and the Four Elements of the South

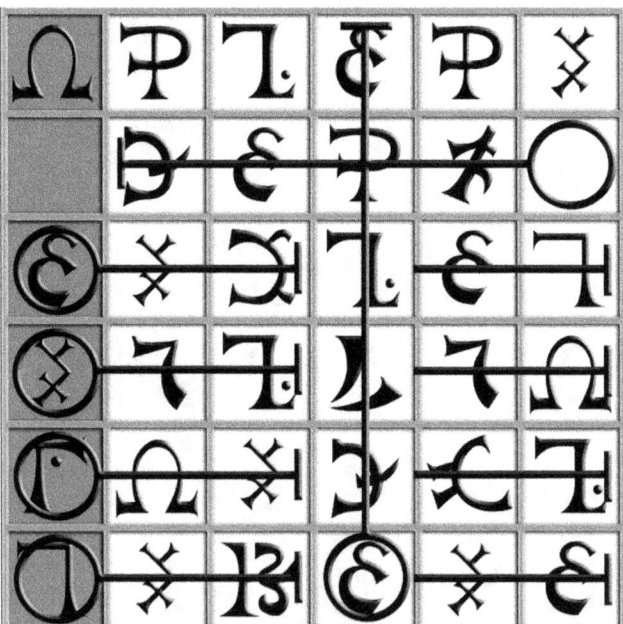

Figure 80. Talisman for the Cacodemons of Living Creatures and the Four Elements of the West

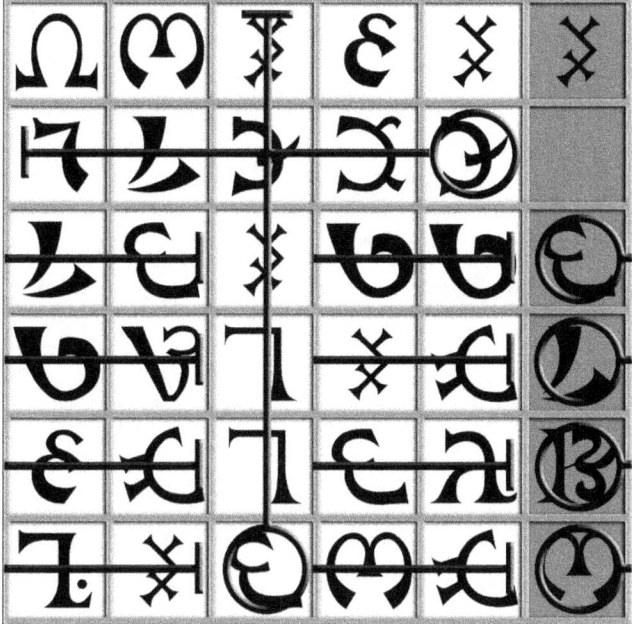

Figure 81. Talisman for the Cacodemons of Living Creatures and the Four Elements of the North

Chapter 12
The Kings and Seniors

The Kings

The names of the four Kings are extracted from each of the quadrants by following a clockwise spiral drawn in the center.

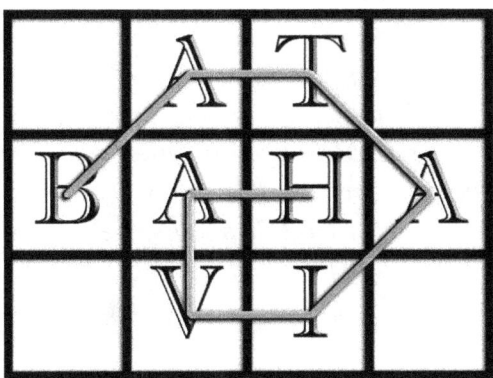

Figure 82. Spiral Showing Bataivah, the King of the East

While their primary attribution is directional the Kings are also elemental in nature, with all four conjured together representing the entire span of nature. Conjured as such, their powers are general and quite extensive. Dee wrote no conjurations for the Kings, so the one that is included here is my own.

Invocation:

Direction	King Name	Names of God
East	BATAIVAH	ORO, IBAH, AOZPI
South	RAAGIOSL	MPH, ARSL, GAIOL
West	EDLPRNAA	OIP, TEAA, PDOCE
North	ICZHIHAL	MOR, DIAL, HCTGA

O you great and mighty King of the [Direction], powerful and faithful to the omnipotent God of our ministry, in the name of the same God, one in three, I say to you, [King], through the divine Names by which you are particularly bound, the Holy Names of God [Name of God 1], [Name of God 2], and [Name of God 3], I, [Your Magical Name], a faithful servant of the our omnipotent God, amicably, earnestly, and confidently demand and beseech you that you appear within this Table of Art and Sigil of God, and thereafter attend to my commands.

I command you to appear, to perform, and to complete, goodly, plainly, intelligibly, and perfectly, according to your Virtue, Power, and Office, and according to the capacity of your Ministry, entrusted and committed to you by the almighty God, by these Holy Names [Name of God 1], [Name of God 2], and [Name of God 3].

Through these sacred Names of God [Name of God 1], [Name of God 2], and [Name of God 3].

Amen.

The Seniors

The twenty-four Seniors are called upon to impart, or influence, knowledge and judgment in human affairs. The six Seniors attributed to each direction can be extracted from each quadrant of the Great Table as shown.

The controlling name for the six Seniors of each direction is the King of that direction.

Direction	Senior Names	King Name
East	HABIORO, AAOZAIF, HTMORDA, AHAOZPI, HIPOTGA, AVTOTAR	BATAIVAH
South	LSRAHPM, SAIINOV, LAOAXRP, SLGAIOL, LIGDISA, SONIZNT	RAAGIOSL
West	AAETPIO, ADOEOET, ALNDVOD, AAPDOCE, ARINNAP, ANODOIN	EDLPRNAA
North	LAIDROM, ACZINOR, LZINOPO, ALHGTGA, LIIANSA, AHMLICV	ICZHIHAL

Invocation:

O you six Seniors of the [Direction], powerful and faithful to the omnipotent God of our ministry, in the name of the same God, one in three, I say to you, [Senior 1], [Senior 2], [Senior 3], [Senior 4], [Senior 5], [Senior 6], through the divine Name by which you are particularly bound, the Angelic Name [King], I, [Your Magical Name], a faithful servant of the omnipotent God, amicably, earnestly, and confidently demand and beseech you that you appear within this Table of Art and Sigil of God, and thereafter attend to my commands.

I command you to appear, to perform, and to complete, goodly, plainly, intelligibly, and perfectly, according to

your Virtue, Power, and Office, and according to the capacity of your Ministry, entrusted and committed to you by the omnipotent God, by the Angelic Name [King]. Through the sacred Name of God [King],
Amen.

Chapter 13
The Kerubic Angels

Referring to this first group of sub-quadrant angels as "Kerubic" is Golden Dawn rather than Dee's terminology, as is the use of "Lesser Angels" in the following section, but I have adopted it because it simplifies the taxonomy of the various Angelic groups. The names of the Kerubic angels, or Kerubs, are formed by combining the four letters above the arms of the controlling cross for each sub-quadrant into all four possible distinct combinations. The Names of God that control them are obtained by combining the letters as they appear on the Table (the first of the four names) with the letters from the vertical and horizontal rows on the black cross matching the first letter of the name.

The Angels of Natural Substances

These angels are conjured in order to learn the various properties of particular materials, as well as to consecrate them for magical workings and assist with various alchemical operations. In addition, they rule over these properties and can be called upon to combine or alter them.

Direction	Angels of Natural Substances	Controlling Names of God
East	RZLA, ZLAR, LARZ, ARZL	ERZLA and MRZLA
South	TAAD, AADT, ADTA, DTAA	ETAAD and NTAAD
West	DOPA, OPAD, PADO, ADOP	ADOPA and NDOPA
North	BOZA, OZAB, ZABO, ABOZ	ABOZA and MBOZA

Invocation:

O you four, faithful and truthful ministers of Omnipotent God, your Creator, [Angel 1], [Angel 2], [Angel 3], [Angel 4] who are in the [Direction] part of the world, and are powerful and skilled in the mixing together of natural substances: I, [Your Magical Name], devoted servant of the same, our Creator, and through the omnipotence of the same, our Creator, and through these mystical Names of our God, [Name 1] and [Name 2], humbly require, and vehemently petition, from you, one and all, that you appear within this Table of Art and Sigil of God, and thereafter attend to my commands.

I require that you discharge, implement and make perfect, benignly, plentifully, plainly and perfectly any and all petitions concerning the mixing together of natural substances and other natural secrets, which our Creator hath committed to your understanding, intelligence, and disposition and, as it were, appointed you as His officers and ministers, through these mystic Names of God, [Name 1] and [Name 2].

Through these Holy and Mystical Names of God [Name 1] and [Name 2],

Amen.

The Angels of Transportation

There is some disagreement among Enochian practitioners regarding the function of these angels, as taken literally their conjuration implies that they could be conjured in order to teleport oneself or other objects. I have tried this, of course, and so far have yet to succeed. However, another interpretation of their powers, more suited to Dee's time period, could also be that they serve to protect travelers on journeys such as trips to the New World, which were at the time quite dangerous ocean crossings.

Direction	Angels of Transportation	Controlling Names of God
East	YTPA, TPAY, PAYT, AYTP	EYTPA and AYTPA
South	TDIM, DIMT, IMTD, MTDI	ETDIM and BTDIM
West	ANAA, NAAA, AAAN, AANA	AANAA and BANAA
North	PHRA, HRAP, RAPH, APHR	APHRA and APHRA

Invocation:

O you four faithful and noble angels and Ministers of our Omnipotent Creator, O, [Angel 1], [Angel 2], [Angel 3], [Angel 4], who rule uniquely in the [Direction] part of the world and whom our Creator has provided and given the skill, strength, and power to be able to transport or transfer any man or thing from one place to another, without injury, harm, offense, or damnation to that man or thing, whether the transference is near or far: I, [Your Magical Name], humble and devoted servant of the Omnipotent God our Creator, through the reverent majesty of the same God, our Creator, and through these divine and mystical Names, [Name 1] and [Name 2], I humbly require you and vehemently petition you, one and all, that you appear within this Table of Art and Sigil of God, and thereafter attend to my commands.

I require that you discharge, implement, and make perfect, goodly, truly, plentifully and perfectly, any and all petitions concerning local motion, transporting from place to place, or any other secrets which you were uniquely conceded and committed the authority and disposition by our God, to His praise, honor, and glory, by the divine and mystical Names [Name 1] and [Name 2].

Through these Holy and Mystical Names of God, [Name 1] and [Name 2],

Amen.

The Angels of the Mechanical Arts

These angels are conjured in order to obtain information about or influence technology in general. They have become more and more useful in this latter regard as technology has grown to permeate nearly every facet of our lives in the modern era.

Direction	Angels of Mechanical Arts	Controlling Names of God
East	XGSD, GSDX, SDXG, DXGS	HXGSD and AXGSD
South	NLRX, LRXN, RXNL, XNLR	HNLRX and BNLRX
West	ZIZA, IZAZ, ZAZI, AZIZ	PZIZA and BZIZA
North	ASMT, SMTA, MTAS, TASM	PASMT and AASMT

Invocation:

O you four holy and truthful ministers of Omnipotent God, our Creator, [Angel 1], [Angel 2], [Angel 3], [Angel 4], who are in the [Direction] part of the world, and who hast by our God been charged and committed with His ministry to practice, impart, teach, and communicate perfect skill in all arts mechanical, to the praise, honor, and glory of our God, I, [Your Magical Name], a devoted servant of the same, our God and Creator, faithfully, prudently, and *powerfully desiring to be devout, do humbly require and vehemently petition from all of you, named above, through the omnipotent wisdom of the same, our God and Creator, and through these holy and mystical Names, [Name 1] and [Name 2], that you appear within this Table of Art and Sigil of God, and thereafter attend to my commands.*

I, [Your Magical Name], require that you discharge, implement, and make perfect immediately, truly, plentifully, manifestly, and perfectly any and all petitions concerning the Arts Mechanical as well as other mechanical conclusions or experiments through the divine and mystical Names [Name 1] and [Name 2].

Through these Mystical Names of God [Name 1] and [Name 2], Amen.

The Angels of Secret Discovery

These angels are conjured in order to obtain information that is being kept secret or otherwise hidden. The Heptarchial King Bnapsen has a similar power, in that he can be conjured to learn the secrets of "evil men."

Direction	Angels of Secret Discovery	Controlling Names of God
East	TNBR, NBRT, BRTN, RTNB	HTNBR and MTNBR
South	MAGL, AGLM, GLMA, LMAG	HMAGL and NMAGL
West	PSAC, SACP, ACPS, CPSA	PPSAC and NPSAC
North	OCNC, CNCO, NCOC, COCN	POCNC and MOCNC

Invocation:

O you four wise and truthful Angels of the Omnipotent God, and ministers of our Creator: O you, [Angel 1], [Angel 2], [Angel 3], [Angel 4], who dwell in the [Direction] part of the world, and whom the same, our God, hath assigned and bestowed the great and special office of discovering and understanding the secrets of men of whatever degree, state, or condition: I, [Your Magical Name], the devoted servant of the same God, a careful investigator, but by no means curious of the secret endeavors, acts, and events of any type of man unless it might be necessary to the honor and glory of God our Creator for me to see, understand, and discover, do humbly require and vehemently petition from you, one and all, through our omniscient God and through these mystical Names [Name 1] and [Name 2], that you appear within this Table of Art and Sigil of God, and thereafter attend to my commands.

I require that you discharge, implement, and make perfect, truthfully, plentifully, and perfectly, any and all petitions concerning the secrets of any men, regardless of state and condition, through these Names of God, [Name 1] and [Name 2].

Through these holy and mystical Names of God [Name 1] and [Name 2],

Amen.

Chapter 14
The Lesser Angels

The Lesser Angels were so called by the creators of the Golden Dawn Enochian system because their names appear below the arms of the crosses formed by the Names of God for each sub-quadrant of the Great Table. Whether or not the position of these angels represents a lower position in the spiritual hierarchy from the "Kerubic" angels is not clear. Generally, Enochian spirits can be classified according to the letters of their names, with names consisting of more letters representing more intelligent, coherent, and powerful entities. By this measure the "Lesser Angels" and the "Kerubic Angels" should be about on par with each other. Angels in both classes have four-letter names and are governed by two five-letter controlling names. Also, according to the powers delineated in the conjurations both classes seem to be of approximately equal strength, though this does depend somewhat on how their descriptions are interpreted.

The Angels of Medicine

These angels are conjured in order to perform healings and cure diseases.

Direction	Angels of Medicine	Controlling Names of God
East	CZNS, TOTT, SIAS, FMND	IDOIGO and ARDZA
South	TOCO, NHDD, PAAX, SAIX	OBGOTA and AABCO
West	OPMN, APST, SCIO, VASG	NOALMR and OLOAG
North	AIRA, ORMN, RSNI, IZNR	ANGPOI and UNNAX

Invocation:

O you Angels of Light [Angel 1], [Angel 2], [Angel 3], [Angel 4], dwelling in the [Direction] part of the universe, powerful in the administering of the strong and healthy medicine of God and in the dispensing of cures: In the name of the omnipotent, Living, and true God, I, [Your Magical Name], by the grace of the Almighty God of the Celestial Realms, and through the reverence and obedience which you owe to the same, our God, and through these, His divine and mystical Names, [Name 1] and [Name 2], I vehemently and faithfully require of you, one and all, that you appear within this Table of Art and Sigil of God, and thereafter attend to my commands.

I summon you by the Names of God, [Name 1] and [Name 2], to perform, to accomplish, and to complete any and all requests, abundantly, excellently, thoroughly, pleasantly, plentifully, and perfectly, through every possible medicine and through the peculiar strength and power of your office and ministry.

Through the Sacrosanct Names of God [Name 1] and [Name 2], Amen.

The Angels of Gold and Precious Stones

These angels function as treasure-finding spirits such as are found in many of the old grimoires. Apparently medieval Europe was a vastly different world than the one in which we live today, in that finding treasure that had been hidden away for some reason was not a completely unheard of event. However, in addition to finding hidden treasures these angels can also locate veins of ore, making them useful for mining, and can be consulted regarding the magical properties of jewels and metals.

Direction	Angels of Gold and Precious Stones	Controlling Names of God
East	OYVB, PAOC, RBNH, DIRI	ILACZA and PALAM
South	MAGM, LEOC, VSSN, RVOI	NELAPR and OMEBB
West	GMNM, ECOP, AMOX, BRAP	VADALI and OBAUA
North	OMGG, GBAL, RLMV, IAHL	ANAEEM and SONDN

Invocation:

You four Angels of Light, faithful in the ministry of God our Creator, [Angel 1], [Angel 2], [Angel 3], [Angel 4], lords in the [Direction] part of the universe, and who, out of the peculiar gifts and dispensations of God, are powerful and learned in the lore of ore-veins, the finding of metal and treasure hoards, the uses and virtues of metals, the coagulation and magical properties of jewels, the places where metals and jewels are gathered, as well as their natures, properties, virtues, and uses, both secret and arcane: I, [Your Magical Name], the humble and devoted servant of the omnipotent, living, and true God, through the inevitable power which is known to the same, our God, in these Names, [Name 1] and [Name 2], to whom you owe reverence and obedience, I vehemently and confidently require of you, one and all, that you appear within this Table of Art and Sigil of God, and thereafter attend to my commands.

I beseech thee, one and all, to complete and make perfect any and all petitions for intended deeds, most swiftly, manifestly, certainly, immaculately, and plentifully, concerning your particular skills, strengths, faculties, and powers over metals and jewels. By the speaking of the divine Names, [Name 1] and [Name 2], I call and command you, one and all.

Through the speaking of the holy and mystical Names of God, [Name 1] and [Name 2],

Amen.

The Angels of Transformation

These angels are conjured for the general purpose of transforming one thing into another. This is a very general and effective power for all sorts of magical operations, since the creation of change in accordance with will generally involves transforming the nature of *something*.

Direction	Angels of Transformation	Controlling Names of God
East	ACCA, NPNT, OTOI, PMOX	AOURRZ and ALOAI
South	XPCN, VASA, DAPI, RNIL	IAAASD and ATAPA
West	ADRE, SISP, PALI, ACAR	RZIONR and NRZFM
North	MSAP, IABA, IZXP, STIM	OPMNIR and ILPIZ

Invocation:

O you four good and true Angels of God our Creator, [Angel 1], [Angel 2], [Angel 3], [Angel 4], who rule in the [Direction] part of the world, who received of God in your creation the singular strength, true knowledge, and perfect absolute power of Transformation as your duty and office, that you might impart and make manifest unto men, as preordained by the same, our God, this true knowledge and perfect power, to the praise, honor, and glory of God. Therefore I, [Your Magical Name], the devoted servant of the same, our God and Creator, truly, diligently, and faithfully desiring to praise, honor, and glorify in God, do vehemently demand and confidently beseech you, one and all, to bring to pass and amplify among men this your aforementioned true knowledge, through these mystical Names of God, [Name 1] and [Name 2]. I, [Your Magical Name], demand that you appear within this Table of Art and Sigil of God, and thereafter attend to my commands.

I, [Your Magical Name], demand that you, one and all, immediately and without delay, perfectly accomplish, manifestly discharge, plainly complete, and plentifully make perfect any and all petitions, by whatever means necessary, that concern or respect your skill, knowledge, and 0power of Transformations, through these Names of our God, here rehearsed, [Name 1] and [Name 2]. Amen.

Through these sacred and mystical Names of God [Name 1] and [Name 2],

Amen.

The Angels of Living Creatures and the Elements

These angels are conjured in order to obtain information about, or influence, living things of all kinds. This includes such beings as elemental spirits, which these angels have the power to control and send forth in order to accomplish various tasks suited to their natures.

Direction	Angels of Living Creatures	Controlling Names of God
East	ABMO, NACO, OCNM, SHAL	AIAOAI and OIIIT
South	PACO, NDZN, IIPO, XRNH	MALADI and OLAAD
West	DATT, DIOM, OOPZ, RGAN	UOBXDO and SIODA
North	OPNA, DOOP, RXAO, AXIR	ABALPT and ARBIZ

Invocation:

O you Angels of God, flowing with truth and goodness, I call you, [Angel 1], [Angel 2], [Angel 3], [Angel 4], who rule in the [Direction] part of the world: so that each one of you, out of the four great elements or sources of the world might wield the duty or office peculiar to him, and his unique skill, knowledge, power, and authority: O you, [Angel 1], bright angel that liveth in the Air of the [Direction], you who hath vision of all its diverse qualities and who perfectly perceives what uses God created in them for Man; and you, O illustrious [Angel 2], who liveth in the Water of the [Direction], who truly knoweth its quality and use; and you, O distinguished [Angel 3], who liveth in the Earth of the [Direction], you who knoweth exactly it varied qualities and to what uses it was created by our God; and finally you, [Angel 4], shining angel of God, who liveth in the most secret Fire of the [Direction], and who hath plentiful knowledge of its efficacy and vital properties; O all of you, faithful to God and ministers of our Creator, you who dwelleth in the [Direction] part of the world, you who knoweth the arcane secrets of the four elements, conceded, assigned, and deputed to you by our omnipotent Creator, and who, to the praise, honor, and glory of God and out of your great charity towards the human race art able to impart and make manifest these great things, and by the approval of God, bring forth those things that are asked of you.

Therefore I, [Your Magical Name], a Lover and Seeker for these secrets, to the praise, honor, and glory of our God, in the Name of the same, our God and Creator, I humbly supplicate you, one and all. And through these holy Names of God, [Name 1] and [Name 2], I require and confidently petition that you appear within this Table of Art and Sigil of God, and thereafter attend to my commands.

And through these holy Names of God, [Name 1] and [Name 2], I require that you benignly consent, clearly discharge, lovingly fulfill, and plentifully make perfect any and all petitions respecting and concerning your aforementioned unique offices, knowledges, and powers.

Through these reverend and mystical Names of God [Name 1] and [Name 2],

Amen.

Chapter 15
The Cacodemons

The Cacodemons are an often-neglected portion of the Enochian system. Dee himself made mention of them only in his invocations, and then only in passing. Groups like the Golden Dawn and Aurum Solis paid them no attention whatsoever, at least if we are to believe the surviving published materials. Essentially, much of this omission may be due to the limited perspective that "the Cacodemons are evil." This is really not clear from the original source material, and if we are to believe the angels' communications to Dee and Kelley, in fact the entire Enochian system is in harmony with God's creation.

Whereas the basic nature of the Great Table angels is creative or constructive, that of the Cacodemons is destructive or chaotic. Through the limited worldview of the Medieval and Renaissance periods, angels = creation = good and Demons = destruction = evil, and this is almost certainly why Dee is not on record as having had anything to do with them. Dee's Christian faith was most likely too strong and too orthodox to allow him to think far enough outside the dogma of the Church to realize that the Cacodemons are a necessary part of the universe. Destruction is a part of nature, though it must be undertaken with great care.

While it may seem strange that the Cacodemons are summoned by the names of God, albeit reversed, this was the norm for grimoires of Dee's period and earlier. It was assumed that since God was all-powerful, the Names of God could be called upon to accomplish all things, especially controlling and binding demons of the underworld. The Names of God that are used to summon the Cacodemons are the reversed forms of those used to summon the Lesser Angels. There appear to be no corresponding Cacodemons for the offices of the Kerubic angels. Cacodemons should always be evoked, that is, called into the Holy Table and Sigillum Dei Aemeth, rather than invoked. When evoking Cacodemons, you replace the word VAOAN in the First Key with the word VOOAN, though apparently they mean the same thing in English.

I do not generally recommend working with the Cacodemons to any but the most experienced magician. When dealing with the destructive aspects of nature there is simply too much that can go wrong. Furthermore, I have found that Cacodemons do not seem to exhibit great organization or intelligence, and if summoned improperly I could easily imagine them just as likely to act upon the magician as they are upon the object of the spell. Because of this, your Enochian temple should be as complete as possible before undertaking a ritual involving the Cacodemons, and you should certainly have and use the Sigillum Dei Aemeth, which possesses strong containment properties. Dee wrote no conjurations for the Cacodemons, so I have written my own, patterned on the invocation of the corresponding Lesser Angels.

The Cacodemons of Medicine

These demons are summoned to cause diseases. They are the only Cacodemons whose powers are mentioned along with the invocation for the corresponding Lesser Angels.

Direction	Cacodemons of Medicine	Controlling Names of God
East	XCZ, ATO, RSI, PFM, XNS, ATT, RAS, PND	OGIODI and AZDRA
South	XTO, ANH, RPA, PSA, XCO, ADD, RAX, PIX	ATOGBO and OCBAA
West	MOP, OAP, CSC, HVA, MMN, OST, CIO, HSG	RMLAON and GAOLO
North	MAI, OOR, CRS, HIZ, MRA, OMN, CNI, HNR	IOPGNA and XANNU

Conjuration:

O you Cacodemons of Darkness [Demon 1], [Demon 2], [Demon 3], [Demon 4], [Demon 5], [Demon 6], [Demon 7], [Demon 8], dwelling in the [Direction] part of the universe, powerful in the causing of diseases and the thwarting of cures: In the name of the omnipotent, Living, and true God, I, [Your Magical Name], by the grace of the Almighty God of the Celestial Realms, and through the reverence and obedience which you owe to the same, our God, and through these, His divine and mystical Names [Name 1] and [Name 2], I vehemently and faithfully require of you, one and all, that you appear within this Table of Art and Sigil of God, and thereafter attend to my commands.

I summon you by the Names of God, [Name 1] and [Name 2], to perform, to accomplish, and to complete any and all commands abundantly, excellently, thoroughly, pleasantly, plentifully, and perfectly, through the peculiar strength and power of your office and ministry.

Through the Sacrosanct Names of God [Name 1] and [Name 2], Amen.

The Cacodemons of Gold and Precious Stones

It was explained to Dee that whereas the Angels of Gold and Precious Stones could find metallic ore, these Cacodemons could bring him "the money, coined." In the modern world there is a clear separation between precious metals and jewels on the one hand and the global financial system on the other. In one experiment I was able to substantially increase the value of my stock portfolio over a three-month period by conjuring these spirits, but it was nonetheless not to the degree that I specified in my charge so further work along those lines is probably necessary before drawing any firm conclusions from a single example.

Direction	Cacodemons of Gold and Precious Stones	Controlling Names of God
East	XOY, APA, RRB, PDI, XVB, AOC, RNH, PRI	AZCALI and MALAP
South	XMA, ALE, RVS, PRV, XGM, AOC, RSN, POI	RPALEN and BBEMO
West	MGM, OEC, CAM, HBR, MNM, OOP, COX, HAP	ILADAV and AUABO
North	MOM, OGB, CRL, HIA, MGG, OAL, CMV, HHL	MEEANA and NDNOS

Conjuration:

You eight Demons of Darkness [Demon 1], [Demon 2], [Demon 3], [Demon 4], [Demon 5], [Demon 6], [Demon 7], [Demon 8], lords in the [Direction] part of the universe, and who, out of the peculiar gifts and dispensations of God, are powerful and learned in the lore of entropy as regards ore-veins, the finding of metal and treasure hoards, the uses and virtues of metals, the coagulation and magical properties of jewels, the places where metals and jewels are gathered, as well as their natures, properties, virtues, and uses, both secret and arcane: I, [Your Magical Name], through the inevitable power which is known to the same, our God, in these Names, [Name 1] and [Name 2], to whom you owe reverence and obedience,

I vehemently and confidently command you, one and all, that you appear within this Table of Art and Sigil of God, and thereafter attend to my commands.

I beseech thee, one and all, to complete and make perfect any and all commands for intended deeds, most swiftly, manifestly, certainly, immaculately, and plentifully, concerning your particular skills, strengths, faculties, and powers over metals and jewels. By the speaking of the divine Names, [Name 1] and [Name 2], I call and command you, one and all.

Through the speaking of the holy and mystical Names of God, [Name 1] and [Name 2],

Amen.

The Cacodemons of Transformation

Given the general nature of the Cacodemons, it would seem that the Cacodemons of Transformation are conjured in order to accomplish the transformation of a target from a state of order to one of disorder or outright collapse. In effect, the Angels of Transformation build up, while the corresponding Cacodemons tear down.

Direction	Cacodemons of Transformation	Controlling Names of God
East	CAC, ONP, MOT, APM, CCA, ONT, MOI, AOX	ZRRUOA and IAOLA
South	CXP, OVA, MDA, ARN, CCN, OSA, MPI, AIL	DSAAAI and APATA
West	RAD, ASI, XPA, EAC, RRE, ASP, XLI, EAR	RNOIZR and MFZRN
North	RMS, AIA, XIZ, EST, RAP, ABA, XXP, EIM	RINMPO and ZIPLI

Conjuration:

O you eight Cacodemons of God our Creator, [Demon 1], [Demon 2], [Demon 3], [Demon 4], [Demon 5], [Demon 6], [Demon 7], [Demon 8], who rule in the [Direction] part of the world, who received of God in your creation the singular strength, true knowledge, and power of entropy as regards transformation as your duty and office, that you might impart and make manifest unto men, as preordained by the same, our God, this true knowledge and perfect power. Therefore I, [Your Magical Name], the devoted servant of the same, our God and Creator, truly, diligently, and faithfully do vehemently demand and confidently command you, one and all, to bring to pass and amplify among men this your aforementioned true knowledge, through these mystical Names of God, [Name 1] and [Name 2]. I, [Your Magical Name], demand that you appear within this Table of Art and Sigil of God, and thereafter attend to my commands.

I, [Your Magical Name], demand that you, one and all, immediately and without delay, perfectly accomplish, manifestly discharge, plainly complete, and plentifully make perfect any and all commands, by whatever means necessary, that concern or respect your skill, knowledge, and power of Transformations, through these Names of our God, here rehearsed: [Name 1] and [Name 2].

Through these sacred and mystical Names of God, [Name 1] and [Name 2],

Amen.

The Cacodemons of Living Creatures and the Elements

As any living creature survives by virtue of maintaining a state of internal order separate from the world around them, it is difficult to deduce the function of these Cacodemons from that of the corresponding Lesser Angels. Perhaps they can be used to kill or injure living things, though it would seem to me that the Cacodemons of Medicine might be more suited for such an operation. Another thought is that they could be conjured in order to summon up and command elemental spirits of a more destructive nature than those controlled by the Lesser Angels.

Direction	Cacodemons of Living Creatures	Controlling Names of God
East	CAB, ONA, MOC, ASH, CMO, OCO, MNM, AAL	IAOAIA and TIIIO
South	CPA, OND, MII, AXR, CCO, OZN, MPO, ANH	IDALAM and DAALO
West	RDA, ADI, XOO, ERG, RTT, AOM, XPZ, EAN	ODXBOU and ADOIS
North	ROP, ADO, XRX, EAX, RNA, AOP, XAO, EIR	TPLABA and ZIBRA

Conjuration:

O you Cacodemons of God, flowing with darkness and power, I call you, [Demon 1], [Demon 2], [Demon 3], [Demon 4], [Demon 5], [Demon 6], [Demon 7], [Demon 8], who rule in the [Direction] part of the world: so that each one of you, out of the four great elements or sources of the world might wield the duty or office peculiar to him, and his unique skill, knowledge, power, and authority: O you, [Demon 1] and [Demon 5], thundering Cacodemons that liveth in the Air of the [Direction], you who embody its diverse qualities and who perfectly perceive what uses lie therein for Man; and you, O storming

[Demon 2] and [Demon 6], who liveth in the Water of the [Direction], who truly knoweth its quality and use; and you, O mighty [Demon 3] and [Demon 7], who liveth in the Earth of the [Direction], you who knoweth exactly its varied qualities and to what uses it was created by our God; and finally you, [Demon 4] and [Demon 8], blazing Cacodemons of God, who liveth in the most secret Fire of the [Direction], and who hath plentiful knowledge of its efficacy and destructive properties; O all of you who dwelleth in the [Direction] part of the world, you who knoweth the arcane secrets of entropy as regards the four elements, conceded, assigned, and deputed to you by our omnipotent Creator, and who art able to impart and make manifest these awesome things and bring forth those things that are asked of you. Therefore I, [Your Magical Name], in the Name of our God and Creator, command you, one and all.

Through these holy Names of God, <Name> and <Name>, I require that you appear within this Table of Art and Sigil of God, and thereafter attend to my commands.

And through these holy Names of God, [Name 1] and [Name 2], I require that you discharge and make perfect this any and all commands respecting and concerning your aforementioned unique offices, knowledges, and powers.

Through these reverend and mystical Names of God [Name 1] and [Name 2],

Amen.

Chapter 16
The Charge

The charge to the spirit is your statement of intent that communicates the exact outcome you want your ritual to produce. Because rituals can be performed for just about any purpose you will need to write the Charge yourself for any ritual that you perform, and there are several key factors that you need to keep in mind when doing so. Much of this material was covered in greater detail in Mastering the Mystical Heptarchy, but it is included here for the sake of completeness. No matter what class of spirit you are working with, you need to know how to properly construct a charge in order to work magick effectively.

I generally explain spirits using the Aristotelean model under which the universe is envisioned as consisting of both Matter and Form. Matter refers to the subatomic particles of which substances are composed and Form refers to how those particles are arranged. At the quantum level, the arrangement of every particle is governed by fields of probability waves that are described in physics by what are called Schroedinger functions. There is some debate among quantum physicists as to whether subatomic particles occupy any particular point in space or simply exist as nonlocal probability waves prior to their interaction with some sort of measuring device.

Whichever of these interpretations is correct, neither demonstrates that the physical world is "illusionary" or somehow made of thoughts, as certain New Age groups like to contend. What it means is that when you interact with an object, what your body is actually touching is a magnetic field rather than a solid object. As the electron shells that form the exterior layer of atoms and by extension molecules are negatively charged, they naturally repel each other at close distances. This repulsion is what we experience when we touch solid matter — but there is nothing illusionary about a magnetic field! If you have ever had your finger pinched by a pair of neodymium magnets you will know exactly what I am talking about. Similarly, powerful enough magnets can lift objects weighing many tons, such as cars and steel girders.

In fact, the debate over whether reality is composed of thoughts or fields of energy has a long history in the esoteric systems of Asia. Supporters of a thought-based model described reality as Maya, or illusion, while supporters of the energy field model described reality as Shakti, or power. The Maya side of the debate for the most part won out, but the irony there is that modern science and especially quantum mechanics have now shown that the Shakti view is the correct one. Everything, even apparently solid matter, is in fact constructed out of energy, as shown by the accuracy of Albert Einstein's most famous formula $E=mc^2$. The Maya concept does have some relevance to how we interpret material reality, in that the reality we experience is constructed by our brains from the various sensory information that we receive. Working with the various qualities of mind can give us much more control over how we interpret that reality than what we generally assume is possible, but it is a serious error to extend this to mean that the physical world is made up of nothing more than these thoughts. If you are about to be hit by a bus, thinking the right sort of thoughts is not going to result in you avoiding injury. Jumping out of the way is a much better strategy.

The important thing to understand about spirits, such as the angels of the Great Table, is that they consist of pure Form rather than

Matter, just like the consciousness of every individual magician, and thus are capable of interacting directly with the probability waves of any particular region of space. Those probability waves then influence the likelihood of particular outcomes when the particles within the region subject to this influence manifest as material objects. This influence is called a Probability Shift and is the basic mechanism by which all practical magick works. According to my experimentation over many years, a powerful magician can produce probability shifts of 100 to 1 or more, which can result in some quite impressive ritual successes.

Working with spirits such as those of the Great Table allows magicians to increase these probability shifts even further. If we declare a variable M as the probability shift that the magician can produce and a second variable S as the probability shift that a particular spirit can produce, the result of the magician conjuring the spirit should be a shift of M + S. So if the magician has trained to the point where his or her consciousness can produce a 20 to 1 shift but needs a 100 to 1 shift for a particular ritual to succeed, the solution is to summon a spirit that can produce a shift of at least 80 to 1. 20 plus 80 yields 100, which should result in a successful outcome if the spell is cast properly. The Kings and Seniors seem to have S ratings of around 100 or so according to my probability tests, about on par with the Heptarchial Kings and Princes. This means that they are capable of producing strong results for even beginning magicians, and as they are summoned in groups they can pool their powers together quite effectively.

A common question regarding spirits is how they can possibly have any sort of independent existence if multiple magicians can summon the same spirit at the same time. Some have contended that this demonstrates spirits are simply psychological projections that originate in the mind of each magician, but the reality is more complex. Spirits are beings of Form, and are thus non-local entities. They exist within the field of probability functions that underlie material reality rather than occupying a particular place and time. In practice, conjuring a spirit is more like tuning your mind to a particular radio frequency than inviting a friend over for coffee. Like a radio signal, the spirit can be in many places at once, and it is from the connection between the mind of the magician and the consciousness of the spirit that overall magical probability shifts arise.

The function of the conjurations and ritual procedures is to establish such a connection in as clear a manner as possible. Once this is accomplished, the charge can be delivered to the spirit. It is necessary to communicate this charge as clearly and succinctly as possible. Some of the old grimoires explain that this is necessary because the spirits will always try to mislead the magician out of animosity, but the truth is that spirits are simply literal-minded and magick always seeks the path of least resistance. With the exception of the Cacodemons, I have never come across a Great Table spirit that was hostile to me. However, I have experienced a number of cases when I got what I asked for rather than what I wanted, especially back when I first started working with the Enochian system.

In the Enochian system, the length of a spirit's name will tell you roughly how "smart" they are. In the Heptarchial system, the Kings and Princes all have seven-letter names, so there is little difference between them in this respect. However, there is much more variation among the spirits of the Great Table. More letters means higher intelligence, and more intelligence gives you greater leeway in terms of the exactness of your charge. For example, the Cacodemons have three-letter names and can be powerful when used properly but are also particularly stupid in practice. They will do exactly as they are told – no more, no less. On the other hand, one of the advantages of working with Great Table spirits such as the Kings (eight letters) and Seniors (seven letters) is that they have the ability to divine the intent of a charger rather than merely its literal meaning. Nevertheless, a well-constructed charge will still help them focus on exactly what you want them to do and prevent any misunderstandings.

A charge should consist of two parts, a series of Injunctions and a series of Limitations. The former explains what you want the spirit to do, and the latter explains what you do not want the spirit to do. As a simple example, perhaps you need money and decide to summon a spirit to bring you five thousand dollars. There are a number of ways in which this intent could manifest, and many of them result in outcomes that you do not want. A death in the family could result in an inheritance. You or one of your children could be injured in a traffic accident and receive a settlement that covers little more than your medical bills. You could have a house fire that results in a settlement from your homeowner's insurance of the requested amount. Your car could be totaled in an accident, again bringing you the desired sum but requiring you to spend it on a new vehicle. So a properly constructed charge in this case would be something to the effect of this:

I hereby command that you bring me the sum of five thousand dollars within one month (injunction), without causing harm or damage to myself, my loved ones, or my property (limitation).

Every injunction should be given a specific amount of time in which to work. Without time limits on spells you can sometimes lose track of a spell that you have "running" and as a result the probability shift you can produce will be decreased. If the spell is given a time limit it will either terminate when its objective is achieved or when the specified time runs out. This is necessary because while the magical probability shift results from the connection between you and a particular spirit, that channel can only produce a total probability shift of a particular magnitude. Think of your field of consciousness as a computer running programs. It can multitask, but as it does the processing power devoted to each program decreases. This decrease is mostly linear, so that if you have an overall M of 20 and are trying to keep five spells running at once, each will be operating with an effective M of around 6 or so.

A good way around this multitasking problem is to conjure a different spirit for each distinct task. In this situation your personal magical power M will still be divided among the spells that you have running, but the power of each spirit will not. Going back to the previous example, if a magician with M of 20 has five spells running involving different spirits, each with S of 100, the resulting M for each spell will be (M/5) + S, yielding probability shifts of 106 to 1. As you can see, especially with multiple spells, working with spirits is quite advantageous for any magician and can result in much greater effective power than even the finest sorcerer could achieve using only his or her mind and aptitudes. This is why practically all magical traditions involve working with spirits – because it really does produce tangibly better results.

In order to get the best possible results you should not specify the means by which your objective should be accomplished and rely only on the limitations contained as the second part of your charge to exclude specific undesirable outcomes. This is because you want to make sure that the objective of the spell is not accomplished in some way that undermines the result, but at the same time you want to keep as many paths open as possible for the effect to manifest. Often the best way that something can manifest in your life is not obvious, so it is better to focus on the end result in constructing your magical intent than to try and micro-manage the details of how that intent comes into being.

You should always make a note of your precise charge in your magical journal along with as many details as possible regarding the rite itself for every operation you perform. Often after performing a ritual the last thing I want to do is write about it in my journal, but on occasions when I skip this step I often find myself regretting it later when planning my next operation. If a spell seems to have failed, you can then look back over your charge and see if anything happened that fit the literal instructions you gave but not your true intent. Similarly, if a spell seems particularly effective you will want to keep track of the charge so that you can use it as a model for subsequent operations. In addition, the details that you record concerning your ritual procedures and impressions will help you determine any unexpected variables that might correspond to successful or unsuccessful workings. Honing your practice in this manner according to measurable, real-world results will allow you to progress as a magician in the most efficient, effective manner possible.

Chapter 17
Closing the Temple

Once you have summoned the proper spirit and delivered your charge, the final step is to send the angel forth to accomplish your magical objective and close the temple. In traditional grimoire evocations, spirits are dismissed using a License to Depart, but no such license is present in the Dee material. I particularly like the following that my magical working group has been using for quite a few years. It is intended to work as a sort of "bookend" to the Fundamental Obeisance used as the preliminary invocation for opening the Great Table. The references to True Will are explicitly Thelemic and are shown in italics because a Christian magician may want to omit them, though Saint Augustine's comment that one should "love, and do what thou wilt"[9] implies to me that this concept is not necessarily incompatible with Christian magick.

You Angels of Light, I, [Your Magical Name], by the power of the True, Almighty, and Living God, I hereby bid you

---
9. Augustine of Hippo, In Epistolam Loannis ad Parthos.

to depart and accomplish your appointed tasks, in the service of my True Will and to the Glory and Honor of our aforementioned True God to whom you owe loyalty and obedience.

I, [Your Magical Name], hereby free the forces constrained, focused, and directed during this operation, that they may go forth and work their various powers upon the manifest universe, for thus is all True Magick and Perfect Power born.

By the power of my True Will here embodied by the Magical Name [Your Magical Name],

Amen.

So mote it be.

In our group workings the individual who performed the conjuration gives the License to Depart up to AMEN, and the rest of the group responds with "So mote it be." A solitary magician may wish to include or drop this final statement as desired. When working on my own I generally include it.

If you are working without the ceremonial forms, your ritual is essentially complete at this point. Finish by knocking once on the Holy Table and stating "I now declare this temple duly closed." When working with the ceremonial forms you will want to close the temple ceremonially before making this declaration. As the AOEVEAE and MADRIAX rituals are designed to encapsulate the evocation itself, they should simply be concluded as shown in Appendix A. prior to the declaration. If you are working with the Golden Dawn ritual forms, the manner in which you conclude the operation depends upon its objective.

Today the various Golden Dawn orders generally teach that rituals should be concluded using both the Lesser Banishing Ritual of the Pentagram and the Lesser Banishing Ritual of the Hexagram. As I mentioned in Chapter 5, I find this to be sub-optimal for most magical objectives because it completely shuts down the ritual as soon as you close the temple. Giving a practical charge more time to operate than the thirty to sixty minutes that are dedicated to a typical ceremonial working will dramatically increase your chances of success. This is accomplished by omitting the Lesser Banishing Ritual of the Hexagram from the closing of your ritual altogether.

For rituals with a target other than yourself you should close with the Lesser Banishing Ritual of the Pentagram. As the pentagram symbolizes the microcosm, this ritual will serve to clear your consciousness of the macrocosmic elements invoked during the rite but allow those elements to continue to operate after you close the temple. It cuts the link between your mind and the spell and, much as stated in the License to Depart, sends the macrocosmic forces back to their proper place so that they can get to work on accomplishing your objective.

For rituals targeting yourself or both yourself and an external target you should close with just the Qabalistic Cross. This serves to balance and ground your consciousness without dismissing the microcosmic elements that you invoked during the rite. Many spells are of this type – for example, if you cast a spell to get a better job you want opportunities to come your way but you also want the magick to affect your body language and attitude so that you seem particularly impressive when a potential employer sets up an interview.

If you are using the Thelemic Star Ruby and Star Sapphire to replace the Lesser Rituals of the Pentagram and Hexagram the same rules apply. Close with just the Star Ruby for a ritual with an external target or the Star Ruby's form of the Qabalistic Cross if the spell targets yourself or both yourself and an external target. I normally use the closing form of this Qabalistic Cross, ending rather than starting with "APO PANTOS KAKODAIMONOS," but I leave that to your discretion based on how you generally perform the ritual.

After performing the closing ceremonial forms, knock once on the Holy Table and declare the temple closed. Your ritual is now complete. At this point, you will want to keep the ritual out of mind while the angels work to accomplish your objective. Some authors contend that in order for a spell to work you must forget the objective completely, but this is difficult in practice and constitutes serious overkill. You can freely remember your working so long as you avoid obsessing or worrying about its outcome. Worry and obsession will undermine a spell just about every time, but simply thinking about it on occasion is harmless.

Chapter 18
Conclusion

Magick should always be a progressive science. While many of its techniques are grounded in the past, the best and most effective way to ensure continual future improvement is a formal regimen of experimentation and refinement. The Great Table serves as an excellent example of this process, in that many divergent methods have been developed for working with it over the course of the last century and a half. Each of these versions has its proponents who claim good results, but at the same time care must be taken that these newer syncretic systems do not stray too far from their original foundation.

For a long time the Golden Dawn Enochian system has been considered the standard by which Enochian work is judged, even though it is not clear to me that this was the original intent of Mathers and Wescott when they first developed their version. They hoped to assemble Dee and Kelley's work into a usable and coherent structure, and they had to do it without any of the tools of the modern information age that we modern researchers take for granted. It may be that their system became the "gold standard" simply because it was so intricate and complex that for so long no one could imagine putting in the amount of work it would take to build a similar alternative. Aleister Crowley himself once wrote that his only regret in his long magical career was that he had never been able to put together a comprehensive edition of the Enochian work, perhaps because even he found the task too daunting.

The original Enochian material is in fact far less complex than the Golden Dawn system seems to imply. Many of the most difficult to master portions consist of speculation built upon speculation, some of it derived from dubious sources like the Treatise on Angel Magic. This makes it difficult to classify the Golden Dawn system as incorrect or inaccurate, as it is impossible to know how much experimentation went into its creation due to the secrecy practiced by magical orders of the time. It is at the very least divergent from the original Dee material, a set of correspondences and methods that took on a life of their own in the decades following their first invention. Still, as modern magicians with access to advanced information technology, it is now possible for us to go back to the original material, perform a comprehensive review of its contents, and proceed to incorporate in a systematic and experimental manner those modern components that improve the Enochian system's effectiveness.

It is my hope that both this book and Mastering the Mystical Heptarchy will help to fill in some of the pieces of the puzzle that link the Enochian system to the Solomonic grimoire tradition from which it emerged, as the best way to get to know any esoteric system is to understand its origin in as comprehensive a manner as possible. Furthermore, I hope it will encourage more modern magicians to take up the Enochian practice and share their results widely with other practitioners, as the building of a knowledge base for magick akin to that found in the physical sciences is largely dependent upon a large body of such fundamental research.

Scott Stenwick
Minneapolis, MN
2013

Appendix A
Basic Ritual Forms

The Lesser Ritual of the Pentagram

This ritual can be found in just about any introductory book on ritual magick, particularly those covering the Golden Dawn and Thelemic traditions. While I am including the text of the ritual and some brief notations here for the sake of completeness, if you are a beginning magician you should do some additional research regarding how to do the visualizations, vibrations, breathing, and so forth correctly. It should be committed to memory rather than read out of this book or any other.

1. Stand facing east. With the thumb of your right hand touch your forehead and intone:

    ATEH

    (ah-TAY)

    Then trace down the center of your body to your genital area and intone:

MALKUTH
(mal-KOOT)

Trace back up to the center of your chest then over to your right shoulder and intone:

VE GEBURAH
(VAY geh-boo-RAH)

Then trace across to your left shoulder and intone:

VE GEDULAH
(VAY geh-doo-LAH)

Finally, clasp your hands over the center of your chest and intone:

LE OLAHM, AMEN
(LAY oh-LAHM, ah-MEN)

This first section is called the Qabalistic Cross and can be performed on its own as a basic centering exercise. As you trace, visualize a cross of glowing white brilliance forming over your body, representing the Qabalistic Tree of Life and linking the spheres of Kether, Tiphareth, Yesod, and Malkuth on the middle pillar along with Geburah and Chesed at the right and left shoulders.

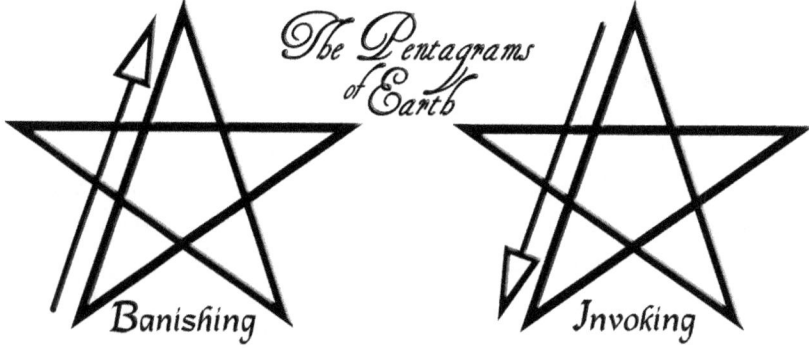

2. In the east, trace the appropriate Pentagram of Earth and vibrate:

YHVH
(yah-WAY or Yod Heh Vav Heh)

The pentagram should be visualized as formed from living fire.

3. Turn to the south. Trace the appropriate Pentagram of Earth and vibrate:

   ADNI
   (ah-doh-NYE).

4. Turn to the west. Trace the appropriate Pentagram of Earth and vibrate:

   AHIH
   (eh-hi-YAY).

5. Turn to the north. Trace the appropriate Pentagram of Earth and vibrate:

   AGLA
   (ah-guh-LAH).

6. Return to face the east. Extend your arms in the form of a cross and intone:

   Before me RAPHAEL (rah-fay-EL),
   Behind me GABRIEL (gah-bree-EL),
   On my right hand MICHAEL (mee-kye-EL),
   On my left hand URIEL[10] (oo-ree-EL).
   For about me flames the pentagram,
   And in the column stands the six-rayed star.

As you vibrate the name of each Archangel, visualize the appropriate figure standing in the corresponding direction. Raphael in the east wears a yellow robe and holds a cadeuceus wand, Gabriel in the west wears a blue robe and holds a chalice, Michael in the south wears a red robe and holds a flaming sword, and Uriel in the north wears a black robe and holds a scythe.

For the final two lines, you first visualize a pentagram forming over your body and then on the last line visualize yourself standing within a vertical hexagonal pillar of light inscribed with a hexagram.

---

10. *Most magical orders teach the final Archangel name as AURIEL rather than URIEL. Either will work, though I like to use the latter name for Enochian operations because John Dee notes URIEL as the fourth Archangel rather than AURIEL.*

For the pentagram visualization, imagine yourself as Leonardo Da Vinci's Vitrivian Man with an upright pentagram inscribing the circle in the drawing. For the hexagram visualization, imagine your entire body within a round column of light extending from floor to ceiling and beyond. The hexagram then inscribes the cross-section of the pillar at a right angle relative to the vertical plane of the pentagram.

7. Repeat step 1, the Qabalistic Cross.

The Lesser Ritual of the Hexagram

Like the Lesser Ritual of the Pentagram, this ritual can be found in most introductory books on Golden Dawn and Thelemic magick. As with the Lesser Ritual of the Pentagram you will want to commit it to memory. Also, before using this ritual you will want to do some additional research above and beyond the instructions given here if you are unfamiliar with it. The main pitfall to watch out for is authors who teach that you should open or close rituals using only the banishing form. I have observed that in many cases this method can undermine your ability to work effective practical magick.

1. Stand facing east following the performance of the Lesser Ritual of the Pentagram. Intone the following:

    INRI — Yod Nun Resh Yod.
    Virgo, Isis, mighty mother,
    Scorpio, Apophis, destroyer,
    Sol, Osiris, slain and risen,
    Isis, Apophis, Osiris,
    IAO.

    This section is called the Keyword Analysis.

2. Give the Sign of Osiris Slain, extending both arms in the form of a cross. Say:

    Osiris slain![11]

    Then give the Sign of the Mourning of Isis. With open hands, bend both elbows at 90 degree angles, raising the right forearm to point up and dropping the left forearm to point down. The right palm should be up and facing forward and the left should be down and facing backwards. Turn slightly to your left and look down. Say:

    The Mourning of Isis!

    Then give the Sign of Apophis and Typhon, raising both arms straight above your head and holding

---

11. The traditional Golden Dawn teaching regarding the first four statements in this section is to add "The Sign of" to the beginning of each. In practice I find this to be choppy and awkward, so when using this ritual I perform it as shown here.

them apart at an angle of about sixty degrees. The wrists should be straight, the hands open, and the palms toward each other. Say:

> Apophis and Typhon!

Then give the Sign of Osiris Risen. Cross your arms on your chest, left over right, like an Egyptian mummy. The hands should be open with your right palm on your left shoulder and your left palm on your right shoulder. Say:

> Osiris risen!

Repeat the Sign of Osiris Slain and say:

> L – V – X – LUX.

Repeat the Sign of Osiris Risen and say:

> The light of the Cross.

This section is called the Signs of LVX.

3. Trace the appropriate Hexagram of Fire in the east as you vibrate:

> ARARITA.

The two upward triangles should be visualized in red.

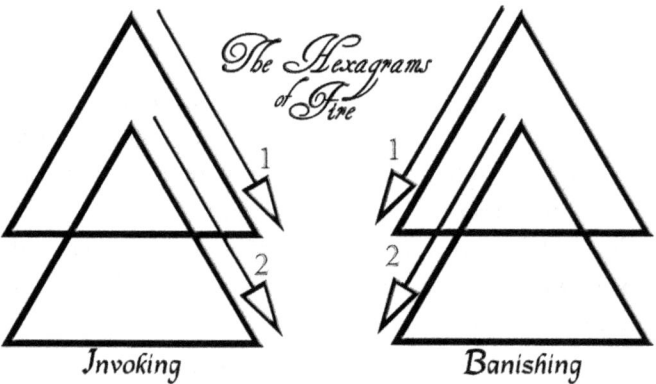

The Hexagrams of Fire

Invoking　　　　　　　Banishing

4. Turn to the south. Trace the appropriate Hexagram of Earth in the south as you vibrate:

> ARARITA

The upward triangle should be visualized in red and the downward triangle should be visualized in blue.

5. Turn to the west. Trace the appropriate Hexagram of Air in the west as you vibrate:

   ARARITA

   The upward triangle should be visualized in red and the downward triangle should be visualized in blue.

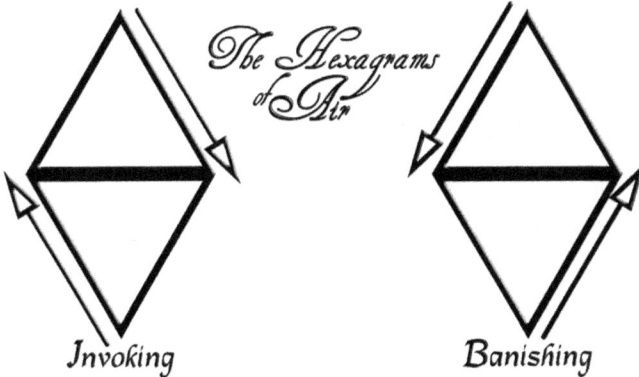

6. Turn to the north. Trace the appropriate Hexagram of Water in the north as you vibrate:

   ARARITA

   The upward triangle should be visualized in red and the downward triangle should be visualized in blue.

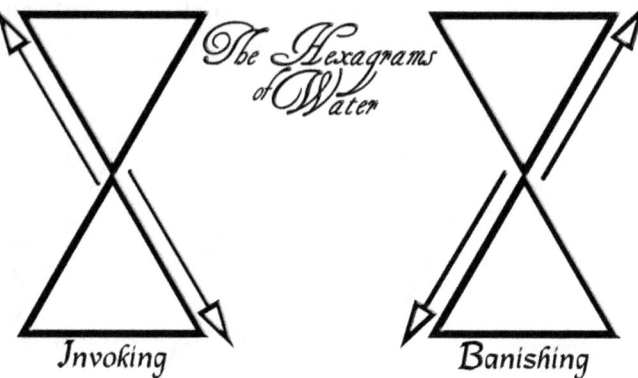

7. Return to the east. Repeat the Keyword Analysis and the Signs of LVX.

The Star Ruby and Star Sapphire

Rather than the Golden Dawn ritual forms, Thelemic magicians may prefer to use the Star Ruby, Aleister Crowley's "improved version" of the Lesser Ritual of the Pentagram, and the Star Sapphire, which corresponds to the Lesser Ritual of the Hexagram. These rituals are not included here but can be found in Crowley's works[12] and also in popular treatments such as Lon Milo Duquette's The Magick of Aleister Crowley.[13] As the Star Ruby is a banishing ritual and the Star Sapphire is an invoking ritual, together they form an operant field just like the LBRP/LIRH combination.

---

12. Aleister Crowley, The Book of Lies (York Beach, ME: Weiser Books, 1986) and Magick: Book Four (York Beach, ME: Weiser Books, 1998).
13. Lon Milo DuQuette, The Magick of Aleister Crowley (San Francisco, CA: Weiser Books, 2003).

AOEVEAE ('Stars') Pentagram Ritual

To replace the Golden Dawn Lesser Ritual of the Pentagram, I have developed an Enochian pentagram ritual that I call the AOEVEAE (a-o-i-ve-ah-EH — "stars" in Angelic). A number of writers have come up with Enochian pentagram rituals of this sort and they all share certain similarities. It is pretty clear that the most logical names to use when tracing the pentagrams are the threefold names of God from Dee and Kelley's Great Table (ORO IBAH AOZPI, MPH ARSL GAIOL, OIP TEAA PDOCE, and MOR DIAL HCTGA) and the most logical equivalents to the Archangels are the Kings of the four directions (BATAIVAH, RAAGIOSL, EDLPRNAA, and ICZHIHAL).

When attributing the names to the directions I use the directional arrangement from the 1587 Tabula Recensa.[14] The text shown here may be adapted to fit the traditional Golden Dawn arrangement of the Great Table by swapping the names associated with the west and south, so that you vibrate OIP TEAA PDOCE in the south and MPH ARSL GAIOL in the west, and swap the directions attributed to RAAGIOSL and EDLPRNAA when calling the Kings.

Start the ritual by standing in the center of your temple facing east, or to the west of the altar facing east if the Holy Table is present. Wear the Enochian PELE ring. If you wish to use a magical weapon, a dagger is probably the most appropriate for the banishing form, while a wand is best for the invoking form, but keep in mind that this is a modern practice and Dee and Kelley used neither. The ritual text follows:

1. With your finger or magical weapon, trace from your left hip to your right shoulder while vibrating:

    NANTA

    (NAHN-ta — Earth)

    from your right shoulder to left shoulder while vibrating:

    HCOMA

    (he-KO-ma — Water)

    from your left shoulder to right hip while vibrating:

---

14. DuQuette, *Enochian Vision Magick* (San Francisco, CA: Weiser Books, 2008), 135-137

EXARP

(EX-arp — Air)

from your right hip to your forehead while vibrating:

BITOM

(BI-tom — Fire)

and finally from your forehead back to your left hip while vibrating:

EHNB

(EH-nub — Spirit)

Then clasp your hands over your heart and vibrate:

JAIDA

(ja-I-da — "The Highest")

Visualize the pentagram traced over your body in bright electric lavender.

2. In the east, trace the Banishing Pentagram of Earth while vibrating:

ORO IBAH AOZPI

(Oh-roh-ee Bah-ah-oh-zod-pee)

The pentagrams should be visualized as formed from burning flames and as vividly as possible.

3. Turn to the north. In the north, trace the Banishing Pentagram of Earth while vibrating:

MOR DIAL HCTGA

(MOR DI-al hek-TGA).

4. Turn to the west. In the west, trace the Banishing Pentagram of Earth while vibrating:

OIP TEAA PDOCE
(o-IP TE-ah-ah PDO-ke).

5. Turn to the south. In the south, trace the Banishing Pentagram of Earth while vibrating:
MPH ARSL GAIOL (MEH-peh AR-sal ga-i-OL).

6. Turn back to face the east. Extend your arms to form a cross and vibrate:
RAAS I BATAIVAH
("In the East is BATAIVAH" — ba-ta-i-VAH),
SOBOLN I EDLPRNAA
("In the West is EDLPRNAA" — ed-el-per-na-AH),
BABAGE I RAAGIOSL
("In the South is RAAGIOSL" — ra-AH-gi-oh-sal),
LUCAL I ICZHIHAL
("In the North is ICZHIHAL" — ik-zod-hi-HAL).

7. Make one full spin counter-clockwise while vibrating:
MICMA AO COMSELH AOIVEAE
("Behold the Circle of Stars"
— MIK-ma AH-o KOM-seh-lah a-o-i-ve-a-EH)

Then clasp your hands over your heart while vibrating:
OD OL, MALPRG, NOTHOA
("And I, a Through-Thrusting Fire, in the Midst."
— OD OL, MAL-perg, NOT-ho-ah).

If you are using this ritual in conjunction with the MADRIAX hexagram ritual which follows, it should be inserted here.

8. With your finger or magical weapon, trace from your right hip to your left shoulder while vibrating:
EHNB
(EH-nub — Spirit)

from your left shoulder to your right shoulder while vibrating:
BITOM
(BI-tom — Fire)

from your right shoulder to left hip while vibrating:

EXARP
(EX-arp — Air)

from your left hip to your forehead while vibrating:

HCOMA
(he-KO-ma — Water)

and finally from your forehead back to your right hip while vibrating:

NANTA
(NAHN-ta — Earth)

Then clasp your hands over your heart and vibrate:

JAIDA
(ja-I-da — "The Highest")

Visualize the pentagram traced over your body in dark, deep purple.

This is the banishing form of the ritual. The invoking form is the same except that the pentagrams should be traced as the Invoking Pentagram of Earth.

In the invoking form, the directional names remain the same. However, they should be traced to the quarters in clockwise rather than counter-clockwise order. Also, the final spin should be counter-clockwise to align with your initial clockwise rotation.

MADRIAX ('O Ye Heavens') Hexagram Ritual

To replace the Golden Dawn Lesser Ritual of the Hexagram, I have developed an Enochian hexagram ritual that I call the MADRIAX ("o ye heavens" in Angelic).

In this revised ritual the four elements are attributed to the four quadrants of the Great Table based on the colors from Kelley's original vision of the Watchtowers[15] and the elemental attributions taken from the later "round house" vision[16]. The names vibrated are those of the Kings from the Heptarchia Mystica:

> Fire = East = BABALEL (Mars)
> Air = South = BNASPOL (Mercury)
> Water = West = BYNEPOR (Jupiter)
> Earth = North = BALIGON (Venus)

If you wish to modify this ritual so as to conform to the zodiacal scheme used in the Golden Dawn Lesser Ritual of the Hexagram you should change these attributions as follows:

> Fire = East = BABALEL (Mars)
> Earth = South = BALIGON (Venus)
> Air = West = BNASPOL (Mercury)
> Water = North = BYNEPOR (Jupiter)

The use of planetary names with the elemental unicursal hexagram represents the union of the planetary and elemental realms, the microcosm and macrocosm. The "above" and "below" points of the ritual are then attributed to BNAPSEN (Saturn) and BLUMAZA (Luna). The figures traced for these points are the usual planetary hexagrams, not the unicursal. When working with the Holy Table the figures form a column running from the heavens to the earth with the hexagram on the Holy Table itself at its midpoint.

The final figure used in this ritual is attributed to BOBOGEL (the Sun). It is combined with the invoking unicursal hexagram of Earth to symbolize the invocation and grounding of the solar force. The ritual text is as follows:

---

15. Meric Causaubon, ed. *A True and Faithful Relation of What Passed for Many Years Between Dr. John Dee and Some Spirits* (New York, NY: Magickal Childe, 1992), 168
16. Ibid, 355-361

1. With your finger or a tool such as a wand trace the Invoking Unicursal Hexagram of Earth over yourself while vibrating:

    BOBOGEL
    (BO-bo-gel)

    This tracing is done is the following manner:

    forehead -> left hip -> right shoulder -> genitals -> left shoulder -> right hip -> forehead.

    This hexagram is visualized in yellow-gold as opposed to the green that is normally used for elemental earth, and it is always traced in the invoking form, even for the banishing form of the ritual.

2. In the east, trace the invoking unicursal hexagram of Fire in red as you vibrate:

    BABALEL
    (BA-ba-lel).

    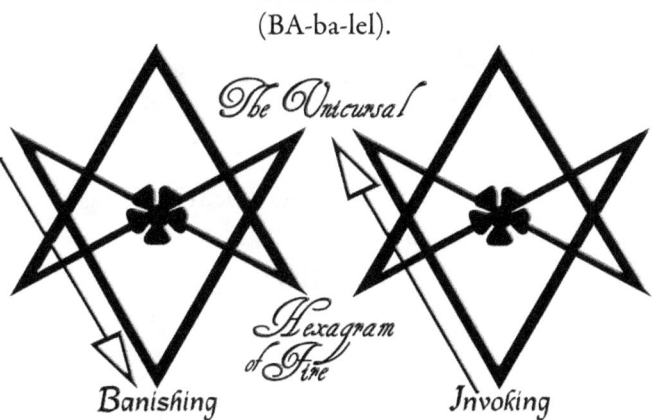

3. In the south, trace the invoking unicursal hexagram of Air in white as you vibrate:

    BNASPOL
    (BNAS-pol).

4. In the west, trace the invoking unicursal hexagram of Water in green as you vibrate:

    BYNEPOR
    (BY-neh-por).

5. In the north, trace the invoking unicursal hexagram of Earth in black as you vibrate:

    BALIGON
    (BA-li-gon).

Banishing   Invoking

6. Above you, trace the hexagram of Saturn in bright lavender as you vibrate:

    BNAPSEN
    (BNAP-sen).

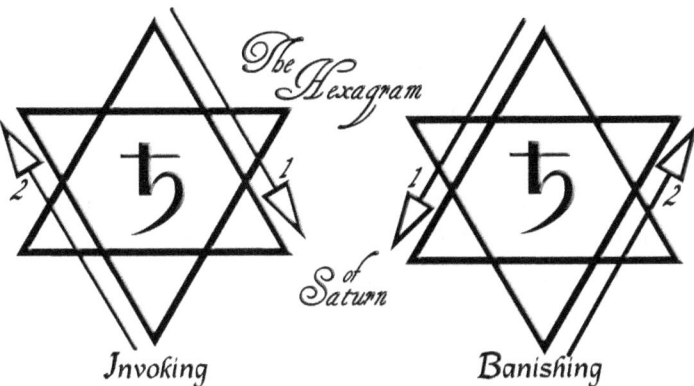

Invoking   Banishing

7. Below you, trace the hexagram of the Moon in deep violet as you vibrate:

    BLUMAZA
    (blu-MA-zah).

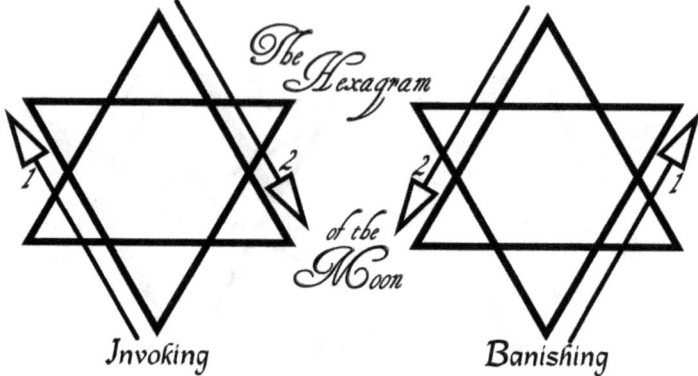

Invoking · Banishing

8. Extend your arms and make one full clockwise rotation (or circumambulation of the temple if you are using the Holy Table) as you vibrate:

> TA CALZ I OROCHA
> (TA CAL-zod I o-RO-ka —
> "as above the firmament so beneath you",
> probably the best Enochian rendering of
> "as above, so below").

Then clasp your hands over your heart for a moment and hold the full visualization of the rite in your mind.

9. For the invoking form of this ritual, hold your hands in front of you with the palms facing outwards and then separate them as though opening a heavy curtain as you vibrate:

> MADRIAX CARMARA, YOLCAM LONSHI
> (MA-dri-ax kar-MA-ra, YOL-cam LON-shi
> — "O ye heavens of Carmara, bring forth power").

Carmara is the eighth Heparchial King who rules over the other seven.

10. The ritual work for which you opened the field goes here.

11. At the conclusion of the ritual work, hold your hands in front of you and to either side with palms facing inwards, and then bring them together as though closing a heavy curtain as you vibrate:

MADRIAX CARMARA, ADRPAN LONSHI
(MA-dri-ax kar-MA-ra, AH-dra-pan LON-shi
— "O ye heavens of Carmara, cast down power").

This is the invoking form of the ritual. For the banishing form, you would turn to each direction going in a counter-clockwise order (East -> North -> West -> South -> East), trace banishing hexagrams as shown (aside from the opening Earth hexagram which should always be traced in the invoking form), and make the final rotation/circumambulation counter-clockwise.

This ritual works with the AOIVEAE to open and close magical fields just like the Lesser Ritual of the Pentagram/Lesser Ritual of the Hexagram combinations. However, they are designed slightly differently from the other similar rituals found in the tradition in order to streamline magical operations. The main innovation I wanted to incorporate was to encapsulate my workings within both rituals rather than repeating either of them to close down a rite. As a result, the basic structure works like this.

A. AOIVEAE steps 1 to 7.
B. MADRIAX steps 1-9.
C. MADRIAX step 10 is the Enochian ritual itself.
D. MADRIAX step 11.
E. AOIVEAE step 8.

So according to this structure (A) and (B) are the opening, (C) is the ritual work itself, and (D) and (E) constitute the closing.

NAZ OLPIRT ('Pillars of Light') Energy Work Exercise

One of the areas that modern magicians sometimes neglect is the energetic state of the subtle body, or body of light. I have found that practices such as Hatha Yoga and Qigong make a great deal of difference in terms of the amount of magical force you can bring to bear upon a situation and thus your ability to create change successfully. In the Golden Dawn tradition, a common practice is the Middle Pillar Exercise, which associates various names of God with specific points on the subtle body and as a result empowers those areas with the energies of the associated godforms. In the Thelemic tradition, a similar practice is the Elevenfold Seal, found in Aleister Crowley's Liber V vel Reguli. This is a similar exercise based upon relating the Enochian elements to the elemental natures of the seven chakras of Eastern mysticism.

Start off by standing in a normal, relaxed pose. Keep your spine straight and imagine your head suspended by a thread from above. Breathe slowly and easily through the nose into your diaphragm. Place your tongue so that it is touching the roof of your mouth and keep it there except when vibrating the words of the ritual. Make sure you hold the tongue in that position when breathing in. The gestures are made with the hand or finger rather than any sort of magical weapon.

1. Make a clockwise circle above your head and intone three times:

    MADRIAX

    ("the Heavens")

    Visualize a sea of luminous brilliance above you, beyond and encompassing all colors.

2. Touch the center of your forehead (ajna chakra) and intone three times:

    IAD

    (i-AHD – "God")

    Visualize energy akin to pure, clear light forming at this point, sending its rays outward to the four cardinal directions. Do not completely drop the visualization of luminous brilliance above you. You are adding to your visualization, not replacing it. This instruction holds true for all the following steps.

3. Touch your throat (vishuddha chakra) and intone three times:

   EHNB
   ("Spirit")

   Visualize a sphere of bright lavender light forming at this point.

4. Touch the center of your chest (anahata chakra) and intone three times:

   EXARP
   ("Air")

   Visualize a sphere of vibrant white energy forming at this point.

5. Touch your solar plexus (samsara chakra) and intone three times:

   BITOM
   ("Fire")

   Visualize a sphere of glowing red energy forming at this point.

6. Touch the lower abdomen just below the navel (svadasthana chakra) and intone three times:

   HCOMA
   ("Water")

   Visualize a sphere of green energy forming at this point.

7. Touch the perineum (muladhara chakra) and intone three times:

   NANTA
   ("Earth")

   Visualize a sphere of solid black energy forming at this point.

8. Drop both hands to your sides and intone three times:
   CAOSGO
   (ka-OS-go — "the Earth")

   Visualize the completion of a circuit that begins above you in the heavens, descends below you into the deep earth down the front of your body and then ascends upwards to the heavens along the back of your body.

9. As you visualize the circulating energy, start with your hands at about the level of your perineum, palms turned upwards, and then raise them to the level of the top of your head as you inhale. Then turn the palms downward and drop them back to the level of the perineum as you exhale.

10. To conclude the exercise, make the Sign of Osiris Risen, crossing your arms over your chest, and intone:
    TA CALZ I OROCHA
    ("As above the firmament so beneath you")

    as you visualize any excess energy you have focused at each of the points of your body descending below your feet into the vast darkness of the deep earth, breaking the circuit. Feel a wave of relaxation sweep over you from your head down to your feet, sweeping any remaining tension into the deep earth along with the grounded energy.

Appendix B
Comselh Ananael
Great Table Evocation Ritual

Comselh Ananael is the name that my magical working group chose when we began doing group ritual work in 2002. Since that time we have explored both the Tree of Life and the Enochian universe, and worked extensively with elemental, planetary, and zodiacal forces. Our work with the Angels of the Great Table was performed using the following ritual, derived from the template found in chapter 5. The ritual has been optimized numerous times over the years and we have found this version to be quite effective for both individual and group operations.

As we work the system from the Thelemic perspective, the ritual structure reflects that rather than the Christian perspective of John Dee and Edward Kelley. Still, much of the methodology is true to the original spirit of the work, even when it incorporates modern ceremonial forms.

0. The Temple

The ritual space is set up as explained in Chapter 5. A scrying stone or mirror is placed on the altar cloth above the center of the Sigillum Dei Aemeth. If possible the four smaller Seals should be placed under each of the altar table's four legs. The closer the Temple can be to the Enochian ideal, the better the system will work.

There are two officers in this ritual, Magus and Scryer. Magus acts as the Officiant and should wear the Enochian ring and lamen. The officers and all others present should wear white robes. Scryer attempts to contact the conjured spirit or spirits using the mirror or crystal.

The bell chime is placed on western edge of the Table. This should be a chime that can be rung easily with one hand. Scryer will be ringing it when the Angel or Angels appear, so it must not require much attention to operate. Because of this, its exact position should be left to Scryer's discretion. A low stool for Scryer is placed to the west of the altar. It should be of such a height that the stone or mirror is at Scryer's eye level.

Talismans for the angels being summoned are placed on the floor in the appropriate positions around the Holy Table. These should be reasonably large, since Magus must stand upon them with both feet when reciting the conjuration. The designs for these talismans are found in Chapter 9.

I. Opening

All form a circle around the altar. Magus initially stands directly west of the altar and Scryer stands directly east. Magus inhales fully, placing the banishing dagger at his or her lips. The air is then expelled as the dagger is swept backwards.

Magus:

Bahlasti! Ompehda!

Magus then performs the AOEVEAE up to the closing as explained in Appendix A, moving around the Table and casting in the direction of Scryer who concentrates on receiving the evoked energies. All present rotate accordingly, so that the entire circle of assembled magicians turns like a wheel as Magus moves to face each quarter. The idea here is to conjure a line of force that originates with Magus, passes over or through the stone or mirror, and is received by Scryer at each of the Temple's four quarters.

Magus:

We take refuge in Nuit,
the blue-lidded daughter of sunset,
the naked brilliance of the voluptuous night sky,
as we issue the call
to the awakened nature of all beings,
for every man and every woman is a star.

All:

AUMGN.

Magus:

We take refuge in Hadit,
the secret flame that burns
in every heart of man
and in the core of every star,
as we issue the call
to our own awakened natures,
arousing the coiled serpent about to spring.

All:

AUMGN.

Magus:

We take refuge in Heru-Ra-Ha,
who wields the wand of double power,
the wand of the force of Coph Nia,
and whose left hand is empty
for he has crushed a universe and naught remains,
as we unite our awakened natures
with those of all beings everywhere and everywhen,
dissolving all obstacles and healing all suffering.

All:
> AUMGN.

Magus:
> For pure will,
> unassuaged of purpose,
> delivered from the lust of result,
> is every way perfect.

All:
> All is pure and present
> and has always been so,
> for existence is pure joy;
> all the sorrows are but as shadows;
> they pass and done;
> but there is that which remains.
> To this realization we commit ourselves
> pure and total presence.
> So mote it be. [17]

II. The Magical Field

Magus performs the MADRIAX up to the closing as explained in Appendix A. As with the AOEVEAE, all present rotate accordingly.

Magus:
> MADRIAX CARMARA, YOLCAM LONSHI!

Magus makes the Sign of Rending the Veil, placing hands back to back and then drawing them apart as though opening a heavy curtain.

III. The Preliminary Invocation

All make the Sign of Apophis and Typhon facing the center of the table.

---

[17] This section of the opening following the AOEVEAE is adapted from the Refuge and Bodhichitta practices of Vajrayana Buddhism, but has been modified so as to fit with Thelemic cosmology.

Magus:
> *Holy art Thou, who art Universe,*
> *Holy art Thou, who art in Nature formed,*
> *Holy art Thou, the Vast and the Mighty,*
> *Source of Darkness, Source of Light.* [18]

All make the Sign of Silence, then clasp hands over hearts.

Magus recites the Revised Oration to God as explained in Chapter 5.

Magus:
> *O Almighty and Omnipotent MAD,*
> *Lord and Creator of the universe,*
> *we devoted worshippers of the Highest*
> *most earnestly invoke*
> *and call upon your divine power,*
> *wisdom, and goodness.*
>
> *We humbly and faithfully*
> *seek your favor and assistance to me*
> *in all my deeds, words, and thoughts,*
> *and in the promotion, procuring,*
> *and mingling of your praise, honour, and glory.*
>
> *Through these, your twelve mystical Names:*
> *ORO, IBAH, AOZPI, MPH, ARSL, GAIOL,*
> *OIP, TEAA, PDOCE, MOR, DIAL, HCTGA,*
> *we conjure and pray most zealously*
> *to your divine and omnipotent majesty,*
> *that all your Angelic* spirits might be called*
> *from any and all parts of the universe*
> *through the special domination*
> *and controlling power of your holy Names.*
>
> *Let them come most quickly to us.*
>
> *Let them appear visibly, friendily,*
> *and peacefully to us.*
>
> *Let them remain visible according to our will.*

---

18. *This revised wording for the Golden Dawn adoration of the Lord of the Universe is adapted from the rituals of the Open Source Order of the Golden Dawn.*

> Let them vanish from us
> and from our sight when we so request.
>
> Let them give reverence and obedience
> before you and your twelve mystical Names.
>
> We command that they happily
> satisfy me in all things by accomplishing
> each and every one of my petitions,
> if not by one means, then by another,
> goodly, virtuously, and perfectly,
> with an excellent and thorough completeness,
> according to their virtues and powers,
> both general and unique,
> and by your united ministry and office,
> O God,
>
> Amen.
>
> So mote it be.
>
> * Substitute "Cacodemonic" for "Angelic"
when summoning Cacodemons.

All:

AMEN. AMEN. AMEN.

Magus rings bell chime.

IV. The Conjuration

Scryer moves to the west of the altar and is seated at the Holy Table, gazing into the stone or mirror. Magus stands behind Scryer and all other participants remain in a circle around the Table.

Magus recites the First Key, in Angelic followed by English, and Scryer then recites the Second Key, in Angelic followed by English, as explained in Chapter 7.

Magus performs the Greater Invoking Ritual of the Hexagram for the element corresponding to the angels being summoned, as explained in Chapter 8. Alternately, the Greater Invoking Ritual of the Pentagram could be performed with each of the elemental pentagrams traced to the appropriate alchemical direction, or the Revised Opening by Watchtower could be employed for this same purpose. Again, all present rotate accordingly except for Scryer, who remains seated.

[More Keys]

Magus then steps onto the talisman and recites the appropriate conjuration for the angels being summoned, depending upon the objective of the rite, as explained in Chapter 10. If necessary, this action is repeated for each of the four quarters, calling upon the angels of each direction corresponding to the objective of the rite. Magus always starts conjuring to the east and ends in the north, moving clockwise and casting across the Holy Table.

Following the conjuration, all begin to chant the controlling names for the angels being conjured as they visualize the divine light descending into the stone or mirror. When Scryer sees a vision, he or she rings the bell chime and the chant ends.

V. Charge / Communication

The contents of this section depend on the nature of the ritual as explained in Chapter 10. Either questions should be asked of the summoned angels through Scryer, as Dee and Kelly did when they received the original system, or the angels should be charged with a particular task. In the latter case, be sure to make note of the exact wording of the Charge.

VI. The License to Depart

Magus gives the License to Depart as explained in Chapter 11. This version of the License is slightly different from the one found in that chapter but will work just as well.

Magus:

O thou Angels of Light,
because thou hast-diligently
answered unto our demands,
and hast been very ready and willing
to come at our call,

> we do here license thee to depart
> unto thy proper place;
> without causing harm or danger
> unto man or beast.
>
> Depart, then, I say,
> and be thou very ready
> to come at our call,
> being duly exorcised and conjured
> by these sacred rites of magick.
>
> We charge thee to withdraw
> peaceably and quietly,
> and the peace of the Almighty,
> Eternal, True, and Living God
> be ever continued between us.
>
> AMEN.
>
> *Substitute "Cacodemons of Darkness" when dismissing Cacodemons.

All:

> So mote it be!

Magus then concludes the MADRIAX as explained in Appendix A.

Magus:

> MADRIAX CARMARA, ADRPAN LONSHI!

Magus makes the Sign of Closing the Veil, bringing both hands together with palms facing as though closing a set of heavy curtains. Scryer then rises and joins the circle, standing opposite Magus.

VII. Closing

All:

> May the benefit of this act
> and all acts be dedicated
> unto the complete liberation
> and supreme enlightenment

> *of all beings everywhere,*
> *pervading space and time.*
> *So mote it be.*
> *May the benefits of practice,*
> *ours and others,*
> *come to fruition ultimately and immediately*
> *and we remain in a state of presence.*
> *AH!* [19]

Magus concludes the AOEVEAE as explained in Appendix A.

Magus:
> *I now declare this temple duly closed.*

One knock with banishing dagger. The rite is at an end.

---

[19]. As in the Opening, this section is adapted from Vajrayana Buddhism.

Bibliography

Causaubon, Meric, ed. *A True and Faithful Relation of What Passed for Many Years Between Dr. John Dee and Some Spirits* (New York, NY: Magickal Childe, 1992)

Crowley, Aleister. *777 and Other Qabalistic Writings* (San Francisco, CA: Red Wheel/Weiser, 1986)

Crowley, Aleister. *Magick: Book Four* (San Francisco, CA: Weiser Books, 1998).

Dee, John. *A True and Faithful Relation of What Passed for Many Years Between Dr. John Dee and Some Spirits* (Whitefish, MT: Kessinger, 2010)

Duquette, Lon Milo. *Enochian Vision Magick* (San Francisco, CA: Weiser Books, 2008)

DuQuette, Lon Milo. *The Magick of Aleister Crowley* (San Francisco, CA: Weiser Books, 2003).

Hay, George, ed. *The Necronomicon: The Book of Dead Names* (London, UK: Skoob Books, 1993)

James, Geoffrey. *The Enochian Evocation of Doctor John Dee* (San Francisco, CA: Weiser Books, 2009)

Kraig, Donald Michael. *Modern Magick* (St. Paul, MN: Llewellyn, 1988)

Laycock, Donald C. *The Complete Enochian Dictionary* (San Francisco, CA: Weiser Books, 2001)

Leitch, Aaron. *The Angelical Language Volumes I and II* (St. Paul, MN: Llewellyn, 2010)

Peterson, Joseph, ed. *John Dee's Five Books of Mystery* (San Francisco, CA: Red Wheel/Weiser, 2008)

Phillips, Osborne and Denning, Melita. *Mysteria Magica* (St. Paul, MN: Llewellyn, 2004).

Regardie, Israel. *The Golden Dawn* (St. Paul, MN: Llewellyn, 2002).

Turner, Robert. *Elizabethan Magic* (Salisbury, UK: Element, 1990)

Tyson, Donald, ed. *Agrippa's Three Books of Occult Philosophy* (St. Paul, MN: Llewellyn, 1992)

Tyson, Donald. *Enochian Magic for Beginners* (St. Paul, MN: Llewellyn, 2008).

Tyson, Donald. *Tetragrammaton* (St. Paul, MN: Llewellyn, 2003).

About the Author

Scott Michael Stenwick was born in Minneapolis, Minnesota in 1969. A natural storyteller from early childhood, he was drawing pictures and assembling them into simple narratives before he could read or write. In elementary school he was exposed to computers when his school acquired an Apple II in 1977 and has been writing and programming ever since. He developed an interest in esoteric studies as a teenager following in the footsteps of his great-grandmother, a professional astrologer and medium, and began practicing ritual and ceremonial magick.

Scott attended Saint Olaf College in Northfield, Minnesota and graduated in 1991 with a degree in psychology. In college he worked on two novels in addition to his studies but eventually decided that neither was suitable for publication without substantial revision. After graduation he went to work in the computer field and built a career as a software developer and information technology consultant. In this capacity he has worked for several Fortune 500 companies and designed and developed numerous business applications.

Scott lives in Minneapolis with his wife and two daughters. After years of solitary magical and mystical work, he joined Ordo Templi Orientis in 1995 and became a Freemason in 1997. In addition, he is part of a smaller magical working group that has been in operation since 2002 and performed numerous experimental workings seeking to advance the general body of magical knowledge.

Contact Scott Stenwick at:
E-Mail: ScottM@iphouse.com

or

Scott@plethora.net

Facebook: Scott Michael Stenwick

Blog: Ananael.blogspot.com

Website: ScottStenwick.wordpress.com

Index

A

A-mi-ran, 92-93
Aaozaif, 29
Aaron Leitch, 78, 82
ABRAHADABRA, 131-132
ADNI, 122, 213
Adonai, 120, 122
ADRPAN, 126, 229, 240
Aeon of Horus, 34
Aethyr Keys, 85
Aethyrs, 21, 33
AG, 94
AGLA, 120, 213
Agrippa, 19, 25, 34, 142, 244
AH, 241
AHIH, 119, 213
Air Dagger, 125, 127

Air of Air, 136
Aire, 85
Aires, 17, 21, 85
Ajna, 121, 230
Akasha, 51
AL, 121
Albert Einstein, 200
Aleister Crowley, 13, 32-33, 48, 53, 56, 66, 75, 81, 90, 117-118, 210, 219, 230, 243
ALIM, 121
Almighty God, 174, 184, 193
AMEN, 64, 73-74, 174, 176, 178, 180-182, 184, 186-187, 189, 193, 195-196, 198, 206, 212, 238, 240
AMIRAN, 92-93

Ananael, 79, 92-93, 233, 246
Ananael Qaa, 79
Angel Madimi, 73
Angel Magic, 27, 48, 139, 210
Angelic Key, 17, 86-87, 89, 92-93, 95-98, 100-101, 103-110
Angelic Letter, 77
Angelic Name, 175-176
Angelic Pronunciation, 77
Angelic Spirits, 72, 74, 237
Angels E H N B, 90
Angels of Atziluth, 25
Angels of God, 186, 188
Angels of Gold, 97-98, 100-101, 185, 194
Angels of Light, 184-185, 205, 239
Angels of Metals, 157-159
Angels of Tablet of Union, 90
Animal Soul, 23
Aoeveae, 14, 56, 59, 66, 69, 71, 206, 220, 234, 236, 241
AOIVEAE, 222, 229
AOZPI, 71-72, 74, 127, 220-221, 237
Apocalypse, 33-34
Apocalypse Working, 34
Apophis, 130, 215-216, 236
Apple II, 245
ARARITA, 216-217
Archangel, 213
Archangels, 51, 75, 220
Archetypal World, 22
Aries, 51
Aristotelean, 199
Ark of Knowledge, 88
ARSL, 49, 71-72, 74, 81, 127, 220, 222, 237
Arts Mechanical, 180-181
ARZL, 31
Asia, 200
Assiah, 22-24
ATEH, 120, 211
Atziluth, 22-25
AUMGN, 235-236
Auriel, 51
Aurum Solis, 13, 33, 144, 191
Avtotar, 29

B

BABAGEN, 105-106
BABALEL, 224-225
BAG-le, 94-95, 97-103
BAGLE, 94-95, 97-103
Bahlasti, 234
BALIGON, 224, 226
Banishing AOEVEAE Pentagram Ritual, 56
Banishing Dagger, 124-126, 234, 241
Banishing Field, 65
Banishing Pentagram of Earth, 221-222
Banner, 47-48
Banners, 19, 46-48, 125
Basic Ritual Forms, 211
Bataivah, 28-29, 52, 136, 173, 220, 222
BAZ-me-lo I-ta, 98-99
Bitom, 129, 221-222, 231
Black, 17, 30, 32, 46-47, 51, 53, 69, 85, 128-130, 144, 177, 213, 226, 231
Black Cross, 17, 30, 51, 53, 69, 85, 129, 144, 177

Blacke, 46
BLUMAZA, 224, 227
Bnapsen, 181, 224, 227
BNASPOL, 224, 226
BOBOGEL, 224-225
BOLP, 110
Book Four, 243
Book of Dead Names, 243
Book of Revelation, 34
Bose-Einstein, 22
Breathe, 230
Briah, 22-24
Bring, 16, 25, 32, 104, 123, 187-188, 194, 196, 198, 202-203, 228, 230
BRINTS, 110
British Museum, 19, 46, 48
BUFD, 98-99
BUSD, 108
BYNEPOR, 224, 226

C

CAB, 87
Cacodemonic, 74, 238
Cacodemons of Darkness, 193, 240
Cacodemons of God, 196-198
Cacodemons of Gold, 97-98, 100-101, 194
Cacodemons of Living Creatures Fire, 110
Cacodemons of Metals, 165-167
Calls, 23, 71, 77, 117
Cancer, 51
CAOSGO, 98-100, 106, 110, 232
Capricorn, 51
Carmara, 228-229, 236, 240
Carpet, 45-46
Cast, 20, 31, 40, 50, 65, 125-126, 201, 207, 229
Castles, 17, 46
Causaubon, 243
Celestial Realms, 184, 193
Centering Field, 65
Ceremonial Forms, 61, 64, 67, 206-207, 233
Chaldean Oracles of Zoroaster, 128
Charge, 32, 50, 59, 75, 194, 199, 202-206, 239-240
Chesed, 212
Chiah, 23
Chinese Qigong, 125
CHIS, 89, 92, 94-98, 100-101, 104, 107, 109
Christian, 132, 191, 205, 233
Church, 192
Circle of Stars, 222
Circumambulations, 49, 131
Close, 59, 75, 85, 124, 200, 205-207, 215, 229
Closing, 50, 59, 119-120, 205-207, 228-229, 234, 236, 240
Cloth, 45-47, 129, 234
CNOQUOL RIT, 97
Communication, 15, 69, 239
Comselh Ananael Great Table Evocation Ritual, 233
Concourse of Forces, 26
Conjuration, 25, 49-50, 59, 145, 179, 193-194, 196-197, 206, 234, 238-239

Conjurations, 25, 32-34, 46, 48-50, 52, 58-59, 70, 91, 133, 135, 145, 174, 183, 192, 202
Coph Nia, 235
Correspondences, 210
Creative World, 22
Creatures, 27, 62-63, 93, 95, 98, 107-110, 161-163, 169-171, 187, 197
Cross, 17, 22, 29-32, 51, 53, 59, 69, 80, 85, 129, 142-144, 177, 207, 212-216, 222
Crowley, 13, 32-33, 48, 53, 56, 66, 75, 81-82, 90, 117-118, 120, 210, 219, 230, 243
CRPL, 94
Cullor, 46
Cup, 124-125, 128
CZNS, 31

D

Dagger, 124-128, 220, 234, 241
QAAON, 96
DAS, 95, 100, 102-103, 105-108, 110
Day, 21, 28, 57, 70, 102, 114-115
Day - Sunrise, 115
Day - Sunset, 116
DE, 92
Demons, 27, 30, 86, 136, 191-192, 194
Demons of Darkness, 194
Denning, 244
Destruction, 191-192
DIAL, 49, 71-72, 74, 82, 129, 220-221, 237
Dittany of Crete, 118
Divine, 16, 25, 48, 69, 72-75, 123, 174-175, 179-181, 184, 186, 193, 195, 202, 237, 239
Divine Power, 72-73, 237
Donald Michael Kraig, 66
Donald Tyson, 19, 33
Dr. John Dee, 13, 48, 83, 243
Dragon, 99, 126
Drop, 206, 230, 232
Duquette, 219, 243

E

E X A R P, 90
Earth of Earth, 91
Earthy, 90
East, 25, 28-29, 46, 48-52, 56-59, 71, 91-92, 97-98, 103, 107, 118-119, 123-124, 126-127, 129-130, 136, 141, 145, 147, 149, 151, 153, 155, 157, 159, 161, 163, 165, 167, 169, 173, 211-213, 215-216, 218, 220-222, 224-225, 229, 234, 239
Eastern, 119, 230
Edlprnaa, 136, 220, 222
Edward Kelley, 13, 17, 233
Egyptian, 122, 131, 216
Eheieh, 119
EHNB, 129, 221-222, 231

Eighteenth Angelic Key, 110
Eighteenth Key, 110
Eighth Angelic Key, 98
Eighth Key, 98, 105
Element, 22, 26-27, 51, 57, 90, 117-118, 123-124, 129, 136, 238, 244
Elements, 13-14, 21-27, 46, 51, 55, 57, 64, 69, 90, 114, 117-118, 123-126, 128-132, 135, 139, 161-163, 169-171, 187-188, 197-198, 207, 224, 230
Elevenfold Seal, 230
Eleventh Angelic Key, 103
Eleventh Key, 103
Elias Ashmole, 49
Elizabethan Magic, 244
Elohim, 121
EMF, 139-140
Energy, 21-22, 56, 65, 69-70, 72, 119, 140, 200, 230-232
Energy Work Exercise, 56, 69, 230
Enochian Apocalypse, 33
Enochian Chess, 26
Enochian Evocation, 141, 244
Enochian Evocation of Doctor John Dee, 244
Enochian Initiation, 24
Enochian Lamen, 37
Enochian Lamens, 52
Enochian Magic, 19, 33, 244
Enochian Magick, 1, 3-4, 13, 15, 17, 19, 21, 23, 25, 27, 29, 31, 33-37, 39, 41, 43, 45, 47, 49, 51, 53, 55, 57, 59, 61, 63, 65-67, 69, 71, 73, 75, 77, 79, 81, 83, 85-87, 89, 91, 93, 95, 97, 99, 101, 103, 105, 107, 109, 111, 113, 115, 117, 119, 121, 123, 125, 127, 129, 131, 133, 135, 137, 139, 141, 143, 145, 147, 149, 151, 153, 155, 157, 159, 161, 163, 165, 167, 169, 171, 173, 177, 179, 181, 183, 185, 187, 189, 191, 193, 195, 197, 199, 201, 203, 205, 207, 209, 211, 213, 215, 217, 219, 221, 223, 225, 227, 229, 231, 233, 235, 237, 239, 241, 243, 245, 247
Enochian Meltdown, 33
Enochian PELE, 220
Enochian Ring, 36, 56, 124, 234
Enochian Rings, 52
Enochian Tables, 48
Enochian Temple, 35, 38, 46, 52-53, 56, 62, 86-87, 91, 119, 124-125, 192
Enochian Vision Magick, 243
Ensign, 42-45
Ensign of Jupiter, 43
Ensign of Mars, 43
Ensign of Mercury, 44
Ensign of Saturn, 44
Ensign of Venus, 42
Ensigns, 27, 41, 45, 52, 125
Ensigns of Creation, 27, 41, 52, 125
Enterer, 131
Europe, 185
European, 24, 47
Eve, 47
Evocation, 56, 86-87, 117, 141, 206, 233, 244
Exarp, 129, 221, 223, 231

F

FAFEN, 92, 104
FAXS, 109
Fields, 14, 65-66, 199-200, 229
Fiery Odors, 117
Fifteenth Angelic Key, 107
Fifteenth Key, 107
Fifth Angelic Key, 95
Fifth Key, 95
Fire of Air, 136
Fire of Fire, 91
Fire Wand, 124, 126
First Angelic Key, 86-87
First Leaf, 86
First Quarter, 117
Five Books of Mystery, 244
Five Books of Mystical Exercises, 35
FMND, 31
Formative World, 22
Fortune, 245
Fountain, 62
Four Horsemen, 33
Four Kings, 25, 27, 135, 173
Fourteenth Angelic Key, 106
Fourteenth Key, 106
Fourth Angelic Key, 93
Fourth Key, 93
Freemason, 246
Friday, 114-116
Full Moon, 117

G

Gabriel, 51, 213
GAIOL, 49, 71-72, 74, 81, 127, 220, 222, 237
Galbanum, 117
Garden of Eden, 46
Geburah, 212
Geoffrey James, 38, 141
Geomancy, 27, 139
George Hay, 83
German, 47, 78
Ghost, 140
Gimel, 81
Glory, 63-64, 72-73, 98-99, 108, 110, 180, 182, 187-189, 206, 237
Gmicalzoma Enochian, 78
GNAY, 100-102
God of Justice, 88
Godhead, 69-71
Goetic, 27, 86
GOHUS, 92-93, 104
Gold, 27, 36, 52, 97-98, 100-101, 185, 194, 210
Golden Dawn Enochian, 18, 20, 26, 51-52, 135-136, 183, 209
Golden Dawn Key, 90, 105
Golden Dawn Key Order, 90, 105
Golden Dawn Lesser Banishing Ritual, 56
Golden Dawn Lesser Ritual, 220, 224
Golden Dawn Lesser Rituals, 59
Golden Dawn Table, 19
Golden Dawn Tradition, 51-52, 64, 81-82, 123, 230
Great Table Conjurations, 25, 48-

49, 70, 91, 133, 135
Great Table Kings, 33
Great Table of Tyson, 19
Great Table Ritual Template, 55-56
Great Table Talismans, 50, 141, 145
Great Work, 5, 16
Greater Invoking Ritual, 238
Greater Ritual, 57, 118, 123-124
Greeks, 21
Green, 45-47, 122, 128, 130, 225-226, 231
GROSB, 105-106
Groups, 13, 18, 24-25, 27, 31, 34, 50, 70, 85, 91, 114, 118, 136, 141, 177, 191, 200-201

H

H. P. Lovecraft, 34, 83
Habioro, 29
Hadit, 235
Hatha Yoga, 230
Hay, 83, 243
Hcoma, 129, 220, 223, 231
HCTGA, 49, 71-72, 74, 82, 129, 220-221, 237
Heart Center, 37
Heavens, 63-64, 95, 123, 224, 228-230, 232
Heavy Odors, 117
Hebrew, 22, 46-47, 77, 80
Hebrew Consonant, 80
Heh, 23, 82, 212
Hekas, 126
Heparchial King, 228
Heptarchia Mystica, 13, 16-17, 35, 49, 139, 141, 224
Heptarchial King Bnapsen, 181
Heptarchial Kings, 34, 80, 139, 201
Hermes Temple, 82
Hermetic, 19, 22-23, 25-26, 123, 131, 135
Hermetic Order, 19, 26
Hermetic Qabalah, 22-23, 25, 131, 135
Heru-Ra-Ha, 235
Hexagram of Air, 217, 226
Hexagram of Earth, 216, 224-226
Hexagram of Fire, 216, 225
Hexagram of Water, 217, 226
Hexagram Ritual, 224
Highest, 22, 63, 73, 88, 93, 103-104, 106-111, 221, 223, 237
Hipotga, 29
Holy, 35, 38-41, 45-50, 52, 56, 58-59, 63-64, 71-72, 74, 86-88, 91, 119, 125-127, 129-130, 174, 178, 180-182, 186, 189, 192, 195, 198, 206-207, 220, 224, 228, 234, 237-239
Holy Names, 63, 72, 74, 174, 189, 198, 237
Holy Names of God, 174, 189, 198
Holy Ones, 88
Holy Tables, 52
HOMIL COCASB, 92
Hoodoo, 15
Horus, 34, 123
Hours, 113-117, 135
Htmorda, 29

I

IAD, 78, 87, 98, 230
IAIDA, 78, 103-110
IAO, 215
IBAH, 71-72, 74, 127, 220-221, 237
Iczhihal, 135-136, 220, 222
ILS, 107-110
Incense, 117-118
Injunctions, 73, 202
INRI, 215
Intellect, 23
Interior Images, 4
Intone, 56, 211-213, 215, 230-232
Intuition, 23
Invoking, 56, 65-66, 70, 75, 86, 120, 123-124, 127-129, 219-220, 223-226, 228-229, 238
Invoking Field, 65
Invoking MADRIAX Hexagram Ritual, 56
Invoking Pentagram of Active Spirit, 129
Invoking Pentagram of Air, 127
Invoking Pentagram of Earth, 129, 223
Invoking Pentagram of Fire, 127
Invoking Pentagram of Passive Spirit, 129
Invoking Pentagram of Water, 128
Invoking Unicursal Hexagram of Earth, 224-226
Invoking Wand, 124, 129
IOYE, 110
Isis, 215
Israel Regardie, 66, 81, 123

J

JAIDA, 87-88, 221, 223
James, 19, 38, 141, 144, 244
Jesus, 132
John Dee, 13, 17, 32, 35, 48-49, 72, 83, 233, 243-244
Joseph H. Peterson, 5
Joseph Peterson, 14
Judgment, 27-28, 102, 136, 175
July, 62
Jumping, 200
June, 17
Just, 24, 32, 34-35, 46, 73, 78, 91-92, 105, 107-108, 127-128, 192, 199, 201, 207, 211, 219, 229, 231, 239
Juyce, 46

K

KA, 88-89, 95, 103, 106
Kaph, 131
Kelly, 35-36, 41, 239
Kelvin, 22
Kerubic, 27, 30-32, 177, 183, 192
Kerubic Angels, 27, 30-31, 177, 183, 192
Kerubs, 177

Kessinger, 243
Kether, 119, 212
Keys Thirteen, 105
Keyword Analysis, 132, 215, 218
King Bataivah, 28
Kingdom, 110, 118, 120
Knowledge, 27-28, 88, 136, 175, 187-188, 196-198, 210, 246
Kraig, 66-67, 244
Krakow, 62

L

Lamen, 35-37, 56, 234
LAP, 87-89, 103-110
LARZ, 31
Last Quarter, 117
Latin, 48
Lava, 22
Law, 34, 88
LAY, 49, 212
LBRH, 64-66
LE OLAHM, 212
Leaf, 83, 86
Leaves, 17, 82-83, 86
Leaves of Liber Loagaeth, 17, 82-83, 86
Leitch, 78, 82-83, 244
Leo Vinci, 78, 82
Leonardo Da Vinci, 214
Lesser Angel, 32
Lesser Angels of Medicine, 31
Lesser Banishing Ritual, 56, 59, 70, 206-207
Lesser Hexagram, 66
Lesser Invoking Ritual, 56
Lesser Pentagram, 66
Lesser Rituals, 51, 59, 65, 124, 207
Liber, 17, 32, 75, 81-83, 86, 90, 117-118, 120, 136, 230
Liber Chanokh, 32, 81-82, 90
Liber Loagaeth, 17, 82-83, 86
Liber O, 75, 118, 120
Liber V, 230
Libra, 51
License, 59, 123, 205-207, 239-240
Life-Force, 23
Light, 62-63, 69, 71-73, 82, 110, 123, 126-128, 130, 184-185, 205, 213-214, 216, 230-231, 237, 239
Limitations, 202, 204
LIRB, 66
LIRH, 64-67, 219
LIRP, 65-66
Living Creatures, 27, 107-110, 161-163, 169-171, 187, 197
Living God, 205, 240
Lon Milo Duquette, 219
London, 243
Lovecraft, 34, 83
Lover, 189
LU, 87-88
Luna, 224
LUX, 216

M

MAD, 73, 87-88, 92-93, 96, 103-110, 237
Madriax, 14, 56, 59, 66, 71, 206, 222, 224, 228-230, 236, 240
Magical Name, 73, 174-175, 178-182, 184-185, 187, 189, 193-194, 196, 198, 205-206
Magician, 14-15, 18, 23, 26, 33, 36, 50, 52, 57-59, 65-66, 69-71, 75, 117-118, 132, 135, 192, 201-206, 211
Magick, 1, 3-4, 13-15, 17, 19, 21, 23, 25, 27, 29, 31-37, 39, 41, 43, 45, 47-49, 51, 53, 55, 57, 59, 61, 63, 65-67, 69-71, 73, 75, 77, 79, 81, 83, 85-87, 89, 91, 93, 95, 97, 99, 101, 103, 105, 107, 109, 111, 113, 115, 117, 119, 121, 123, 125, 127, 129, 131, 133, 135, 137, 139, 141, 143, 145, 147, 149, 151, 153, 155, 157, 159, 161, 163, 165, 167, 169, 171, 173, 177, 179, 181, 183, 185, 187, 189, 191, 193, 195, 197, 199, 201-203, 205-207, 209-211, 213, 215, 217, 219, 221, 223, 225, 227, 229, 231, 233, 235, 237, 239-241, 243-245, 247
Magick of Aleister Crowley, 219, 243
Magickal Childe, 243
MAHD, 73
Malkuth, 118, 120, 212
MALPRG, 87, 96, 222
Man, 48, 62-63, 101-102, 179, 182, 188, 197, 214, 235, 240
Manus, 118
Master, 96, 210
Mathers, 26, 32, 209
Matter, 14-15, 21-22, 77, 129, 199-201
Maurine Stenwick, 5
Maya, 200
ME, 5, 21, 34, 48, 62-64, 73-74, 78, 88-89, 91-92, 94, 103-104, 106-111, 120, 132, 140-141, 182, 197, 202-203, 205, 209, 213, 237-238
Medicine, 27, 31, 50, 92-93, 95-96, 139, 141, 155-157, 163-165, 184, 192, 197
Medieval, 185, 191
Melita, 244
Mem, 82
Meric, 243
Michele Rockne, 5
MICMA, 92, 105-106, 222
Middle East, 124
Middle Pillar Exercise, 70, 230
MN, 16, 210, 244
MOM, 100
Monday, 114-116
Moon Earth, 114, 117
Moon Saturn, 115-116
MOR, 49, 71-72, 74, 82, 129, 220-221, 237
Mountains, 62
Mourning of Isis, 215
MOZ OD, 110
MPH, 49, 71-72, 74, 81-82, 127, 220, 222, 237
MT, 243
Much, 14, 19, 21, 25-27, 33, 40, 45-

46, 49, 64, 70, 81-82, 128, 130, 140, 145, 191-192, 199-200, 202-203, 207, 210, 233-234
Myrrh, 117

Mysteria Magica, 244
Mystical Names of God, 178, 180-182, 186-187, 189, 195-196, 198

N

Name of God, 73, 118-122, 174, 176
Nanta, 129, 220, 223, 231
NAPEAI SOBOLN, 105
Natural Substances, 27, 92-93, 95-96, 147-149, 178
Nature, 22, 24-25, 31, 128, 130, 174, 186, 191-192, 195, 197, 235, 237, 239
NAZ OLPIRT, 14, 56, 69, 230
Naz Olpirt Enochian, 14
Necronomicon, 34, 83, 243
Nephesch, 23
Neschamah, 23
Nevertheless, 202
New Age, 200
New Moon, 117
New World, 179

New York, 243
NI, 97
Night, 102, 114, 116, 235
NIISO, 98-103
Ninth Angelic Key, 100
Ninth Key, 100
NON-kap, 103
Non-Thelemites, 132
NOR, 88, 94
NOR MO-lap, 94
NOR QUASAHI, 94
Northern Hemisphere, 98
Northfield, 245
NOTHOA, 87, 222
Nuit, 235
Nun, 215
NY, 243

O

OIP, 71-72, 74, 128, 220, 222, 237
OL, 87, 101-102, 106, 222
OL SONF VORSG, 87
Olibanum, 117
OLN, 98-99
OMEBB, 79
Omnipotent Creator, 179, 188, 198
Omnipotent God, 174-176, 178-181

Omnipotent MAD, 73, 237
Omnipotent Majesty, 72, 74, 237
Ompehda, 234
Onycha, 117
Open Source Order, 130
Opening Key, 86
Opening Keys, 56, 85-86, 113
Opening The Temple, 56, 61, 67, 70

Operant Field, 56, 64-66, 219
Oration, 71, 237
Ordo Templi Orientis, 246
ORO, 47, 71-72, 74, 90, 127, 220-221, 237
Osborne, 244
Osiris, 123, 131, 215-216, 232

Over, 17, 20-21, 26, 28, 33, 46, 65, 67, 69, 71, 77-78, 88, 93, 105, 131, 139-140, 178, 186, 194-195, 200-201, 204, 209, 212-213, 216, 221-223, 225, 228, 232-233, 235, 237
OX, 98-99

P

PAMBT, 110
PANPIR MALPIRGI, 92-93
Pantacle, 39, 124-125, 128-129
PAROKETH, 120, 125, 131
PDOCE, 71-72, 74, 128, 220, 222, 237
Peh, 82, 131
Peh Resh Kaph Tau, 131
Pentagram of Active, 118, 129
Pentagram of Active Spirit, 118, 129
Pentagram of Earth, 118, 129, 212-213, 221-223
Pentagram of Passive Spirit, 118, 129
Pentagram Ritual, 56, 69, 220
Pentagrams, 57, 118-125, 129-130, 220-221, 223, 238
Pentagrams of Active Spirit, 119-120
Pentagrams of Air, 122
Pentagrams of Earth, 122
Pentagrams of Fire, 121
Pentagrams of Passive Spirit, 120
Pentagrams of Water, 121
People, 16, 24, 33, 52, 125, 136
Perfect Happiness, 5, 16
Perfect Power, 187, 196, 206

Phases, 70, 117, 135
Philosophers of Nature, 24-25
Physical Manifestations, 139
Pillars of Light, 230
PIR DES, 88
Planetary Days, 113, 117
Planetary Hours, 114-116, 135
Plato, 22
Positions of Sigillum Dei Aemeth, 41
Power, 14, 25, 32, 70-74, 88-89, 93, 97-98, 106, 140, 174, 176, 179, 181, 184-188, 193-194, 196-197, 200, 203, 205-206, 228-229, 235, 237
Prayer of Enoch, 56, 62, 74
Preliminary Invocation, 56, 69-71, 113, 205, 236
Preliminary Invocations, 69
Preparation, 50, 56
Prince, 28, 145
Princes, 17, 34, 49, 80, 139, 141, 201-202
Probability Shift, 20, 35, 140, 201, 203

Q

QAA, 78-79, 87, 103-110
Qabalistic, 21, 24-25, 27, 31, 59, 71, 75, 118-120, 207, 212, 214, 243
Qabalistic Cross, 59, 207, 212, 214
Qabalistic Tree of Life, 119-120, 212
Qabalistic Worlds, 21, 24-25, 27, 31, 71
Qigong, 125, 230
Quadrant, 26-29, 31, 46, 48, 50, 80, 90, 92, 136, 141, 144, 175
QUAH, 79

R

Raagiosl, 136, 220, 222
Raphael, 18, 51, 213
Regardie, 66, 81-82, 123-124, 244
Reguli, 230
Renaissance, 25, 113, 191
Resh, 81, 131, 215
Revelation, 34
Revised Fundamental Obeisance, 56, 73
Revised Opening, 57, 123, 125-126, 239
Revised Oration, 237
Rivers, 62
Robe, 37, 56, 213
Ruach, 23
Rulership, 27
RZLA, 31

S

Sacrosanct Names of God, 184, 193
Sagittae, 75, 118
Saint Augustine, 205
Saint Olaf College, 245
Salisbury, 244
Samekh, 81
Samuel Liddell MacGregor Mathers, 26
San Francisco, 243-244
Sands, 62
Saturday, 114-116
Schroedinger, 199
Scorpio, 215
Seals, 234
Second Angelic Key, 86, 89
Second Key, 56-57, 87, 90, 238
Second Keys, 86
Second Leaf, 86
Secret Discovery, 27, 107-110, 153-155, 181
Seeker, 189
Seer, 62
Self, 23, 62
Semitic, 47
Senior, 175
Senoirs, 29
Set, 16, 33, 35, 38, 50, 52-53, 56, 66, 70, 72, 80, 91, 94, 122,

129, 136, 210, 234, 240
Seventeenth Angelic Key, 109
Seventeenth Key, 109
Seventh Angelic Key, 97
Seventh Key, 97
SG, 81
Shakti, 200
Shewstone, 45
Shin, 132
Shu, 122
SIAS, 31
Sigil Marks, 141-144
Sigillum, 39-41, 45, 50, 123, 125, 139-140, 192, 234
Sigillums, 52
Sign of Air, 122
Sign of Apophis, 130, 215, 236
Sign of Closing, 119, 240
Sign of Earth, 122
Sign of Fire, 121
Sign of Osiris Risen, 131, 216, 232
Sign of Osiris Slain, 215-216
Sign of Rending, 119, 131, 236
Sign of Silence, 130, 237
Signs of LVX, 216, 218
Silence, 86, 130, 237
Silk, 45-47
Six Seniors, 28-29, 175
Sixteenth Angelic Key, 108
Sixteenth Key, 108
Sixth, 96
Sixth Angelic Key, 96
Sixth Key, 96
Skoob Books, 243
Skoob Esoterica, 83
Sloane, 19, 48

SOBOLN, 100, 105, 222
Sol, 215
Sound, 34, 78, 80-82
Source of Darkness, 130, 237
Source of Light, 130, 237
South, 25, 46, 48-51, 57, 71, 81, 93-94, 98, 104-106, 108, 119, 123, 127-130, 136, 146, 148, 150, 152, 154, 156, 158, 160, 162, 164, 166, 168, 170, 213, 216, 220, 222, 224, 226, 229
Space, 46-48, 50, 57, 65, 113, 123, 130, 135, 200-201, 234, 241
Spirit Pentagram, 118
Spirits, 21, 26-27, 31-32, 34, 46, 58-59, 65, 69, 72, 74-75, 91-92, 96-97, 103, 107, 117-118, 139-140, 183, 185, 187, 194, 197, 199-205, 234, 237, 243
St. Paul, 244
Star Sapphire, 56, 59, 66, 207, 219
Stars, 220, 222
Stella Matutina, 82
Storax, 117
Sub-quadrant, 26-27, 30-31, 90, 92, 136, 139, 141, 177, 183
Summum Bonum, 5
Sun of Spirit, 130
Sun Passive Spirit, 114
Sun Water, 114
Sunday, 114-116
Sunrise, 114-116
Sunset, 114-116, 235
Supernal, 126-128
Supporters, 200
Svadasthana, 121, 231

T

TA, 87-89, 92, 94-95, 97, 99-100, 103, 126, 228, 232
Table of Tyson, 19-20
Tables, 11, 17, 48, 52, 63-64, 90, 114
Tablet, 28-29, 51-53, 69, 85, 90, 129
Tablet of Union, 51, 53, 69, 85, 90, 129
Tablet ORO, 90
Tai Chi Chuan, 125
Talismans, 41, 49-50, 58-59, 141-142, 144-145, 234
Taoist, 69
TAS-tax YL-si, 109
Tau, 131
TEAA, 71-72, 74, 128, 220, 222, 237
Temple, 14, 35, 38, 40, 46, 48, 50, 52-53, 56, 59, 61-62, 65-67, 70, 82, 85-87, 91, 99, 119, 123-128, 130, 139, 192, 205-207, 220, 228, 234-235, 241
Temple - Ceremonial, 56
Temple - Devotional, 56
Temple Arrangement, 35, 91
Tension, 14, 232
Tenth Angelic Key, 101
Tenth Key, 101
Tetragrammaton, 19, 23, 33, 244
Thaumaturgy, 14-15
The Angelical Language, 78, 82, 244
Thelemic, 118, 132, 205, 207, 211, 215, 219, 230, 233
Thelemic Star Ruby, 207
Thelemite, 48
Thelemites, 34
THILD DAS, 95
Third Angelic Key, 92
Third Key, 92
Third Leaf, 86
Thirteenth Angelic Key, 105
Thirteenth Key, 105
Thirty Aires, 17, 21, 85
Thomas Brenden, 5
Three Books of Occult Philosophy, 19, 25, 34, 142, 244
Throat, 231
Through-Thrusting Fire, 88, 222
Thursday, 114-116
Tiphareth, 120, 131, 212
TORGU, 94
TOTT, 31
Touch, 200, 211, 230-231
TOX DSI-vam, 106
Trace, 118-119, 124, 129, 211-213, 216-217, 220-222, 225-227, 229
Transformation, 27, 103-106, 159-161, 167-169, 186-187, 195-196
Transformations, 187, 196
Transportation, 27, 97-98, 100-101, 149-151, 179
Treatise, 27, 139, 210
Tree of Life, 25, 70, 118-120, 131, 212, 233
True, 5, 16, 24-25, 39, 62-64, 73, 80, 83, 85-86, 88, 93, 103-104, 106-111, 184-187, 193, 196, 204-206, 231, 233, 240, 243
True God, 184-185, 193, 206

True Magick, 206
True Seal of God, 39
True Will, 205-206
True Wisdom, 5, 16, 62
Tuesday, 114-116
Tuning, 57, 113, 201

Turner, 244
Twelfth Angelic Key, 104
Twelfth Key, 104-105
Twenty-Four Seniors, 25, 27, 136, 175
Typhon, 130, 215-216, 236

U

ULCININ, 100
Unicursal Hexagram of Earth, 224-226
Union, 14, 51, 53, 69, 85, 90, 129, 224

Universe, 21-22, 71, 73-74, 127, 130, 184-185, 192-194, 199, 206, 233, 235, 237
Uriel, 51, 213

V

VAOAN, 86-88, 192
VaOReSaJi, 81
Vast, 35, 53, 130, 232, 237
VAUN NA NAEEL, 92
Vav, 23, 81, 212
VAX, 105
VAY, 212
VE GEBURAH, 212
VE GEDULAH, 212
Veil of Paroketh, 120, 125
Vibrate, 47, 71, 118-119, 132, 212-213, 216-217, 220-223, 225-228

VII, 240
Virgo, 215
Virtue, 47, 174, 176, 197
Vitrivian Man, 214
Voice, 33, 53, 62, 97, 103, 107, 127
Voice of Fire, 127
VONPH, 105
VOOAN, 86-88, 92-93, 192
VORS KLA, 92
VORSG, 81, 87
VORSK, 81
VOVIN, 126
Vowel Sound, 80, 82

W

Wand, 123-124, 126-127, 129, 213, 220, 225, 235
Watchtower Keys, 58, 85-86, 90-91, 105, 107, 113
Watchtower Ritual, 126, 128
Watchtowers, 17, 46, 224

Water of Water, 91
Wednesday, 114-116
Wescott, 26, 32, 77, 209
West, 25, 46, 48-52, 56-59, 71, 91, 95, 100-101, 105-106, 109, 119, 123, 126, 128-130, 136, 146, 148, 150, 152, 154, 156, 158, 160, 162, 164, 166, 168, 170, 213, 217, 220-222, 224, 226, 229, 234, 238
Western, 14, 113, 234
Western Esoteric Tradition, 14
White, 37, 46-48, 73, 127-128, 130, 212, 226, 231, 234
Whitefish, 243
Whitney Holiday, 5
Wisdom, 5, 16, 62-63, 72-73, 93, 181, 237
Woe, 102
Working, 13, 15, 21, 23-25, 28, 32-34, 36-37, 46-50, 52, 57, 66-67, 73, 80, 86-87, 90-91, 113-114, 118, 123, 131-132, 135, 192, 199-207, 209, 224, 233, 246
World, 14, 21-23, 26, 33-34, 65-66, 72, 128, 178-180, 182, 185-186, 188, 194, 196-198, 200
Wynn Wescott, 26, 77

Y

Yahweh, 122
Years, 23-24, 33, 46, 52, 77, 105, 124, 201, 205, 233, 243, 246
Yechidah, 23
Yesod, 212
Yetzirah, 22-24
YHShVH, 132
YHVH, 23-24, 72, 122, 132, 212
Yod, 23, 212, 215
Yod Heh Vav Heh, 212
Yod Nun Resh Yod, 215
Yogic, 69

Z

ZACAR, 89, 92, 94, 97, 103-110
ZAMRAN, 87-89, 94, 97, 99, 103-110
ZIMZ, 87
ZIRN, 97
ZLAR, 31
Zod, 80
ZORGE, 87, 103-110

Magickal Works from Pendraig Publishing

Radomir Ristic
Balkan Traditional Witchcraft

Raymond Buckland
Buckland's Domino Divinaton
*Fortune-Telling with Döminös
and the Games of Döminös*

Buckland's Practical Color Magick

Eric De Vries
Hedge-Rider
Witches and the Underworld

Ed Fitch
Magical Rites from the Crystal Well
The Classic Book for Witches and Pagans

Veronica Cummer
Masks of the Muse
*Building a relationship
with the Goddess of the West*

Sorgitzak: Old Forest Craft
*Stories and messages
from the gods of Old Europe*

Dancing the Blood
Sorgitzak II

To Fly By Night
An Anthology of Hedgewitchery

Eric De Vries
Hedge-Rider
Witches and the Underworld

Starr Casas
The Conjure Workbook
Vol I Working the Root

Reading with Old Style Conjure Cards
Vol I Working the Root

Scott Stenwick
Mastering the Mystical Heptarchy
Vol I of the Mastering Enochian Magick Series

Ellen Evert Hopman
Scottish Herbs and Fairy Lore

Peter Paddon
Enchantment
The Witch's Art of Manipulation by Gesture, Gaze and Glamour

Visceral Magick
Bridging the Gap Between Magic and Mundane

A Grimoire for Modern Cunningfolk
A Practical Guide to Witchcraft on the Crooked Path

The Crooked Path
Selected Transcripts from the Crooked Path Podcast

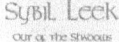

Christine Jones
Sybil Leek:
Out of the Shadows

Robin Artisson
The Flaming Circle
A Reconstruction of the Old Ways of Britain and Ireland

The Horn of Evenwood

The Resurrection of the Meadow

Witching Way of the Hollow Hill
The Gramarye of the Folk Who Dwell Below the Mound

Ann Finnin
The Forge of Tubal Cain
Southern California Witchcraft, Roebuck, and the Clan of Tubal Cain

Fiction Novels from Pendraig Publishing

The Demon's Apprentice Series
by Ben Reeder

The Demon's Apprentice *Book 1*
The Page of Swords *Book II*

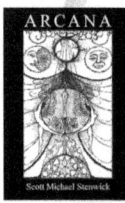

Arcana
by Scott Stenwick

The Wrath of Amun
by Claudia Dillaire

The Tale of Tyrfing
by Sokarjo Stormwillow

Golden Illuminati
by Raymond Buckland

The 13th Moon
by Ilana Sturm

The Glastonbury Chronicles
by S.P. Hendrick

Uneasy Lies the Head *Volume I*

The Sword of the King *Volume II*

Coin of the Realm *Volume III*

The Rose Above the Sword *Volume IV*

The Blood of Kings *Volume V*

The Barley and the Rose *Volume VI*

Tales of the Dearg-Sidhe
by S.P. Hendrick

Son of Air and Darkness *Volume I*

Great Queen's Hound *Volume II*

The Pale Mare's Fosterling *Volume III*

www.ingramcontent.com/pod-product-compliance
Lightning Source LLC
Chambersburg PA
CBHW071148160426
43196CB00011B/2046